Children in Colonial America

CHILDREN AND YOUTH IN AMERICA
General Editor: James Marten

Children in Colonial America
Edited by James Marten

Children in Colonial America

EDITED BY

James Marten

WITH A FOREWORD BY

Philip J. Greven

New York University Press

NEW YORK AND LONDON

NEW YORK UNIVERSITY PRESS
New York and London
www.nyupress.org

Library of Congress Cataloging-in-Publication Data
Children in colonial America / edited by James Marten ; with a foreword by
Philip J. Greven.
p. cm.
Includes bibliographical references and index.
ISBN-13: 978-0-8147-5715-4 (cloth : alk. paper)
ISBN-10: 0-8147-5715-4 (cloth : alk. paper)
ISBN-13: 978-0-8147-5716-1 (pbk. : alk. paper)
ISBN-10: 0-8147-5716-2 (pbk. : alk. paper)
1. United States—Social life and customs—To 1775. 2. United States—
Social conditions—To 1865. 3. Children—United States—History—16th
century. 4. Children—United States—History—17th century.
5. Children—United States—History—18th century. 6. America—Social
life and customs. 7. America—Social conditions. 8. Children—America—
History—18th century. I. Marten, James Alan. II. Title.

E162.C47   2006
305.230973'0903—dc22   2006019831

New York University Press books are printed on acid-free paper,
and their binding materials are chosen for strength and durability.

Manufactured in the United States of America

c 10 9 8 7 6 5 4 3 2 1
p 10 9 8 7 6 5 4 3 2 1

Contents

DOCUMENTS

PART IV Becoming Americans

DOCUMENTS

Foreword

Philip J. Greven

Why study childhood? As the essays in this volume demonstrate, there is much to be learned about the complex and varied experiences of children and adolescents in the seventeenth- and eighteenth-century British American colonies. The range of contexts is impressive—from the indigenous peoples of the east coast and Mexico to the Dutch-born children of Plymouth colony to children and adolescents in New England, the middle colonies, and the southern colonies and to the African-born offspring of slaves in the Caribbean. All of these geographical contexts shaped the life experiences of the children and the adults whose lives are being explored in this volume. The range of issues investigated is equally impressive. The detailed information in these essays about the lives of children enriches our understanding of many aspects of the extraordinarily diverse contexts characteristic of colonial America.

In terms of these particular vignettes, there is much to appreciate and to use to expand our understanding of life and thought, of values and behavior, in the multiple settings in which children's lives unfolded over a very long span of time. These essays are like individual patches in a very complicated academic quilt—each a vital and yet distinctive contribution to a much larger design. But what, one must ask, is the larger design itself like? Knowing what we now know, can we begin to envision the image of the quilt itself or of multiple quilts reflective of these multiple contexts?

The often complicated process of stitching together the histories of children and youth in early America can be seen in my own work. When I began to do the research that in 1977 was published as *The Protestant Temperament: Patterns of Child-Rearing, Religious Experience, and the Self in Early America* (which I ought to have entitled *Protestant Temperaments*—

plural rather than singular), I did not have a clear picture of the overall design of my inquiry. I only had a series of questions that needed answers. In the end, though, after I had followed countless life histories throughout the British colonies from the early seventeenth century to the late eighteenth and early nineteenth centuries, I came to realize that indeed there were themes that connected the various pieces of evidence that I had collected. The patches of information, often tiny and seemingly inconsequential, actually did combine to create patterns out of the life experiences of a vast number of males and females of all ages, from infancy to old age.

Ultimately, I discerned three distinct patterns that helped make sense of the information that I had gathered—three groups that I called the evangelicals, the moderates, and the genteel. In each section of the book, an exploration of childhood experiences was followed by an exploration of adulthood, the assumption being that the experiences of childhood were of fundamental importance for an understanding of the life experiences and the mindsets of adults in each of these three groupings. The individual patches multiplied and became an integral part of a much more complex quilting, with three distinct modalities of human thought and life taking shape throughout the seventeenth and eighteenth centuries in the British American colonies. The patterns that emerged ultimately helped me make better sense of the religious and political experiences and beliefs that so many historians have explored so thoroughly without ever realizing how rooted these experiences and beliefs were in the childhoods of successive generations of British Americans.

Subsequently, I made another surprising discovery that enabled me to explore the implications of disciplining children. I had planned to write a book on apocalyptic Protestants from the seventeenth century to our own times. The first exploration to see print was my essay " 'Some Root of Bitterness': Corporal Punishment, Child Abuse, and the Apocalyptic Impulse in Michael Wigglesworth."[1] In the course of this research, however, I began to realize that, over the course of four centuries, evangelical Protestants had consistently advocated breaking children's wills and recommended the use of physical means for accomplishing this goal. Corporal punishment of children thus became the focal point of my inquiry, and I ended up writing *Spare the Child: The Religious Roots of Punishment and the Psychological Impact of Physical Abuse.* Once again, childhood held the key to an understanding of a very complicated set of emotional, intellectual, political, and religious dimensions of adulthood. Indeed, without an understanding of the implications of discipline in childhood, these aspects of adulthood would remain mysterious and unconnected. The apocalyptic impulse itself was rooted in the traumas of childhood pain and suffering resulting from harsh and often brutal physical punishments.

In the course of my researches, much like a number of the authors who contributed to this anthology, I found the insights of psychologists, family therapists, sociologists, political scientists, and others working on issues relevant to childhood and adulthood in the twentieth century profoundly important in terms of my own understanding of the evidence that I had gathered from the seventeenth century to the present. The past can be understood best when we have a clear understanding of our own present, it appears. When I reexamined my earlier work and wrote the essay called "The Self Shaped and Misshaped: *The Protestant Temperament* Reconsidered," I acknowledged the interconnections between the past that I once had explored and the present in which I now lived. Whereas I had once believed that the past of the seventeenth and eighteenth centuries had few or no implications for an understanding of the present, I now know better.[2]

By being aware of the larger designs of the patterns rather than merely focusing upon the details that constitute the actualities of individual life experiences, historians have the opportunity to make major contributions to our understanding of life in the twenty-first century as well as in centuries past. The continuities often are astonishingly important. Certainly in terms of the religious experiences of people within the Protestant communities—from fundamentalist to evangelical to mainstream to liberal—the continuities are impressive and merit our closest attention.

As part of the growing historiography on children and youth, *Children in Colonial America* contributes to our understanding not only of the past but also of our present. The essays provide many insights for readers who are imaginative and who can take these individual patches and stitch them into their own larger and more complex quilts of scholarship.

NOTES

1. Philip J. Greven, "'Some Root of Bitterness': Corporal Punishment, Child Abuse, and the Apocalyptic Impulse in Michael Wigglesworth," in James A. Henretta, et al., eds., *The Transformation of Early American History: Society, Authority, and Ideology* (New York: Knopf, 1991).

2. Philip J. Greven, "The Self Shaped and Misshaped: *The Protestant Tempera-ment* Reconsidered," in Ronald Hoffman, et al., eds., *Through a Glass Darkly: Refl-ections on Personal Identity in Early America* (Chapel Hill: Published for the Omohundro Institute of Early American History & Culture, Williamsburg, Vir-ginia, by the University of North Carolina Press, 1997), 348–69.

Acknowledgments

My sincerest thanks and appreciation go to Philip J. Greven for graciously agreeing to write the preface; the anonymous outside reader, whose practical comments strengthened the manuscript in large and small ways; Eric Zinner and NYU Press for their support of the Children and Youth in America series, of which *Children in Colonial America* is the inaugural volume; Despina Gimbel, Emily Park, and the rest of the staff at NYU Press, who ushered the book through the production process; Emily Wright, for her crisp and thorough copyediting; and, most important, the authors of the essays for their creativity and cooperation and for sending me their essays on time—more or less!

Thanks are also extended to the South Carolina Historical Society and the University of Virginia Press for permission to publish extracts from the Letterbook of Eliza Lucas Pinckney and from Hunter Dickinson Farish, ed., *Journal & Letters of Philip Vickers Fithian, 1773–1774: A Plantation Tutor of the Old Dominion*, respectively.

Introduction

James Marten

There were many childhoods in colonial America. Race and ethnicity, region and religion, and economic and social distinctions shaped a wide variety of material conditions and styles of childrearing. As in so many other fields of colonial history, New England has dominated the literature on the history of childhood, at least partly because her early residents documented their lives so well. Yet historians have recently begun to expand beyond the rocky soil of New England to other regions in the New World.

Indeed, in *Huck's Raft,* his recent synthesis of American children's history, Steven Mintz argues that regional variations in the principles and experiences of childrearing were "a defining feature of colonial childhood."[1] His graceful survey offers telling glimpses of childhood in the major regions and among the many ethnicities of colonial America, including the ways in which those experiences and ideas changed between the early seventeenth and the mid-eighteenth century. Puritans were the first Westerners to think seriously about the place of children in society because their sons and daughters—and *their* sons and daughters—would bear the burden of preserving their "city on a hill." Their close family relationships and, at least during the first generation or two of the typical New England town, tight community bonds, ensured that parents and children were rarely out of one another's sight and never out of one another's thoughts. The entire Puritan enterprise depended on their successful childrearing. That intensity emerges in this passage from a famous Puritan book for children, which describes a boy seemingly without hope for salvation:

There seemed to be little hopes of doing good upon him, for he was a very monster of wickedness, and a thousand times more miserable and vile by his sin, than by his poverty. He was running to hell as fast as he could go, and was old in vice when he was but young in years: one scarcely hears of one so like the devil in his infancy, as was this poor child. What sin was there, that his age was capable of, which he did not commit? What by the corruption of his nature, and the abominable example of little beggar-boys, he was, indeed, arrived at a great pitch of impiety. He would call names, take God's name in vain, curse, swear, and do all kinds of mischief; and as to any thing of God, he was worse than a heathen.[2]

This unblinking chronicle of a young child's capacity for evil is the sort of thing that gives the Puritans a rather harsh reputation. It appeared in one of the first children's books written in English, James Janeway's *A Token for Children,* published in England in the 1670s and in America in 1700. Modern readers might gasp at the subject matter in a book purportedly for children, but it was popular in both England and the American colonies. The stories followed a simple formula: each told the tale of a dying child. Inspired to righteousness by the deaths of siblings, by natural piety, or by the enormity of their own sins, they sickened and died at peace with their maker, showing no fear and encouraging their mourners to live Godly lives.

Not surprisingly, then, the children of colonial New England are commonly believed to have been so emotionally and psychologically repressed, so weighed down by the Protestant notion of original sin and battered by high expectations and narrow assumptions that they were unable to live a "real" childhood. Indeed, the handful of surviving portraits of colonial children—including the painting on the cover of this book—represent children as straight-backed and dour, dressed in modest suits and gowns. In them, Puritan boys and girls appear as nothing but "miniature adults." Moreover, given the sometimes high mortality rates for children and others, especially in the southern colonies, and the largely agricultural economy, which required hard work from every family member, there seemed to be very little in the way of a true childhood anywhere in colonial America.

Although there are kernels of truth in these and other stereotypes, they are exaggerations of the beliefs and experiences of a very small percentage of the population of colonial America. Historians have relieved the Puritans of some of the worst stereotypes (they were hardly the cold, emotionless parents of legend), but Mintz does point out that New Englanders created childhoods that were much different from those of children living in the South. Early in the colonial period, the extraordinary threats to the health of children and adults in Virginia and Maryland created a fluid, confusing situation of orphaned children, combined families, and under-age property owners. As the southern economy developed and the mortality rate declined, children and youth in the planter class came to enjoy relative leisure and far less pressure to sustain their parents' religious values. Nevertheless, the priority placed on passing estates down through families placed a different kind of pressure, almost entirely economic, on southern planter children.

At the other end of the plantation spectrum, of course, were the slaves, whose children began working at the age of five or six—and entered the fields as full hands by the age of twelve—and suffered alarming mortality rates throughout the colonial period and into the nineteenth century. Those who survived grew older, but, in many ways, never "grew up," since they enjoyed few of the rights of grown whites. Slave children, it probably goes without saying, endured more hardship and enjoyed less of an actual "childhood" than any other group of youngsters in colonial America. Yet Mintz and other historians firmly argue that they and their parents fought to form stable families characterized by love and grief; some slave children even found time to play.

Yet another group of children with unique experiences were the sons and daughters of American Indians, who, like Europeans, applied their unique values to childrearing. One of the most remarked upon aspects of Indian childhood—which Anglo-Americans commented upon whenever they encountered natives during two hundred years of "first contacts"—was its remarkable freedom from physical discipline, from physical labor, from any serious institutional restraints. Most Europeans blamed ignorance or laziness for the relatively light touch of Indian parents, but Native American childrearing practices purposefully sought to instill pride, independence, and courage, rather than timidity.

Many other cultures rose in colonial America—the Dutch in New Amsterdam, the Quakers in Pennsylvania and New Jersey, the Caribbean-born planters and slaves of the Carolinas, the indentured servants toiling on tobacco plantations in the Chesapeake, to name just a few—and each developed its own approaches to children and to childhood.

Purpose and Scope of the Anthology

The essays that follow, while bowing somewhat to historians' traditional interest in New England, seek to delineate the diversity of colonial childhoods. But an even more important premise of this volume is that the histories of the American colonies and of American children can be better understood if they are considered together rather than separately. As a result, although each section confronts a set of concerns typically emphasized by historians in one field or the other, the authors combine the sensibilities of both groups.

Since the 1960s and 1970s race has been central to scholarship on colonial America, and part 1, "Race and Colonization," owes a debt to such classics as Edmund Morgan's *American Slavery, American Freedom* and to the dean of historians of Native Americans during the colonial period, James Axtell. The pieces on Mexico, New England, and Jamaica show how Western Europeans employed schools, churches, and slavery to overwhelm indigenous peoples and to control the "immigrants" stolen into slavery by reshaping the lives of Native American and African children. The essays in part 2, "Family and Society," are guided by a few prominent themes in the historiography of childhood—sibling relationships, child abuse, and family networks—but their authors place those issues solidly in their colonial contexts (in the elite families of South Carolina, for instance, training children into adulthood took on forms that would have been familiar to the English gentry but were also quite distinctly "colonial"). Part 3, "Cares and Tribulations," also reflects the concerns of children's historians. The familiar stories of Pilgrims, Puritans, and Quakers—among the most studied colonial populations—are deepened with essays on children imperiled by the process of immigration in the 1620s, the continuing threats to children's health in the mid-1700s, and the familial-religious, legal-religious, and familial ramifications of mental disability. Finally, part 4, "Becoming Americans," unites two of the most distinctive issues raised by historians in the two fields: colonial historians' investigation of the conditions and ideologies that encouraged British subjects to metamorphose into Americans; and children's historians' interest in the socialization of children into the communities in which they live. Placing the latter in the context of the former offers a fresh perspective on both.

Historiographical Contexts

Whatever their emphasis, all of the essays are firmly rooted in the historiographies of colonial America and of childhood. Up to the 1950s, the colonial historian Jack P. Greene recently declared, scholars "had no doubt" about what they should write about: elections, wars, and revolutions; economic and social transformations; great personalities in politics, art, and culture. Indeed, John Demos, writing in 1970, just as the traditional historical topics were beginning to lose their dominance, claimed that his own study of families and communities "has not as yet won a wide following among working historians." That would change over the next thirty years. The emergence of the "new history" in the 1960s, according to Greene, "reorder[ed] our priorities about the past," convincing many historians that

> the experiences of women, children, servants, slaves, and other neglected groups are quite as integral to a comprehensive understanding of the past as those of lawyers, lords, and ministers of state; that . . . popular culture is far more revealing than high culture; and that great events are important objects of study only when they open a window upon otherwise obscure aspects of more basic processes of social change.[3]

A 1993 essay by Joyce Appleby showed the extent of that historiographical change. Until after the Second World War, historians of early America were trapped by the necessities of explaining the uniqueness of America and of Americans, and of showing how the largely British colonists clinging precariously to the Atlantic sea coast challenged the most powerful empire on earth to build their own nation. Inspired by social scientists and European social historians, a new generation of American scholars overcame their fixation on nation building and began to explain how colonial America fit into international transformations; investigate the ways in which communities and families dealt with new religious, sexual, and economic ideas; and, inspired by the dramatic transformations of the United States in the 1960s and 1970s, take a fresh look at the colonial period through the roles of women and ethnic minorities. "Investing the typical conditions of everyday existence with an importance they had never known before," wrote Appleby, "historians made society—its geographic setting, its enduring traditions, its productive and reproductive activities—the central focus of historical research." In his sweeping and often humorous essay on the historiography of early America, Gordon S. Wood wrote that "there is scarcely an aspect of human behavior in early America that historians today do not write about—from divorce to dying, from the consumption of goods to child rearing." Nevertheless, except for a few notable exceptions, the colonial period is relatively unexplored by historians of American children, who have focused more on the last 150 years, especially the twentieth century.[4]

Part of the problem may be that there was not just one definition of childhood in the seventeenth and eighteenth centuries. As John Demos has suggested, contemporary pictorial and written representations of the "ages of man" borrowed seasonal metaphors or assigned characteristics based on arbitrary ages unrelated to actual child development. Furthermore, the coming-of-age rituals of virtually all modern American children and youth—graduations, first jobs, etc.—were virtually meaningless in an overwhelmingly rural culture without a large number of social and cultural institutions.[5]

The most difficult populations of children and youth to study during the colonial period—or any period in history, for that matter—are ethnic minorities. Some of these groups were, of course, "premodern" in the sense that they did not have the same traditions of education and literacy as Europeans. More important, however, was the fact that colonialization, and, in the case of Africans, enslavement, either destroyed the traditions and kinds of sources required by historians or rendered the conquered populations uninteresting to the conquering Europeans. In the case of colonial America, few documents and other historical evidence have survived to offer clues about the lives of Native American and African American youngsters, especially from their own points of view. European colonizers frequently commented on the Indians they encountered and the slaves they imported, but painfully few accounts by Native and African Americans have survived the colonial period. This is reflected in the paucity of articles and, especially, books on "minority" children in colonial America. A recent anthology suggests that the history of children in Latin America—where, of course, indigenous peoples were never a "minority" —has been even less investigated than in the rest of the Western hemisphere: "If the history of childhood in Europe and in North America is a late developer, the history and sociology of childhood in Latin America are truly in their infancy." And, as in British North America, most of the work on Latin American children has focused on more recent times.[6]

Attacking the problem from a different direction are historians of children and youth, who have also begun to apply the themes and methods of children's history to early America. The historiography of children dates from the mid-twentieth century, when Phillipe Ariès's *Centuries of Childhood: A Social History of Family Life* caught the attention of social scientists and historians alike with its argument that Western society had barely recognized children as a separate group until the early modern period. Although Ariès—an amateur historian whose work was first published in France—is more often cited than read, *Centuries of Childhood* was a catalyst for the modern study of childhood. Over the last several decades, historians have challenged Ariès's methodology and conclusions but have also marked the publication of his book as the beginning of the modern study of childhood. And Ariès's contention that childhood was not recognized as such until the early modern period resonates for historians of colonial children, who have often inquired about the extent to which their subjects enjoyed recognizable "childhoods."[7]

Children's historians employ a wide range of approaches and interests, which are highlighted in three recent surveys. Mintz, for instance, sought to clear away several popular myths, including the notions that American children have enjoyed peculiarly carefree childhoods in stable, nurturing families, that American childhoods are not affected by class, and the conflicting ideas that American children have, over the generations, enjoyed irrefutable progress or inevitable decline. Like Mintz, Joseph E. Illick acknowledged that there were many "varieties of childhood"—he stressed ethnicity, class, and geography as the chief agents of that diversity—but the overriding purpose of his *American Childhoods* was to show how these factors shaped the ways in which children sought autonomy and their parents prepared them for it. Harvey J. Graff also suggested that American children have followed a number of "conflicting paths" shaped by ethnicity, economics, and gender, among other factors, but, in focusing on the process of growing up, he attempted to provide an analysis of "an integrated human developmental process." More so than most historians, Graff emphasized the words of children themselves—or, more accurately, adult memories of childhood—and virtually ignored major historical events. Finally, in his quick survey of issues facing Western childhood from the Middle Ages through the first quarter of the twentieth century, Colin Heywood argued that children "must be seen as active in determining their own lives and the lives of those around them," or, to use a term favored by social historians of late, that children have "agency" in shaping their own experiences and destinies. He also provided a handy list of topics concerning historians of children and youth—a "repertoire of themes," he called it—that he set up as a series of dichotomies: depravity versus innocence, nature versus nurture, independence versus dependence, age versus gender. The historians whose essays appear in this anthology follow a number of the threads laid out by these historians.[8]

"Constructions" of Colonial Childhoods

It goes without saying that there have always been children, and that those children fill virtually identical biological roles in the societies in which they live. But a notion that has become almost universally accepted by historians of children and youth over the last generation, and one that is stressed in many of the essays that follow, is that, although the presence of children is, of course, a constant in all societies and cultures, "childhood" itself is a "construction," a concept created by humans rather than a state of being governed by inevitable natural laws. In other words, people living in different times and places have accepted a bewildering variety of behaviors from and have projected myriad expectations onto the youngest members of their societies. Those assumptions have and are shaped by countless factors, but most historians have focused on race and ethnicity, class, religion, and gender. Heywood refers to childhood as "a variable of social analysis," and this anthology seeks to explore how the colonial experience in the Americas led to particular constructions of childhood.[9]

Rather than simply describing the lives of children and youth who happen to have lived in American colonies between the late sixteenth and late eighteenth centuries, *Children in Colonial America* addresses two questions. First, how did the colonial experience shape or even alter perceptions and assumptions about children and childhood? Second, how can research on the history of children reorient our knowledge and interpretations of colonial history? Some essays confront these questions only indirectly. Parnel Wickham's piece on "Idiocy and the Construction of Competence," for instance, deals with an issue that was confusing to Puritans in England and America alike. But a number of the essays provide bridges between these two fields of inquiry that strengthen both. By focusing on the children of Plymouth Plantation rather than the adults, for example, John Navin lends texture to our understanding of the tough choices and tougher conditions faced by the Pilgrims. Similarly, Audra Diptee's examination of the young slaves trapped in Jamaica's "colonial project" stretches our knowledge about eighteenth-century attitudes toward children and the ways those attitudes were adapted to match the blunt economy of the plantation system that was central to European mercantilism.

As Tobias Hecht wrote about Indian youngsters in Latin America, "children were a sort of ground zero for the colonial encounter, a point of entry through which Europeans not only interpreted the nature of the indigenous societies but gained access to and sought to change them." As the essays in this volume show, it is not too great a leap to suggest that children were similarly central to the colonial experience throughout North America.[10]

The historiographies of children and of colonial America have, over the last generation or more, developed in often intersecting ways. Historians still write about traditional topics like the coming of the American Revolution, the Enlightenment, and Puritan theology, of course, but they also investigate the day-to-day lives of the peoples of early America. Although the shortage of documentation has often hindered research on colonial children, scholars have nevertheless begun to uncover the ways in which colonial childhoods reflected both European assumptions and "American" values.

The illustrations and primary documents intermingled with the essays complement and expand on the themes and arguments introduced in the essays. They are followed by a brief section of study questions that is inspired by the somewhat outdated but still provocative notion that colonial Americans thought of their children as "miniature adults." Finally, a brief historiographical essay and full bibliographic references for crucial secondary sources cited in the essays can be found in the "Suggested Readings."

NOTES

1. Mintz, *Huck's Raft*, 41. In this essay and throughout the volume, only short citations will be provided for crucial secondary sources. Full citations can be found in the "Suggested Readings" section at the end of the book.

2. James Janeway and Cotton Mather, *Janeway's Token for Children: Being an Exact Account of the Conversion, Holy and Exemplary Lives, and Joyful Deaths of Several Young Children* (London: Religious Tract Society, 1676), http://www.calvaryroadbaptist.org/pages/Token%20-%20a_poor_street_child.htm, accessed May 15, 2005.

3. Greene, *Interpreting Early America*, 3, 4; Demos, *A Little Commonwealth*, xv.

4. Joyce Appleby, "A Different Kind of Independence: The Postwar Restructuring of the Historical Study of Early America," *William and Mary Quarterly*, 3rd Ser., 50 (April 1993): 245–67, quote on 250; Gordon S. Wood, "A Century of Writing Early American History: Then and Now Compared; or, How Henry Adams Got It Wrong," *American Historical Review* 100 (June 1995): 688.

5. Demos, *Circles and Lines,* esp. 15–23.

6. Hecht, *Minor Omissions,* 5.

7. Colin Heywood's brief but wide-ranging survey offers a useful summary of historians' reactions to Ariès. Heywood, *A History of Childhood,* 12–15. For two brief summaries of the historiography of children, one written just as the field was emerging and another, after a generation of historians had explored countless aspects of children's lives, see, Sommerville, "Bibliographic Note: Toward a History of Childhood and Youth," and Cunningham, "Histories of Childhood."

8. Graff, *Conflicting Paths,* 5; Heywood, *A History of Childhood,* 4, 32–40.

9. Heywood, *A History of Childhood,* 4.

10. Hecht, *Minor Omissions,* 11.

Part I

Race and Colonization

Broteer, son of Saungm Furro, had it all when he was born in Guinea, on the west coast of Africa, around 1729. His father was prince of the Dukandarra; despite family tensions caused by jealousies among the prince's several wives, Broteer could look forward to a life of affluence and power. However, his world collapsed before he had the chance to enjoy it. Another band from a distant region, encouraged and armed by European slave traders, invaded Broteer's territory, capturing smaller, less powerful groups and herding them toward the Atlantic coast. His father's attempts to negotiate failed, and when he refused to reveal the location of his people's treasury, he was tortured to death before Broteer's eyes. The rest were marched to the coast, put on a slave ship, and conveyed to America. On the way nearly a fourth died when smallpox broke out on the tiny vessel. Although most of the human cargo was sold in Barbados, Broteer and a few others sailed to Rhode Island. His new American owner, proud to be finally making an investment in the lucrative slave trade, named him Venture; the little boy had suddenly been transformed from a human being into a commodity. He was eight years old.

The historian Wilma King named her book about antebellum slave children *Stolen Childhood: Slave Youth in Nineteenth-Century America* (Bloomington: Indiana University Press, 1995), for obvious reasons: the lives of slave youngsters had been taken from them before they were born. The Native American and African children who appear in the essays in this section were also deprived of their traditional childhoods. Jamaican slave children shared Broteer's virtually complete loss of childhood, while Indian children in Mexico and New England found their childhoods reshaped and their lives reorganized around values and institutions imposed on them and their families by European colonists. These essays, along with the eyewitness account of Native American childrearing and the excerpt from one of the few autobiographies of a native African caught in the web of American slavery, show the complications and tragedies that arose when Europeans, Africans, and indigenous Americans encountered one another. Colonialism unleashed economic and social forces that dramatically altered the assumptions and expectations of slave and native children. Schools not only changed *how* they learned but also *what* they learned; Puritan ideas about religion and gender collided with Native American notions in New England; and the plantation system forced children like Broteer/Venture into harsh economic roles. These processes, and the responses of native and African children to them, highlight the ways in which children became the targets of what one of the authors, Audra Diptee, calls the "colonial project."

Chapter 1

Indian Children in Early Mexico

Dorothy Tanck de Estrada

The nation now known as Mexico was called New Spain from 1521 to 1821 when, in what is considered the colonial period, it was under the rule of the Spanish monarchs. During those three hundred years it became the most valuable possession of Spain, producing in the eighteenth century two-thirds of the world's silver and a population of six million inhabitants —including 112,000 in Mexico City, the largest city in the Americas. Hundreds of different Indian groups formed the majority of the population. Prior to the arrival of the Spaniards, one of these native peoples, the Aztecs, had conquered the central area and spread their language and customs to much of the region.

As Philippe Ariès pointed out in his study of children in eighteenth-century France, knowledge of the society existing prior to that period is necessary in order for historians to understand later developments. In the case of New Spain, many aspects of the highly developed Indian civilization existing before 1521 continued to form a part of family and child rearing practices in later centuries, not only because of the demographic predominance of the natives but also because in a law established in 1555 the Spanish government allowed certain judicial, political, and social structures of the Indians to continue, as long as they were not in opposition to the Catholic faith or the sovereignty of the king.[1]

Thus, the Indians were not expelled from the territory to the frontiers, but rather their pre-Hispanic settlements were recognized as Indian towns, "*pueblos de indios,*" and the Indians were allotted grants of land and given permission to elect their municipal Indian authorities. Approximately two thousand *pueblos de indios* were established in the sixteenth century, interspersed with Spanish settlements; by 1800 there were 4,468 legally recognized Indian towns, located from Chihuahua in the north to Yucatan in the south.[2]

Children in Aztec Mexico (1325–1521)

Ancient pictographic codices and archeological remains only depict scenes of military triumphs, descriptions of sacrifices to deities, lists of monarchs, and registers of tribute, making it difficult to explore the daily life of children in pre-Hispanic times. It was, in fact, after the Spanish conquest of Mexico that information on the social life of the Aztecs was obtained. The Catholic missionaries, realizing that they needed to understand the culture of the conquered in order to transmit the Catholic faith, learned the Aztec language (Náhuatl) and systematically collected data from native informants concerning the religion, government, laws, history, medicine, education, and customs of the Indians. This effort was carried out over a fifty-year period by the Franciscan friar, Bernardino de Sahagún, considered to be the founder of modern ethnography, who transcribed the information in Náhuatl with a resume in Spanish, thereby forming "one of our most precious windows into the structure and patterning of the New World's most advanced indigenous civilization."[3]

Sahagún's sources reveal that mothers and children were highly regarded in Aztec society. Women who died in childbirth were compared to the soldiers who succumbed in battle: each was rewarded with the highest place in the afterlife. The newborn infant also received special attention. The umbilical cord was cut and buried under the hearth, if it was a girl, and in a field of battle, if a boy. All the time the midwife spoke to the baby in the most loving and concerned manner: "Precious necklace, precious feather, precious green stone, precious bracelet, precious turquoise. . . . Thou hast come to reach the earth, the place of torment, the place of pain." Around the twentieth day, after consultation with the soothsayer, the child received its name as registered in the ritual calendar in accord with the month and day of its birth.[4]

At different moments in each child's development, parents who cared for their children at home delivered formal, memorized speeches on the meaning of life and the way the child should behave. When the boy or girl was six years old, the age of discretion, each parent offered a didactic discourse to the offspring.

Here you are, my little daughter, my precious necklace, my precious quetzal feather, my human creation, born of me. You are my blood, my color, in you is my image. Now grasp, listen, you live, you were born, sent to earth by our lord . . . maker of humankind, creator of people. . . . Listen well, my little daughter, my little child, earth is not a place of well-being, there is no joy, there is no happiness. It is said that earth is the place of painful joy, of a joy that hurts.[5]

In these early years, specific chores were given to a boy according to his age. At four, to begin helping his father; at five, to carry wood; at six, to carry heavier things to market; at seven, to learn to fish with nets. These tasks continued, mixed with different types of punishments for bad behavior, such as being beaten with a stick, stuck with cactus spines, or having to inhale the smoke from burned chiles.[6]

Girls followed a similar pattern, learning to use the spindle whorl to twist yarn at age five and perfecting this skill until at thirteen they would grind maize, make tortillas, and learn to cook. At fourteen a girl began to weave maguey or cotton cloth on the back-strap loom, which was generally tied to a tree, a skill she would perfect over the years. Girls also received knowledge of plants and medicinal remedies. Children were urged to bathe frequently in cold water and in the hot vapors of the sweatbath when they were sick.[7]

The sons of the nobles studied and lived in the *calmécac*. Some entered at the age of five and others in early adolescence. A minority learned the sacred rites of the priestly class and most concentrated on legal and military studies. All had to gain understanding of the pictorial codices, decipher the sacred calendar, memorize historical and religious accounts, perfect their rhetorical skills, fast, and do physical penances. Martial arts and ceremonial dance were also part of the instruction. The youths participated in battles, attempting to take prisoners who would be sacrificed so as to guarantee the rising of the sun.

The sons of the commoners, when they were eighteen years old, attended for two years another type of school, the *tepochcalli*, where they trained for war, learned crafts, and carried out agricultural and construction projects. They also memorized ritual songs. Through manual labor and discipline, strong soldiers were prepared by the state. As in the *calmécac*, the students lived within the school.[8]

Adolescents of both sexes between the ages of thirteen and fifteen attended a "House of Song" where elderly men and matrons taught them

Drawing of Aztec children entering the *calmécac* (school for nobles). The teacher is on the left and the father of the boys is on the right.

the sacred chants and they practiced the ceremonial rhythmic steps of the ritual dances. The students lived at home and went to the school a few hours each day. These schools were in every neighborhood and town next to the temple. The adolescents learned to play the drums, flutes, conch shells, and trumpets for the frequent celebrations that lasted many hours and sometimes days. Some dressed as jaguars, eagles, or parrots, with feathered costumes and masks; all danced in unison to the beat of wooden drums. Some performances had up to a thousand participants. The music and song were generally slow and solemn for the nobles, and for the commoners, sometimes lively, humorous, and ribald. In one piece, young men donned masks of old men and danced in a hunched-back way, causing much laughter.[9]

The home was the main educational center until the child was an adolescent. The dwelling consisted of one rectangular room without windows and a door opening onto the street. Apart, in the yard at the back, were a kitchen area and a sweat bath, where flowers, a vegetable garden, and songbirds also were found. Young boys dressed in a coarse knee-length white cape tied in a knot on their right shoulder. For recreation, they played with hard rubber balls, competed in hipball games, used blowguns or sling shots to kill birds, and practiced shooting small bows and arrows. At about age ten a loincloth was added to this attire and the youth let a tuft of hair grow on the back of his head. This was cut when the young man took his first prisoner of war, and if it was still there at the age of twenty he was ridiculed when he met adolescent females. Little girls used a wide, sleeveless tunic and a short wrap-around skirt, both of cloth woven at home. Their hair was worn loose. As the child grew older, her skirt was lengthened and when married she adopted a new hair-do of two rolls of hair that protruded on each side of her head like "horns."[10]

All children were expected to be obedient, humble, and hard working. Their parents not only treated them with care but orally expressed to them love and tenderness, sentiments that are not revealed in the treatment given by other members of society to each other, at least not in ceremonial speeches. Children were considered treasures. Perhaps this was due to another aspect of Aztec thought: the fragility and fleetingness of life and the premonition that human existence was a dream. This fatalistic sentiment, combined with practices of warfare and human sacrifice, may have caused the families to give extreme value and attention to their children. Fray Diego de Duran in the sixteenth century wrote that "they are the people who love their children more than any nation in the world."[11]

Drawing of Aztec boys being taught by their teacher in the *calmécac.*

Indian Children during the Sixteenth Century

Into this society, where warfare and religion were paramount activities, came the Spaniards, who conquered the Indian empire in 1521, bringing to the New World their own forms of military and religious zeal. The first friar who arrived in New Spain was an exceptional Belgian, Pedro de Gante, a close relative of King Charles and a man of genius and self-abnegation. Soon after, in 1524, a group of twelve Franciscans disembarked in Veracruz and walked barefoot to the city of Mexico-Tenochtitlan, where they were greeted by a kneeling Hernán Cortes. These priests were versed in the humanism of Erasmus, in the linguistic research promoted at the universities of Alcalá and Salamanca, and in the first Spanish grammar by Antonio de Nebrija. Many missionaries, upon perceiving the austere life of the Indians, desired to form a Catholic Church similar to that of the primitive Christianity practiced during the first centuries after Christ.[12]

Thus, the early missionaries wanted to isolate the Indians from the Spanish settlers, whom they considered violent, unjust, and immoral, like voracious sharks among minnows. However, the seven thousand Spaniards who populated the region during the sixteenth century amidst an Indian population of millions, wreaked havoc on the native civilization, due to the devastating mortality caused by imported European diseases, such as smallpox, measles, and typhoid, against which the natives had no natural immunity. The number of Indians dropped from approximately sixteen million to two million by the end of the century.[13]

The friars had two main objectives: to convert the Indians to the Catholic faith and to transmit knowledge and useful skills. To accomplish these aims, they learned to preach in the indigenous languages and employed specially taught native children.

New Spain was as linguistically varied as Europe, with twenty major tongues and well over one hundred minor dialects. The friars learned these languages by playing games with the Indian children during the day, discovering the sound and meaning of what they heard, and then, in the evening, writing in alphabetic form the strange words and their Spanish translations. Using Nebrija's grammar as a guide, dictionaries and catechisms in the native languages were published in Mexico City, starting in 1539, "less than a century after the first work in Europe and more than a century before the first book in the British American colonies." Among the

A page from *The Catechism of Pedro de Gante* (ca. 1525) containing symbolic paintings, representing Christian doctrine and prayers, that resembled the Aztec codices.

early books was a guide for Indian parents for giving Christian instruction to their own children, the style of which followed the pattern of the repetitive, metaphorical style of the Aztec didactic speeches.[14]

Pedro de Gante prepared small books containing symbolic colored paintings of the prayers and doctrine, in a form similar to those of the pre-Hispanic codices. With the help of the Indians, the friars also wrote at least twenty theatrical pieces in Náhuatl. Similar to the medieval miracle plays, they were performed from 1533 to 1600. Real trees, live animals, and many actors, singers, and costumes recalled the Aztec performances.[15]

Following the instructions of the king, who recommended converting the children of the Aztec nobility to provide examples for the rest of the population, the Franciscans gathered together the sons of the nobles in their monasteries and taught them religion, music, reading, and writing in Náhuatl and Spanish. Some parents, disapproving of the new religion, hid their sons and sent their servants instead, thereby inadvertently contributing to the ascent of commoners to positions of power and responsibility.

Instruction for the rest of the children was carried out every day outside the church, either in the portals of the monastery, in the cemetery, or
in special chapels in the atrium. The rudiments of faith and prayers were
taught in the native languages. "Even in poorer parishes where there are
no boys who know how to read, at prime and vesper time other poor boys
come to teach them how to say the Pater Noster and Ave Maria and in this
way they have learned not only the Psalms, but also antiphonal chants." In
large schools, five hundred to a thousand students received instruction in
carpentry, sculpture, painting, and architecture.[16]

The youngsters, in turn, translated the sermons prepared by the priests.
At other times, an Indian boy translated the words of the preacher as he
spoke. Young boys became the "teachers and preachers of their own parents and elders, traveling in the region, discovering and destroying the
idols and taking them away from their nefarious practice." Three boys in
Tlaxcala, Cristobalito, Antonio, and Juan, who were martyred when they
denounced idolatrous rites, were immortalized in print, both in Náhuatl
and Spanish, as examples to be revered, and were compared to the child
martyrs of fourth-century Spain, Justo and Pastor.[17]

The bishop of Tlaxcala, the Dominican Julián Garcés, who had spent
ten years in contact with the natives, wrote to the pope in 1536 praising the
abilities of the Indian children and the piety of all the adults:

> The children of the Indians [. . .] learn more rapidly and with greater joy
> than the Spanish children the articles of faith in their order and the other
> prayers. [. . .] They are not chattering or quarrelsome, nor stubborn nor
> restless, nor arrogant, nor reproachful, nor peevish, but agreeable, and very
> obedient to their teachers.
>
> They are very intelligent, so that they can be easily taught anything.
> When they are ordered to count, or read or write, paint, perform any type
> of manual or artisan work or art, they show great clarity, quickness and
> facility of mind in learning the basic principles.
>
> No one objects, no one mumbles, nor complains, because all of the care
> and concern of the parents is to procure [sic] that their sons make good
> progress in the teachings of Christianity. They learn perfectly ecclesiastical
> song, as well as that of the organ and Gregorian chant and harmony to such
> a degree that foreign musicians are not needed.[18]

Pope Paul III responded a year later with a papal bull in which he
reminded everyone that Christ had commanded the apostles to teach all

nations without exception and declared that nothing justified depriving the Indians, who were reasonable men, of the faith, of their liberty, and of their property.

The most outstanding institution for Indians in the sixteenth century was the College of the Holy Cross, opened by the Franciscans in Tlatelolco, a neighborhood of Mexico City, in 1536. There, seventy boarding students, from twelve to seventeen years of age, received instruction in Latin grammar, rhetoric, logic, aspects of philosophy and theology, music, and herbal and therapeutic medicine. Some later became scribes for Bernardino de Sahagún and served in high government posts in the pueblos.[19]

Daily Life of Native Children

These institutions touched the lives of only a few individuals. For most Indian children, and, for that matter, for all children in New Spain, the rest of North America, and Europe, the struggle for survival formed the most important parts of their daily lives. Before the second half of the nineteenth century, infant mortality was frequent; one in four babies failed to survive the first year of life. Death continued to pursue small children, for another fourth died before reaching the age of ten. Only half of all infants reached adolescence. These high rates of infant and child mortality, combined with periodic epidemics, meant that for centuries the population of the Western world did not increase, resulting in the fact that by 1800 the annual growth of population was only half of 1 percent.[20]

In New Spain, perhaps because of a better climate, at the end of the eighteenth century population growth was at 1 percent per year among all classes. Despite this, most families still suffered the loss of one or more of their offspring at an early age, often of intestinal or respiratory infections. Even the noble families of European descent in New Spain lost many of their children.[21]

In times of epidemics, families of deceased infants were not required to pay the usual burial fees. Or, in normal times, in order not to pay for burial, "the [Indian] church singers alone bury the child, so as to avoid paying the parish fees." Children were the most apt to die in the epidemics because they had no natural immunity, as did the adults who had survived previous plagues. Often a toy used by the child was buried with him and he was dressed as an angel, his cadaver covered by rosemary and other sweet-smelling herbs.[22]

Because of the high mortality of infants, families in New Spain were small. In Mexico City the average size of an Indian family was approximately 4.1 and for non-Indians, 3.2. Indian children assisted their parents in chores, agriculture, and herding, but in rural areas and small towns did not leave home to work in other activities until they married, at the average age of 20.7 for young men and 18.5 for women. However, in one urban center, the city of Oaxaca, one half of the Indian boys left home by age ten, to work as servants in Spanish houses or to learn a trade as an apprentice, but most children of non-Indians in that city did not leave home at such an early age.[23]

In the colonial period, the Indian infant was neither enveloped in swaddling clothes nor placed in a cradle. Rather, infants were laid in hammocks, or their mothers carried them all day wrapped in a shawl behind their backs. Children were generally baptized within a week after birth. In the sixteenth century, most received names such as Maria, Ana, Juan, and José. Among the natives, the name of Juan was the most popular during three centuries. From 1600 to 1800, parents usually did not name their children after themselves, but in accordance with the name of the saint on whose feast day they were born or baptized, a practice perhaps reinforced by the pre-Hispanic custom of giving the child a name corresponding to his birth date in the ritual calendar. The name of the saint was often combined with that of Mary or Juan. This resulted in a great variety of names, some of which were quite unusual. The names of some Indian boys registered in the schools reflect this practice: Dorotheo Cesario, Pío Quinto (Pius the Fifth), Benancio, Eusebio Victoriano, Hermenegildo, Policarpo, Leocadio, etc.[24]

Children were expected to help their parents in the fields or at home: watching sheep, caring for siblings, spinning wool or cotton thread, aiding the father in his crafts. Probably the happiest moments for boys and girls were the processions, fireworks, and communal meals that took place about eight times a year in the Indian pueblos. Children could belong to some sodalities (called "cofradías," religious organizations whose members were parishioners devoted to the veneration of Christ, the Virgin Mary, or a saint) and, along with the women, helped cultivate and gather flowers to decorate altars, shrines, statues, and the routes of the processions.

The feast of Corpus Christi was one public event in which children participated. During this joyful spring celebration, women and girls strewed flowers at the beginning of the parade, and girls performed special dances while waving colored feathers in the air, to prepare the way for the artisan guilds (including boys who were apprentices), municipal authorities, sodalities, religious orders, and neighborhoods that marched before the priest carrying the Sacred Host. The boys and girls among the spectators along the route cavorted and escaped from the dragonlike figures and cardboard giants representing the four corners of the world that led the parade and were to scare away the devil so that the procession could pass.[25]

Besides Corpus Christi, another favorite time for Indian youngsters was the feast of the patron saint of their home towns. All day and night tremendous fireworks filled the air, accompanied by music, which enlivened the processions, dances, and mock battles of the Moors versus the Christians and of the ancient "Tlaxcaltecas." The latter were reminiscent of pre-Hispanic performances. Each town had a dance master, paid with municipal funds, to train the participants and practice for many hours beforehand. Young boys learned to play the organ, clarinet, drums, and flutes, which could be a source of income in later life. One little girl from Tlaxcala, "prostrate in bed and in agony, without hope of living, made a promise to Holy Mary that if she recovered her health she would dress as a monarch and go out in the dance." On a chair by her bed lay the feathered headdress, rattle, and scepter for the costume of a pre-Hispanic princess, who would dance in the atrium in front of the church. In a nearby town, "the father of another Indian girl opposed her going to dance, but upon walking in his field a poisonous snake almost bit him. Freed from death he promised Mary to allow his daughter to fulfill her desire to dance in the festival of the Holy Virgin."[26]

From the end of the seventeenth century onward, devotion to Our Lady of Guadalupe greatly increased. The Virgin was said to have appeared in 1531 to an Indian, Juan Diego, on a hill outside of Mexico City, and to have left her image painted on his cape, which was preserved in a great basilica built on the site of the apparition. Indian families made pilgrimages to the shrine, "bands of men and women, hand in hand, who, as they approach the sanctuary, dance, making various jubilant pirouettes, some of them also playing their rustic instruments. . . . There is no home here, rich or poor, that does not have an image of this Virgin."[27]

Indian Catholic priests, municipal authorities, and non-Indian clerics wrote the history of this devotion and the role of Juan Diego, along with biographies of other pious Indians. The story of holy Catherine Tekawitha and her Iroquois companions in Canada was also included in the texts, some of which were published. Paintings of the child martyrs of Tlaxcala were commissioned during the eighteenth century. In 1752 an Indian priest petitioned the archbishop to approve the founding of a seminary, headed by Indian professors, to train clergymen. He reminded the prelate that, in fact, it was not really the friars who had converted the natives after the conquest, but the native children. Throughout the colonial period, Bishop Garcés's praise of the talents of Indian students was brought to the attention of the authorities by Indian leaders.[28]

Indian Schoolchildren

Several changes in the administration of Indian schools took place between 1690 and 1770. Formal schooling of Indian youngsters increased after 1690 due to mandates from the king, who ordered that schools be established with funds from the Indian municipal treasuries. For the first time, the decrees specified that reading and writing in Spanish, in addition to Christian doctrine, were to be taught. In addition to these local schools, the Jesuits directed not only colleges but also primary schools in twenty-one settlements throughout New Spain. Thus, all classes of children were educated together in these free urban schools, whose teacher was a Jesuit brother rather than a priest. There were also large schools within the hospitals of the Bethlehemite brothers and numerous private schools in urban areas.[29]

The educational picture changed drastically during the period from 1750 to 1770. The Jesuits were expelled by Charles III in 1767 from all of the Spanish territories, resulting in the exile of four hundred priests from New Spain, one-third of whom were teachers. The government also removed the friars from the Indian towns, replacing them with diocesan priests, who, in turn were fewer in number than those of the religious orders and were not inclined to open primary schools.[30] From 1770 onward, education in the Indian towns came under the direct supervision of the civil government, so that the role of the church was greatly diminished. New decrees ordered that priority be given to the payment of schoolteachers from the Indian municipal funds, with expenditures diminished for religious celebrations. By 1808 there were such schools in 1,015 Indian towns, which represented 26 percent of the total number of pueblos.[31]

Cover of catechism translated into *náhuatl*. Gerónimo de Ripalda and Ignacio de Paredes, translators and editors, *Catecismo mexicano* (Mexico: Imprenta de la Bibliotheca Mexicana, 1758).

At times parents opposed sending their children to school; some disliked that the instruction was in Spanish instead of their own language; others did not want to pay part of the teacher's salary out of their own pocket; and many stressed that they needed their children at home to help with the chores. Gradually, as the municipal treasuries assumed teachers' salaries, opposition lessened. An added incentive for Indian children to study was the royal decree in 1696 that lifted the sixteenth-century prohibition against their becoming priests: it declared that Indians could be ordained and enter all the religious orders, as well as be eligible to occupy governmental positions.[32]

Children were often compared to soft wax that could be molded to any shape—to wet clay that, through education, could be formed into useful vases or, without it, would become unusable pots; or to tender seedlings that could grow into beautiful trees or into scraggly bushes. The boys and girls were not referred to as sinful and condemned beings; religious practices tended toward the festive rather than the penitent and woeful, except during Holy Week.[33]

A typical school day began when elderly men and women, or the teacher himself, went to the homes, rounding up the children to bring them to class. Dressed in short pants and a tunic of cotton or maguey cloth, the boys often wore their hair in a peculiar style, the *balcarrota*, which involved leaving two long strands of hair on each side of the head in front of the ears. A few towns, besides instructing Indian girls in religion, had primary schools for them with lay teachers, often the wife or sister of the schoolmaster. The girls dressed in the skirt and blouse of the Aztec period, with different-colored skirts corresponding to distinct pueblos. The blouses were embroidered, some so elaborately that they were worn by Spanish women in high society. Bright colors were part pf the attire of men and women. Little girls used earrings in the form of butterflies and tied their hair in braids interspersed with red or black ribbons, while their mothers used gold loop earrings.[34]

The favorite games were flying kites, playing with rubber balls (sometimes against a pyramid), using a swing hung on a tree, playing blind man's bluff, blowing pipe guns, spinning tops, riding a hobby horse made of a pole with a horse's head, jumping rope, playing a small guitar, and blowing bubbles. Most of these activities were shown in an engraving used to teach the letters and sounds of the alphabet. Tag, mock bullfighting, miniature wars, somersaults, and juggling were played with friends while the girls had rag dolls and liked hand-clapping games. Children still feared the screech of the owl, which, as in Aztec times, signaled the death of someone or the mournful call of the Crying Woman (the "Llorona") who wandered in the night lamenting and wailing the loss of her children whom she had killed.[35]

In schools designed for Indian children bilingual teachers were found and subjects that interested the parents were taught: religion, prayers, song, and chant. Many children, both Indian and non-Indian, learned only Christian doctrine and, because their parents took them out of school before they learned to write—in New Spain, the English colonies, and Europe, teachers regularly taught reading prior to teaching writing—more people knew how to read than to write. Some children walked long distances to school, crossing rivers and wading in puddles during the rainy season. Many did not attend during the planting and harvest time. Thursday was a half-day and on Saturday the Christian doctrine was recited in a loud voice as the students marched through the streets of the pueblo.[36]

The schoolbooks consisted of the Cartilla, a reading primer of eight pages, filled with letters and syllables, since 1635 published by the thou-

Broadside used for teaching reading with the letters of the alphabet and commonly used syllables. Note the boy playing ball against a pyramid.

sands on cheap paper each year in Mexico City, the profits going to the Royal Indian Hospital. Then the catechism of Father Ripalda was used, printed in Spanish or a native language, and a third book, the Catón, which contained in verse or prose the advice of Cato, the statesman of ancient Rome. Cartilla—Catechism—Catón, the three "C's," were the basic texts.[37]

A fourth book was used in the Indian schools around Mexico City. It was the biography of an Indian woman, Salvadora de los Santos Ramírez, who lived from 1701 to 1762. Written by a Jesuit, it was reprinted by the Indian municipal council of Mexico City in 1784 and 1791. The Indian governors expressed in the prologue of the biography the purpose of the book:

> To provide the schools and Migas [name given to schools for girls] where our children are educated, with a type of Cartilla, in which, while being taught how to read, they learn at the same time, to imitate the Christian virtues, with the sweet, powerful and natural attractiveness of seeing how they were practiced by a person of their same status.[38]

This book promoted ethnic identity, cohesion, and pride among the Indian school children and can be considered the first free textbook published in Mexico.

Good teachers, competent and moral, were difficult to find, because the pay was not very adequate and few men wanted to live in an isolated town. The priests pointed out that often they were drunkards or fugitives, or made the students help them in the fields instead of teaching them. Parents complained that the professors were too strict or not strict enough. It was not uncommon for the students who misbehaved to be whipped, "but only up to six lashes and without drawing blood."[39] The municipal officials of Xochimilco requested that the teacher assigned to their school be

> a person who, in addition to being perfectly trained in the ministries of the faith which he must teach, ha[s] the ability to translate them from the Castilian language to the Mexican. This is almost the principal quality that should be sought in a teacher who must cultivate the little ones in this parish, in addition to possessing *paternal love* so that in a way he can caress them and not cow or intimidate them.[40]

This idea was similar to that contained in the rules for the College for Indian Girls supported by the Jesuits, which stated that the lay Indian women who were the teachers should "educate them more by <u>love</u> than by fear." The parents of the Indian children in Coyoacán praised Don Joaquín Antonio Sumalla: "For more than thirty years, with only the scant stipend with which we have contributed, he has <u>lovingly</u> taught our children and maintained them in the greatest tranquility and peace." In Chiapas, one teacher treated "the little Indians with <u>paternal tenderness</u>, giving them example of virtue by his conduct," while the Spanish authority of the region recommended finding professors who would instruct "the little Indians with patience and *gentleness*."[41]

The author of the first recreational book for children in Mexico expressed this philosophy of education in the very title of the text, *Moral Fables for the Beneficial Amusement of the Children who are in the Primary Schools*, and addressed the boys to whom he told the stories as "persons who are for me very respectable." In the first poem he spoke with love and tenderness for the children of the Indian town where he was living. He announced to the "innocent children [that] in my little fables I give you my *love*," and added in the last line, "in these moral fables I dedicate my *affection* for you." His original fables included Indians and their practices as well as persons from other groups in the Mexican countryside.[42]

These sentiments toward children, present since Aztec times, indicate that some ideas concerning education and schooling were not taken from the Anglo-Saxon and Spanish models but emerged during the construction of a distinct culture, which in the colonial period was a melding of Indian and non-Indian customs. The statements by authors, parents, municipal officials, and teachers in New Spain indicate that "love" "affection," "tenderness," and "gentleness" were qualities that should be present in the ideal teacher, and probably even the Indian children of colonial Mexico themselves wanted that too.

NOTES

1. Although documents dating from Mexico's colonial period contain information about Indian children, it is from the point of view of the teachers, parents, priests, and authorities. Very rarely do individual children with their names appear. "Until now we have not discovered signatures, letters, or quotes from Indian students. Rarely are their voices or notice of their presence perceived, and always through the writings of adults." Dorothy Tanck de Estrada, *Pueblos de indios y educación en el México colonial, 1750–1821* (México: El Colegio de México, 2nd ed., 2000), footnote 137, 394–95. This creates a difficulty in reconstructing children's lives. An attempt has been made to do this in my article "Muerte precoz. Los niños en el siglo XVIII," in *Historia de la vida cotidiana en México. El siglo XVIII: entre tradición y cambio,* coordinated by Pilar Gonzalbo Aizpuru (México: El Colegio de México/Fondo de Cultura Económica, 2005), vol. 3, 213–46, in which the lives and deaths of specific children are described.

Ariès, *Centuries of Childhood,* 9–10; Charles Gibson, *The Aztecs under Spanish Rule: A History of the Indians of the Valley of Mexico, 1519–1810* (Stanford, CA: Stanford University Press, 1964), 32–57; Tanck de Estrada, *Pueblos de indios y educación,* 49.

2. "Pueblos de Indios de Nueva España en 1800," in Dorothy Tanck de Estrada, *Atlas ilustrado de los pueblos de indios: Nueva España, 1800* (México: El Colegio de México/Comisión Nacional para el Desarrollo de los Pueblos Indígenas, 2005).

3. H. B. Nicholson, "Sahagún, Bernardino," *The Oxford Encyclopedia of Mesoamerican Culture: The Civilizations of Mexico and Central America,* ed. David Carrasco (New York: Oxford University Press, 2001), vol. 3, 111; Miguel León-Por-

tilla, *Bernardino de Sahagún. Pionero de la antropologí* (Mexico: Universidad Nacional Autónoma de México, 1999), 39–42, 169–83, 205–12.

4. Frances F. Berdan, *The Aztecs of Central Mexico: An Imperial Society* (New York: Holt, Rinehart and Winston, 1982), 81–83.

5. León-Portilla, *The Aztec Image of Self and Society*, 190–91.

6. Alfredo López Austin, *La educación de los antiguos nahuas* (Mexico: Secretaria de Educación Pública, 1985), vol. 1, 99–107.

7. Ibid.; Friar Ilarione da Bergamo, *Daily Life in Colonial Mexico: The Journey of Friar Ilarione da Bergamo, 1761–1768*, ed. Robert Ryal Miller and William J. Orr (Norman: University of Oklahoma Press, 2000), 125–26; *Historia documental de México* (Mexico: Universidad Nac........ 'utónoma de México, 1974), vol. 1, 67; Pablo Escalante, "Sentarse, guardar la compostura y llorar entre los antiguos nahuas (el cuerpo y el proceso de civilización)," *Familia y vida privada en la historia de Iberoamérica* (Mexico: El Colegio de México, 1996), 443–58.

8. Berdan, *The Aztecs of Central Mexico*, 88–90, 155. López Austin, *La educación de los antiguos nahuas*, vol. 1, 54. Francisco Javier Clavijero, *Historia antigua de México* (Mexico: Editorial Porrúa, S.A., 1991), 201.

9. López Austin, *La educación de los antiguos nahuas*, vol. 1, 85, 90–91.

10. Berdan, *The Aztecs of Central Mexico*, 87; Ignacio Bernal, "The Pre-Columbian Era," *A Compact History of Mexico*, 6th ed. (Mexico: El Colegio de México, 2004), 39; Patricia Rieff Anawalt, "Dress, Costume, and Adornment," *The Oxford Encyclopedia of Mesoamerican Cultures*, vol. 1, 343.

11. López Austin, *La educación de los antiguos nahuas*, vol. 1, 73.

12. John McAndrew, *The Open-Air Churches of Sixteenth-Century Mexico: Atrios, Posa, Open Chapels, and Other Studies* (Cambridge, MA: Harvard University Press, 1965), 31–32; John Leddy Phelan, *The Millennial Kingdom of the Franciscans in the New World*, 2nd ed. (Berkeley: University of California Press, 1970), 32, 44–46, 59–77.

13. McAndrew, *The Open-Air Churches of Sixteenth-Century Mexico*, 14–16. Thomas M. Whitmore, *Disease and Death in Early Colonial Mexico* (Boulder, CO: Westview Press, 1992), 206, 213.

14. Ibid., 70, 74–76; Pilar Gonzalbo Aizpuru, *Historia de la educación en la época colonial: El mundo indígena*, 2nd ed. (Mexico: El Colegio de México, 2000), 227–28.

15. Ibid., 33–34.

16. McAndrew, *The Open-Air Churches of Sixteenth-Century Mexico*, 51, 75, 280.

17. Ibid., 77; Gonzalbo Aizpuru, *Historia de la educación en la época colonial*, 37, 223.

18. *Historia documental de México*, vol. 1, 147–51.

19. Gonzalbo Aizpuru, *Historia de la educación en la época colonial*, 117–20, 126.

20. Michael W. Flinn, *The European Demographic System, 1500–1820* (Baltimore, MD: John Hopkins University Press, 1981), 14–17.

21. Statistics of the number of Indian tributaries from 1790 to 1802, Archivo General de la Nación, *Propios y Arbitrios*, vols. 25 and 35; Doris M. Ladd, *The Mexican Nobility at Independence, 1780–1826* (Austin: University of Texas Press, 1976), 187–228.

22. Gutierre Aceves, "Imágenes de la inocencia eterna," in *El arte ritual de la muerte niña* (Mexico: Artes de México, 1998), 27–50; Luisa Zahino Peñafort, ed., *El Cardenal Lorenzana y el IV Concilio Provincial Mexicana* (Mexico: Miguel Ángel Porrúa, 1999), 216, 864.

23. Juan Javier Pescador, *De bautizados a fieles difuntos; familias y mentalidades en una parroquia urbana: Santa Catarina de México, 1568–1820* (Mexico: El Colegio de México, 1992), 85–186; Marta G. Vera Bolaños, *La población de Ozumba en 1793: Un estudio de demografía histórica* (Zinacantepec, Mexico: El Colegio Mexiquense, 1993), 31, 49, 51; Cecilia Rabell, "Trayectoria de vida familiar, raza y género en Oaxaca colonial," in Pilar Gonzalbo Aizpuru and Cecilia Rabell, eds., *Familia y vida privada en la historia de Iberoamérica* (Mexico: El Colegio de México/Universidad Nacional Autónoma de México, 1996), 101.

24. Ilarione da Bergano, *Daily Life in Colonial Mexico*, 125–26; Rebeca Horn, "Nahua Naming Patterns in Postconquest Central Mexico," in Susan Schroeder, Stephanie Wood, and Robert Haskett, eds., *Indian Women of Early Mexico* (Norman: University of Oklahoma Press, 1997), 108–11, 363; Kevin Terraciano, *The Mixtecs of Colonial Oaxaca: Ñudzahui History, Sixteenth through Eighteenth Centuries* (Stanford, CA: Stanford University Press, 2001), 150–57; Archivo General de la Nación, *Historia*, vol. 495, ff. 238–40.

25. Fray Matías de Escobar, *Americana Thebaida (1729)* (Morelia, Mexico: Balsa Editores, 1970), 83–84, 89–90, 397.

26. Tanck de Estrada, *Pueblos de indios y educación en el México colonial*, 301–7; James Lockhart, *The Nahuas after the Conquest: A Social and Cultural History of the Indians of Central Mexico, Sixteenth through Eighteenth Centuries* (Stanford, CA: Stanford University Press, 1992), 217; Jaime Cuadriello, "Tierra de prodigios: la ventura como destino," *Los pinceles de la historia: El origen del Reino de la Nueva España, 1680–1750* (Mexico: Museo Nacional de Arte, 1999), 216–17.

27. Ilarione da Bergano, *Daily Life in Colonial Mexico*, 142–43.

28. Dorothy Tanck de Estrada, "Ilustración, educación e identidad nacionalista en el siglo XVIII," in *Gran historia de México ilustrada*, vol. 3 (Mexico: Planeta/CONACULTA/INAH, 2001), 28–31.

29. Tanck de Estrada, *Pueblos de indios y educación*, 156–57, 414; Dorothy Tanck de Estrada, *La educación ilustrada, 1786–1836. Educación primaria en la ciudad de México*, 6th ed. (Mexico: El Colegio de México, 2005), 173–74.

30. Tanck de Estrada, *Pueblos de indios*, 160–64; Gonzalbo Aizpuru, *Historia de la educación en la época colonial*, 167–73.

31. Tanck de Estrada, *Pueblos de indios*, 285–86.

32. Ibid., 157, 160–64, 414; Archivo General de la Nación, *Hospital de Jesús,* reports of priests on the schools in Indian towns in Cuernavaca, Oaxaca, and Coyoacán, vol. 110, files number 8, 10, 12; schools in Toluca, vol. 309, file 6.

33. "Constituciones del Real Colegio de Indias de Nuestra Señora de Guadalupe de México," National Library, Madrid, manuscript number 13919; Joh Leddy Phelan, *The Millennial Kingdom of the Franciscans in the New World: A Study of the Writings of Gerónimo de Mendieta (1525–1604)* (Berkeley: University of California Press, 1956), 61.

34. Gonzalbo Aizpuru, *Historia de la educación en la época colonial,* 150; Manuel Esparza, ed., *Relaciones geográficas de Oaxaca, 1777–1779* (Mexico: CIESAS/Gobierno de Oaxaca, 1994), esp. 275–432.

35. *Alphabet and Silabario,* Broadside, ca. 1818; Thompson, "Children in Family and Society," 174; Peñafort, *El Cardenal,* 862.

36. Tanck de Estrada, *Pueblos de indios,* 394–400, 406–7, 412.

37. Dorothy Tanck de Estrada, "La enseñanza de la lectura y de la escritura en la Nueva España, 1700–1821," *Historia de la lectura en México,* 4th ed. (Mexico: El Colegio de México, 2000), 50–52, 68, 71, 83.

38. Antonio de Paredes, *Carta edificante en que el P. Antonio de Paredes de la extinguida Compañía de Jesús, refiere a la vida exemplar de la hermana Salvadora de los Santos, india otomí* (Mexico: Felipe de Zúñiga y Ontiveros, 1784), prologue.

39. Archivo General de la Nación, *Hospital de Jesús,* vol. 110, file 10, f. 7; Archivo General de la Nación, *Historia,* vol. 496, f. 216r.

40. Tanck de Estrada, *Pueblos de indios y educación,* 391.

41. "Constituciones del Real Colegio de Indias de Nuestra Señora de Guadalupe"; Archivo General de la Nación, *Hospital de Jesús,* vol. 110, file 7, emphasis mine; Latin American Library, Tulane University, *Chiapas,* box 2, folder 1, 29–30, emphasis mine.

42. Dorothy Tanck de Estrada and Rebeca Cerda, eds., *Fábulas morales de José Ignacio Basurto, 1802* (México: Editorial Sestante, S.A. de C.V.), 2004, prologue and 13–14, emphasis mine.

Chapter 2

Colonizing Childhood
Religion, Gender, and Indian Children in Southern New England, 1620–1720

R. Todd Romero

While historians have often treated childhood as a marginal topic, Indian children in southern New England were historically important on a number of counts. Indian children were often at the center of ongoing efforts by Native communities to persist as they adapted long-standing social, cultural, and religious practices to the tough realities that arrived with European colonization. Children were also often a focus of colonialism in the region. English colonists—who were frequently obsessed with the fortunes of their own "rising generation"—focused a good deal of their energy on Indian children. Colonial officials saw Indian children as key to the success of missionary efforts. They similarly viewed indentured servitude as a means of civilizing native children, while having the added benefit of providing Anglo-Americans with another source of child labor in a region that often turned to sons and daughters to work in a variety of occupations. As recent scholarship suggests, Anglo-Americans spent a great deal of energy trying to colonize Indian families by regulating marriage practices. Marriage and family were not marginal concerns and instead lay at the heart of colonialism.[1] What we know less about, however, are the contours and experience of Indian childhood in a rapidly changing colonial world where children were important, if often silent, historical actors. Focusing on childhood illuminates the role of religion and gender in the experience of Native American childhood in the region, while also illuminating the centrality of children to cultural persistence and adaptation for both traditionalist and Christian Indian communities.

While the arrival of Europeans sometimes wrought catastrophic changes in Indian country, religion nevertheless remained essential to the experience of childhood for both traditionalist and Christian Natives alike, offering an especially important means of adapting to life in a colonial society. As we will see, oral traditions that circulated throughout the region gave supernatural meaning to social values and gender ideals, while religious practices illustrated the importance of contacting and drawing on spiritual power as a means of defining childhood and the transition to adulthood. In a reflection of the importance of religious practice to the major transitions in an individual's life, Indian parents and kin actively assisted children in cultivating relationships with a range of powerful supernatural entities. With these concerns in mind, I will first address coming of age in traditionalist communities that eschewed Anglo-American missionary efforts before turning to consider indentured servitude's impact on Indian childhood and children's experience in communities that adapted Christianity to Native American understandings of religion.

1

Age was important in Native communities. Indian children accorded respect to elders in numerous ways that reflected deep-seated social values and suggested the importance of age as a marker of status. Given the importance of age, it should not be surprising that childhood was indicated symbolically in numerous ways. Clothing and hairstyle, for example, served to denote sexual maturity, virginity, gender, age, spiritual associations, and tribal affiliation. The organization of space was also shaped by both gender and age. For instance, menstrual wigwams were reserved for women rather than girls, and all-male speaking sessions after some feasts were reserved for men rather than boys. Names served as another index of one's success at becoming an adult. Edward Winslow reported that among the Wampanoags "names are significant and variable for when they come to the state of men and women, they alter them to their deeds and dispositions." Another account explained that a child's name typically came from "the appearances of providences," suggesting that names also evoked religious associations.[2]

Religion was essential to the formation of gender identities and the experience of childhood. For instance, Roger Williams explained how individual skill was understood religiously, claiming that among the Narragansetts "Excellency in Men, Women, Birds, Beasts, &c." were all a reflection of spiritual power. Excellence in a range of everyday activities thus reflected an individual's connection to a religious world that was constantly present. As girls and boys came of age, all of these symbols and associations changed, thus marking a child's physical and spiritual progress towards adulthood and the assumption of adult gender identities.[3] This process was not passive, however. With assistance and encouragement from kin, children actively sought to cultivate relations with supernatural entities to increase their spiritual power, perhaps earning new names and the right to wear adornment and use spaces most often reserved for adult women and men. In all of these ways, childhood was more than just a biological reality. Instead, it was socially and culturally constructed, something that was just as surely framed by individual accomplishments and religious practice as it was reflected in material culture and the organization of space.

Given the fragmentary nature of the sources it is sometimes difficult to discern religious differences among Indian peoples in the region. As we will see below, different peoples sometimes employed different names for seemingly analogous spiritual entities and no doubt possessed a range of distinct practices that were not recorded by colonists, who tended to take an extremely negative view of Native American religion. Nevertheless, Indians in the region engaged in similar rituals and shared a respect for the potential of supernatural power to define individual identity just as surely as it filled the natural world and even the most mundane events with spiritual meaning. In this way, it is possible to discuss the relationship between religion and childhood, while remaining mindful of differences among the region's diverse Algonquian-speaking peoples.

In Indian communities, a rich religious world overflowed with supernatural meaning and was charged with spiritual power. From an early age, children would have been aware that this enchanted world was populated with numerous powerful other-than-human beings that assumed multiple forms and were deeply implicated in the intricacies of everyday life. Wampanoag children, for example, were regaled with numerous stories of the supernatural giants Maushop and Squant. Along with their children, this husband and wife duo was credited with many supernatural feats, such as creating Nantucket from "snuff out of [Maushop's] pipe." Before Maushop smoked it down to snuff, the tobacco in question had originally come from an offering by the Indians who shared the island with the giants. Maushop also put a high value on reciprocity and hospitality in other ways, sharing food with his neighbors. While illustrating the efficacy of spiritual power, such traditions also reinforced social values and gender ideals.[4]

A range of spiritual entities like Keihtan and Hobbomock—to cite Wampanoag examples who were analogous to powerful spiritual entities sought out by other Indians in the region—were similarly capable of supernatural feats and remained extremely important to determining an individual's identity and status in society. While Indians generally sought to cultivate relationships with a powerful deity like Hobbomock, the existence of entities like Squáuanit—"the Woman's God"—and Muckquachuckquànd—"the Children's God"—among the Narragansetts suggested the degree to which the enchanted world mediated the passage from childhood to adulthood and filled gender identities with spiritual meaning.[5]

Reminders of the connections between everyday activities and the enchanted world were constant. For instance, Narragansett children working in the corn and bean fields with their mothers might reflect on the deity Cautantowwit's gift of corn, which gave women's agricultural labor spiritual meaning that would have especially stuck with girls as they watched the women of their village work with great skill. These connections would have probably passed through a Narragansett boy's mind if he stopped short of letting an arrow fly at a crow while he perfected hunting skills that would be key in defining his identity as a man. He would no doubt remember being warned about the potential danger involved in killing the birds. It was Cautantowwit, after all, who appeared as a crow flying from his home in the southwest bearing corn and beans for the Narragansetts to cultivate. If an individual enjoyed a good life then his or her soul might return along the crow's ancient path back to Cautantowwit's domain. By contrast, the souls of malevolent people were left to wander. For obvious reasons, very few people wanted to kill a crow, which might not be simply a crow.[6]

Recognizing the power and importance of the spiritual in the quotidian, both traditionalist and Christian Indian families spent tremendous energy religiously instructing their children. Edward Winslow, for example, related long-standing Wampanoag beliefs about Keihtan, who like the Narragansett Cautantowwit was responsible for creation and was especially important to traditional religious life. Winslow reported that "old men tell them of him, and bid them tell their children, yea, to charge them to teach their posterities the same, and lay the like charge upon them."

Traditions of Keihtan's origins and kin's special attention in assisting children to cultivate relations with a range of supernatural entities like the especially powerful Hobbomock reflected this call to instruct children religiously. The missionary Matthew Mayhew, for example, remarked that on Aquinnah, which was later renamed Martha's Vineyard by the English, "[Indian] parents often out of certain Zeal dedicated their Children to the gods, and educated them accordingly, observing certain Diet, debarring Sleep & c. yet of the many thus designed, but few obtained their desire."[7] While we have more detailed accounts of rituals tied to the passage from boyhood to manhood, Mayhew's observation is important because he indicates that childhood religious instruction was equally important for girls and boys. His account also suggests that not all children were able to successfully cultivate relationships with supernatural entities. Given the importance of these rituals in becoming a woman or man, the seriousness with which parents approached religious instruction was a pragmatic consideration. Such rituals may have become more important in the seventeenth century, offering a powerful tonic against the difficult changes wrought by colonization. Religious practice thus offered an important avenue to adulthood, while also reinforcing an important cultural bulwark against colonization. In this way, the passage from childhood to adulthood was as much about coming of age as it was bound up with the social and cultural renewal of the community.

Children probably approached such ritualized occasions with an understandable mix of trepidation and excitement. For boys, vision quest rituals followed the same general pattern suggested by Mayhew. Particularly vigorous Wampanoag boys, for instance, were singled out for rituals that tested their potential to become *pnieses,* a special group of fearsome warriors and advisors to Indian leaders that embodied masculine ideals and mustered tremendous spiritual power. *Pniese* initiates endured physical trials, underwent sleep deprivation, and ingested special herbs, all of which aimed at contacting Hobbomock. In some ways, these rituals were an extension of early physical training that girls and boys underwent as a means of preparing them for the rigors of everyday life. Physical accomplishment, however, was especially important for boys who endeavored to reach the masculine ideals embodied by successful hunters and warriors. Similar rituals were involved in identifying religious specialists called *powwows.* One of the main objects of these rituals, Hobbomock was an especially potent source of spiritual power who appeared in a number of forms but most frequently as a snake. For this reason, an individual's connection to Hobbomock was often integrated into adornment and material culture, reflecting the potential ability to draw on supernatural power. Spiritually potent warriors might carry a snakelike anthropomorphic war club, while women who enjoyed an association with Hobbomock sometimes ground corn with effigy pestles evocative of the deity.[8] Children were thus surrounded by symbols that were constant reminders that the world was full of supernatural meaning and power, all of which was of signal importance in successfully becoming an adult.

The evidence on the ritualized passage from girlhood to womanhood in southern New England remains scant in comparison to the sources on boys. Like the boyhood vision quest, a girl's first admission into the *Wetuomémese* —a wigwam reserved for women's menstrual seclusion—may have marked her emergence as a woman in a distinctly religious fashion. While scholars have suggested this parallel and argued that women's seclusion was symbolic of female spiritual power, we do not have much evidence of any rituals associated with this important transition. In the absence of such accounts, the practices of other Algonquian-speaking Eastern Woodland Indian cultures remain suggestive. Among Illinois Indians in the seventeenth century, for example, girls were secluded during their first menses. Like Wampanoag boys on vision quests, Illinois girls abstained from food and sought to contact a spiritual entity like Hobbomock. The French trader and official Pierre de Liette observed that if a girl was successful in her quest, as a woman she would be "everlastingly fortunate and achieve the gift of great power for the future." Like Mathew Mayhew's observation of Aquinnah Wampanoags, Liette also noted that cultivating relationships with supernatural entities was not an easy feat. Some would fail in the effort, and thus much was at stake in such ritual passages. In Micmac country, north of New England in what are now the Canadian Maritime provinces and the Gaspé Peninsula, menstruating women were also secluded. According to the French Recollect missionary Chrestien Le Clercq, girls menstruating for the first time were forbidden certain foods and had to use separate cooking vessels. The surgeon Seieur de Dièreville added that contact with menstruating women was considered extremely detrimental to males, causing paralysis and "bewitch[ing]" muskets so that they were useless for hunting or battle.[9] Menstruating women were spiritually powerful and potentially threatening to Micmac men because they could unmake a man, leaving his body useless and causing a form of martial impotence. If his musket failed, what Micmac man could fulfill the masculine ideals embodied by successful hunters and warriors?

While we lack specific evidence for southern New England, together these examples suggest the possible significance of first menses for Indian girls coming of age. The *Wetuomémese* was thus a likely site for girls to cultivate relations within a powerful spiritual world, while remaining secluded from their relatives during this moment of heightened supernatural power. While admittedly speculative, these conclusions are reasonable given evidence that both childhood and womanhood were associated with special spiritual entities, indicating that certain stages of life and gender identities were shaped by religious practice. Spiritual symbols associated with women are similarly suggestive. That women sometimes used material objects that announced an association to Hobbomock was also indicative of their success in encountering the elusive but especially powerful entity.

2

The advent of European colonialism changed the experience of girlhood and boyhood in new ways, as Indian communities sometimes adopted Christianity, became enmeshed in the colonial economy, and suffered the impact of war over the course of a frequently violent period. Religion nevertheless remained central to the experience of childhood and the formation of gender identities for both traditionalist and Christian Indians. The way in which religion shaped childhood subtly changed, however, as novelties like Christian devotions and indentured servitude increasingly influenced Indian childhood.

At the missionary program's height in the years before King Philip's War (1675–76), numerous praying towns, as the missionary villages were known by the late 1640s, could be found in Martha's Vineyard, Nantucket, Massachusetts, and Cape Cod. An estimate by Daniel K. Richter suggests that overall around twenty-three hundred of the twenty thousand Natives in southern New England were living in praying towns on the eve of the war. Christian communities were concentrated in the most heavily colonized areas. Perhaps a quarter of the Indian population in eastern Massachusetts and Plymouth resided in Christian communities, for example. While the mission would continue in all of these areas, King Philip's War had a profound effect on Indian life, especially on the mainland. In Massachusetts Bay Colony, for example, the fourteen prewar praying towns were consolidated into four after the war.[10]

Indians living in praying towns adapted the new religion to traditional understandings of ritual and cosmology, making Christianity Indian at the same time that missionaries endeavored to civilize and christianize the Native neophytes according to European values. Endeavoring to transform traditional Indian lifeways, missionaries put special energy into evangelizing children. The Massachusetts Bay Colony missionary John Eliot, for example, made Indian children a focus of his efforts, putting special effort into catechizing children while also using gifts of apples and biscuits to excite and prepare potential young converts. His missionary colleague Daniel Gookin reported that "by [Eliot's] prudence and winning practice, the children were induced with delight, to get into their memories the principles of the christian religion." Together with efforts to undermine native political and religious leaders, Eliot's approach to Indian children reflected a larger effort to transform Indian society. In this way, the missionary program followed familiar Puritan logic and assumed, as the seventeenth-century commonplace went, that Indians needed to be civilized before they could become Christian. Indian children living in praying towns were often the focal point of cultural transformation, as they were key elements of the mission's future.[11]

Missionaries saw servitude as a means to the same ends. For example, Gookin also suggested that Indian children might be "procured" with "the free consent of their parents and relations" and then "placed in sober and christian families, as apprentices," to prepare boys for a trade and girls for "good house wifery of all sorts." He thus imagined moving boys from traditionally mobile—and, according to Anglo-American standards, inappropriate—occupations like hunting and fishing, and instead binding them to a master and trade. At the same time, girls ideally would be removed from the largely female world of the village and especially women's vital role as the primary agriculturalists in Native society, an occupation that was an important source of female power. For colonists, agriculture was key to property holding, civilization, and independence, all of which lay at the heart of English masculine ideals on both sides of the Atlantic. Gookin's plan thus shared some common missionary goals: transforming Native gender practices and work regimes as a means to civilization and Christianization. After noting that the scarcity of servants made his plan more than amenable to the demands of the colonial economy, Gookin observed that it would be difficult to persuade Indian parents of the essential genius of binding their children to strangers, "for [Indians] are generally so indulgent to their children, that they are not easily persuaded to put them forth to the English."[12] Servitude nevertheless became a part of colonial life for many Indian children early in English settlement.

The first account of missionary efforts in New England, for example, reported that by the 1640s, "Divers of the *Indians* Children *Boyes* and *Girles* we have received into our houses, who are long since civilized and in subjection to us, painfull and handy in their buisnesse," and conversant in English. While the authors may well have overstated Indian acculturation in an effort to trumpet missionary efforts, by the end of the decade John Eliot reported that "young men" were entering into servitude in growing numbers and increasingly found themselves in English courts when they broke their contracts. As colonization further developed, Christian persuasion failed where the colonial economy was succeeding and growing numbers of Indians, especially women and children, became servants. Where Indian parents who favored Christianity sometimes offered to have their children "trained up" among the English in the middle of the seventeenth century, by the early eighteenth century the missionary Experience Mayhew could not find an audience in Narragansett and Niantic country because local Indians "were many indebted to their English, & lived much among them," neither caring for the counsel of their *sachem* Ninnicraft nor willing to listen to the missionary's sermon and promise of Christianity's many gifts. A keen observer of colonial life, Ninnicraft suggested that Mayhew's efforts might be better spent elsewhere. The *sachem* offered that perhaps the missionary should "make the English good in the first place," pointing out religious differences among Rhode Island's English Christians and declaring that praying Indians from Martha's Vineyard were most noteworthy as thieves. Like Ninnicraft's people, both Christian and traditionalist Indian children were increasingly swept into the colonial economy as servants to English families that did not necessarily view pedagogy and religion as imperative in running their household economies. The massive growth of Indian servitude in the decades after King Philip's War (1675–76), has led David Silverman to conclude that "[i]ndentured service . . . was one of the most significant legacies of the English colonization of southern New England's Indians."[13]

For Christian Indian children facing these realities, the old and new remained in counterpoint. In this way, children were at the forefront of cultural change as they adapted long-standing traditions to life in a colonial society. Just as English observers had noted of traditionalist Indians,

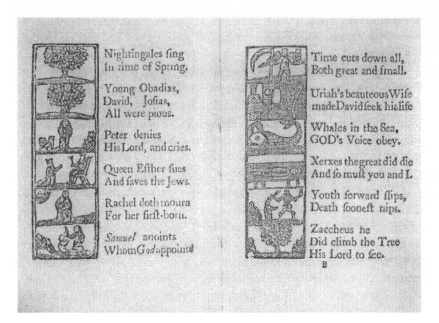

Pages from the *New-England Primer.*

Christian parents expended tremendous energy cultivating their children's religious lives as a means of defining their future identities as women and men. In a continuation of a long-standing conviction regarding the importance of religious practice, in the earliest days of the missionary program in 1647 John Eliot noted that praying Indians in Massachusetts Bay Colony were "carefull to instruct their children" and prepare them for catechism. A similar dynamic was well established on Aquinnah. By the early eighteenth century Experience Mayhew reported that on the island "it has been a Custom amongst our [Christian] *Indians* to teach their Children Forms of Prayers," to a such a degree "that young People among the *Indians* have thought it no Presumption to call upon God for his Mercy, when their Parents have been by, and heard them." While it is hard to know how the practice of prayer was understood by the pious, it most certainly echoed older ways of calling upon spiritual entities. Earlier observers like Roger Williams noted the intensity of traditionalist Indian religious devotions, especially prayer directed at spiritual entities and in community rituals.[14] While the language of salvation may have in some ways complemented or even supplanted a world full of numerous spiritual entities and manifestations, Indian Christians still lived within an enchanted world charged with supernatural meaning.

Religion remained central to defining gender identities and the passage to adulthood in praying towns. As she lay on her deathbed in 1723, the eleven-year-old Hannah Soopasun had an encounter with the divine that recalled traditionalist visions of Hobbomock and other spiritual entities. After requesting that her "Father . . . commit her to God by Prayer . . . she did her self call upon him," and then Soopasun reported seeing "a shining Person clothed in White, standing at the Foot of her Bed." While no doubt intent on addressing the state of her soul and facing the prospect of death, the young Deborah Sissetom also approached prayer in a manner reminiscent of older religious practices used by *powwows* that focused on mustering spiritual power to cure illness. "She said she used to pray in secret to God before she was sick," Mayhew explained, "but she had especially since her sickness prayed earnestly to him." Ultimately, any of her prayers for a return to good health went unanswered, and she died in 1724 at age fifteen. Girls like Soopasun and Sissetom could also look to the examples of especially pious and spiritually powerful women on Aquinnah. At the turn of the century, Hannah Ahhunnut was viewed in her community "as a Woman of Prayer, and one who had an Interest in Heaven, Persons of her own Sex, used to desire her to pray with them and for them" when they were sick. Perhaps revealing his anxiety over women's authority in praying town life, Mayhew added that Ahhunnut only engaged in this religious office if "there were no Men for whom it might be more proper to perform that Office." He nevertheless went on to explain that Ahhunnut "used to perform the same [religious] Duty at Womens Travails also . . . and it has been reported, that she had sometimes very remarkable Answers."[15] While Hannah Ahhunnut may no longer have prayed to the women's god like her traditionalist neighbors, she nevertheless drew on tremendous spiritual power—reflecting her special "Interest in Heaven"—that was respected and sought by other women and, one suspects, both encouraged and a bit feared by the missionary who reported her religious authority with equal parts pride and concern for gendered propriety. Girls coming of age would have no doubt aspired to such examples of religious and moral authority, as prayer and spiritual power gave meaning to womanhood just as surely in Christian communities as it had in traditional villages.

As was the case for girls coming of age in praying towns, the novelties of Christianity blended with a long-standing religious grammar that filled the passage from boyhood to manhood with spiritual meaning. Eleazor

Ohhumuh well illustrated the importance of prayer to Christian Indian youths. Looking back at the teenager's childhood in the late seventeenth century, Ohhumuh's mother reported to Mayhew that "he used frequently of his own accord to pray to God while he was very young, and used also to tell others that they ought to do so." Still a great practitioner of prayer as an adult, Ohhumuh became concerned that "it would not be decent for him to pray vocally where others were present," and he "used to frequently to withdraw himself into obscure Places, whither it was supposed he went to pray in secret to God, being there sometimes found kneeling down, or lying prostrate on the Ground, or otherwise leaning against some Trees, as tho he was praying." Although Abel Wauwampuhque would eventually emerge as a deacon and preacher on the island in the early eighteenth century, Mayhew reported that as a teenager he, "while yet in a State of Nature, inclined to the same youthful Vanities unconverted young Men generally are, and would sometimes drink to Excess; but when it pleased God to work a saving Change in his Heart, there followed there on an evident Change in his Life, he then departed from his sin" and became a Christian man. For the young William Tuphaus, who also came of age in the late seventeenth century, prayer helped define the transition from boyhood to manhood:

> After this Youth had thus prayed, he appeared yet more grave and serious than he had formerly done. He did not any longer carry himself like a young Boy; but rather like some Man of Years, who had his Heart seasoned with the Grace of God: he kept at home and took care of the Affairs of the House when his Father was gone abroad to work, and was as dutiful to his Parents as any Child could be.

The transformative power of religious practice may well have been even more striking to family and friends because it occurred while Tuphaus, at age twelve, was relatively young.[16]

While missionaries like Experience Mayhew expended a great deal of energy stressing how Indian children successfully emulated the genius of English civilization and religion, the accounts of Deborah Sissetom, Hannah Soopasun, Abel Wauwampuhque, and William Tuphaus reveal a very different reality. Like generations of Indian children in the region, they were socialized into gender roles and grew to adulthood through religious practices that drew on diverse sources of spiritual power. That power might be revealed in a white form that arrived as a Christian girl lay praying on her deathbed or as the snakelike form of Hobbomock during a traditionalist boy's vision quest. Whether they came of age in Christian or traditionalist communities, Indians in the region turned to religious practice not only to give supernatural meaning to the passage from childhood to adulthood but also as a familiar source for community renewal and a means of adaptation in a colonial world.

NOTES

1. Philip Greven, *Four Generations: Population, Land, and Family in Colonial Andover, Massachusetts* (Ithaca, NY: Cornell University Press, 1970), 72–99; Glenn Wallach, *Obedient Sons: The Discourse of Youth and Generations in American Culture, 1630–1860* (Amherst: University of Massachusetts Press, 1997), 10–32; Daniel Vickers, *Farmers and Fishermen: Two Centuries of Work in Essex County, Massachusetts, 1630–1830* (Chapel Hill: University of North Carolina Press, 1994), 64–77, 173–75, 323–24; David J. Silverman, "The Impact of Indentured Servitude on the Society and Culture of Southern New England Indians, 1680–1810," *New England Quarterly* 74.4 (2001): 622–66; Ruth Wallis Herndon and Ella Wilcox Sekatau, "Colonizing the Children: Indian Youngsters in Servitude in Early Rhode Island," in *Reinterpreting New England Indians and the Colonial Experience*, ed. Colin G. Calloway and Neal Salisbury (Boston: Colonial Society of Massachusetts, 2003), 137–76; Ann Marie Plane, *Colonial Intimacies: Indian Marriage in Early New England* (Ithaca, NY: Cornell University Press, 2000), 6–13.

2. Edward Winslow, *Good Newes from New England* (London: I. D. for William Bladen and John Bellamie, 1634), 58–59, *Early English Books Online* [hereafter, *EEBO*]; Thomas Morton, *New English Canaan or New Canaan* (1637), ed. Jack Dempsey (Scituate, MA: Digital Scanning, 2000), 28; William Wood, *New England's Prospect* (1634), ed. Alden T. Vaughan (Amherst: University of Massachusetts Press, 1977, reprint, Amherst: University of Massachusetts Press, 1993), 83; Thomas Lechford, *Plain Dealing; or, News from New England* (1642), ed. J. Hammond Trumbull (Boston: J. K. Wiggin and W. M. Parsons Lunt, 1867), 116; Thomas Shepard, *The Clear Sun-shine of the Gospel Breaking Forth upon the Indians in New-England* (London: Printed by R. Cotes for John Bellamy, 1648), 33; Roger Williams, *A Key into the Language of America* (London, 1643), ed. John J. Teunissen and Evelyn J. Hinz (Detroit, MI: Wayne State University, 1973), 96, 115–16, 184–87; John Gyles, "Memoirs of Odd Adventures, Strange Deliverances, Etc." (1736), in *Puritans among the Indians: Accounts of Captivity and Redemption, 1676–1724*, ed. Alden T. Vaughan and Edward W. Clark (Cambridge, MA: Harvard University Press, 1981, reprint, Cambridge, MA: Harvard University Press, 1995), 123.

3. Williams, *Key*, 191; R. Todd Romero, "'Ranging Foresters' and 'Women-Like-Men': Physical Accomplishment, Spiritual Power, and Indian Masculinity in Early Seventeenth-Century New England," *Ethnohistory* 53.2 (Summer 2006).

4. William Baylies, "Account of Gay Head," *Memoirs of the American Academy of Arts and Sciences* 2.1 (1793): 153–54; Benjamin Basset, "Fabulous Traditions and Customs of the Indians of Martha's Vineyard," *Collections of the Massachusetts Historical Society* 1 (1792): 139–40. For the fullest discussion of Maushop and Squant along with a collection of excerpted selections, including the accounts of Baylies and Basset, see William Simmons, *Spirit of the New England Tribes: Indian History and Folklore, 1620–1984* (Hanover, NH: University Press of New England, 1986), 172–234.

5. Williams, *Key*, 189–91; William Simmons, *Spirit of the New England Tribes*, 37–64; Constance Crosby, "From Myth to History; or, Why King Philip's Ghost Walks Abroad," in *The Recovery of Meaning: Historical Archeology in the Eastern United States*, ed. Mark P. Leone and Parker B. Patton, Jr. (Washington, DC: Smithsonian Institution Press, 1988), 183–209; David J. Silverman, "Indians, Missionaries, and Religious Translation: Creating Wampanoag Christianity in Seventeenth-Century Martha's Vineyard," *William and Mary Quarterly* (2005): 141–75; Romero, "'Ranging Foresters' and 'Women-Like-Men.'"

6. Along with the prohibition against killing crows, Roger Williams reported the tradition that explained the supernatural origins of corn and beans; see Williams, *Key*, 164.

7. Winslow, *Good Newes*, 53; Matthew Mayhew, *A Brief Narrative of the Success Which the Gospel hath had, among the Indians of Martha's-Vineyard* (Boston, 1694), 12, *EEBO*.

8. Winslow, *Good Newes*, 55–56; "Isaack De Rasieres to Samuel Bloomaert, c. 1628," in *Three Visitors to Early Plymouth*, ed. Sydney V. James, Jr. (Plymouth, MA: Plimoth Plantation, 1963, reprint, Bedford, MA: Applewood Books, 1997), 78–79. Samuel Lee reported similar rituals for prospective *powwows;* see "Rev. Samuel Lee to Nehemiah Grew, M.D., 1690," in *Letters of Samuel Lee and Samuel Sewall Relating to the New England and the Indians*, ed. George Lyman Kitteredge (Publications of the Colonial Society of Massachusetts, vol. 14, reprint, Cambridge, MA: John Wilson and Son, 1912), 151; Wood, *New England's Prospect*, 105–6; Williams, *Key*, 149, 164; Michael Nassaney, "Archaeology and Oral Tradition in Tandem: Interpreting Native American Ritual, Ideology, and Gender Relations in Contact-Period Southeastern New England," in *Interpretations of Native North American Life: Material Contributions to Ethnohistory*, ed. Michael S. Nassaney and Eric S. Johnson (Gainesville: University Press of Florida, 2000), 412–31; Michael S. Nassaney and Michael A. Volmar, "Lithic Artifacts in Seventeenth-Century Native New England," in *Stone Tool Traditions in the Contact Era*, ed. Charles R. Cobb (Tuscaloosa: University of Alabama Press, 2003), 78–93; Romero, "'Ranging Foresters' and 'Women-Like-Men.'"

9. The accounts of Pierre de Liette, Chrestien Le Clercq, and Seieur de Dière-ville are all excerpted in James Axtell, ed., *The Indian Peoples of Eastern America: A Documentary History of the Sexes* (New York: Oxford University Press, 1981), 57–58, 61, 62–63.

10. Daniel K. Richter, *Facing East from Indian Country: A Native History of Early America* (Cambridge, MA: Harvard University Press, 2001), 95–96.

11. Daniel Gookin, "The Historical Collections of the Indians in New England" (1674), *Massachusetts Historical Society Collections* 1.1 (1792): 168–99.

12. Gookin, "Historical Collections," 219; R. Todd Romero, *Making War and Minting Christians: Masculinity, Religion, and Colonialism in Early New England* (Amherst: University of Massachusetts Press, forthcoming).

13. [Anonymous], *New England's First Fruits* (London: Printed by R. O. and G. D. for Henry Overton, 1643), 3; Shepard, *The Clear Sun-shine of the Gospel*, 28; Experience Mayhew, "A Brief Journal of my visitation of the Pequot & Mohegin Indians . . . 1713," in John W. Ford, ed., *Some Correspondence between the Governors and Treasurers of the New England Company* (London: Spottiswoode & Co., 1896), 98; Plane, *Colonial Intimacies*, 99–105; Herndon and Sekatau, "Colonizing the Children," 137–76; Silverman, "The Impact of Indentured Servitude," 624 (the quoted passage), 622–66.

14. Shepard, *Clear Sun-shine*, 19; Experience Mayhew, *Indian Converts; or, Some Account of the Lives and Dying Speeches of a Considerable Number of the Christian Indians of Martha's Vineyard in New-England* (London, 1727), 176; Williams, *Key*, 107, 189–94, 222.

15. Mayhew, *Indian Converts*, 141.

16. Ibid., 67, 224–25, 229.

Chapter 3

Imperial Ideas, Colonial Realities
Enslaved Children in Jamaica, 1775–1834

Audra Abbe Diptee

Introduction

Although it is popularly conceived that African children were rarely transported across the Atlantic in the slave trade, there is now evidence to
demonstrate the contrary. The demographic studies of slave trade specialists have made it clear that children did, in fact, account for a significant
proportion of the slave population that was transported across the
Atlantic in the late eighteenth century. This is particularly evident when
one contextualizes the demographic patterns of the slave trade in an
Atlantic framework. When the slave trade is compared to other transatlantic migration flows, it is clear that "a higher proportion of children left
Africa than left Europe."[1]

Jamaica was by far the largest importer of enslaved Africans in British
America during the eighteenth century. As a result, the island imported
significant numbers of enslaved African children. The three key areas
from which the enslaved arrived at the island between 1776 and 1800
were the Bight of Biafra, the Gold Coast, and West Central Africa. In the
Bight of Biafra and the Gold Coast, which were the most significant and
second most significant slave-trading regions for the British, children
accounted for 19 percent of all captives leaving each of these regions. In
West Central Africa, the third largest exporter to British colonies, children came in slightly lower proportions and accounted for 16 percent of
the slave trade. Moreover, although the Jamaican plantocracy continued
to rely heavily on slave imports to meet its labor needs during this

period, there was a growing creole (Jamaican-born) slave population that, by the end of the slave trade, accounted for 55 percent of the slave population.[2] Clearly, then, children were an important segment of Jamaican slave society.

The enslaved children of Jamaica, however, were part of a larger world of child laborers in the British socioeconomic system. Historically children have long been used as a productive source of labor in various parts of the world. Eighteenth- and nineteenth-century Britain was no exception. Moreover, there can be little doubt that British ideas about child labor influenced Jamaican colonial thinking about enslaved children on the island. Although Jamaican colonists developed a worldview that was distinctively local (or creole), they continued to be influenced by British ideology. British ideas imported into the island, however, would take new form in Jamaican slave society. In this new environment, British notions about child labor would operate in a highly racialized context. As a result, they would be transformed to support the social and economic priorities of Jamaican colonials—which were "the defense of slavery and white male solidarity."[3] In many ways, it was this racialization of British thinking that is often referred to as the Jamaican "creole" worldview.

Slavery specialists have been giving increasing attention to the historical experiences of enslaved children in the Americas. Most significant would be the pioneering work of Wilma King and the later published work of Marie Jenkins Schwartz—both of which focus on enslaved children born in the United States during the nineteenth century.[4] By giving attention to the experiences of enslaved children, works such as these have allowed for a more nuanced understanding of slavery. To date, there have been few historical works, however, that contextualize the historical experiences of enslaved children within the history of childhood and child labor.

Exploring the history of enslaved children from the perspective of Jamaican colonialism allows for such contextualization. Hence, this article will contextualize the history of the enslaved children of Jamaica in a framework that recognizes that they were part of a larger socioeconomic system that had a long history of using child labor in Britain. The use of child labor, however, was also prevalent in Africa. For this reason, enslaved African children brought to the island would also have their own notions of child labor, and even of childhood. As this paper will highlight, there were a number of competing notions about this issue circulating in Jamaica during the late eighteenth and early nineteenth centuries. A historical exploration that looks at the history of enslaved children in the colonial context, and a wider Atlantic framework, will better situate the history of enslaved children into the narrative of children's history.

British Ideas and the Colonial Reality

For British slave traders, the definition of a child among the recently enslaved was very much shaped by practical concerns. The enslaved children and adolescents brought from Africa were generally sold for less than adults. As a result, a standard method had to be developed in order to categorize adults, adolescents, and children. Jamaican merchants, of course, had no real means for determining the exact age of the enslaved they had available for sale. The impossibility of the task was summed up nicely in a House of Commons debate about implementing age restrictions to the slave trade, when one abolitionist frustratedly asked, "How was their age to be ascertained? What was the *baptismal register* on the Coast of Africa to which they were to go and look into for the ages of all these children?"[5]

In the absence of such documentation, British slave traders came up with their own way to determine which captives they would categorize as children. The most logical and practical gauge was height. As a result, enslaved Africans brought to Jamaica who were "below 4 feet 4 inches" were considered children and sold at a lower price. Historians estimate that Africans who were four feet four inches were approximately fourteen years old.[6]

But the fact that planters used height to determine which of the newly arrived Africans would be considered a child tells us little about how they perceived African children. Interestingly, although historians have traditionally argued that Jamaican planters had a clear preference for adult African males, there is some evidence to suggest that in the late eighteenth century, planters were increasingly willing to purchase young Africans of both sexes.[7] Simon Taylor, the wealthiest planter in Jamaica during the late eighteenth century, repeatedly expressed his interest in "young people chiefly boys and girls." In fact, Taylor as a general rule never bought enslaved persons estimated to be over the age of eighteen. The slaves he requested usually ranged between the ages of ten and sixteen. The Jamaican overseer and pen owner, Thomas Thistlewood, preferred to purchase "men-boys and girls, none exceeding 16 or 18 years old," as he believed that "full grown men or women seldom turn[ed] out well." Similarly, one absentee plantation owner advised his plantation manager that when he was purchasing new slaves he should prioritize the purchase of "young girls & wenches."[8]

Though some planters were specifically requesting young slaves, they were definitely wary of purchasing slaves they deemed to be too young. In fact, Jamaican planters generally believed that the ideal "age" of newly purchased captives should be young people who were *no less* than four feet four inches in height (i.e., approximately fourteen years or older). Merchants in Jamaica often complained that of the enslaved transported to the island "the grown people were too old and the young people too small." Despite this, however, young African children were available for sale on the island. In 1792, in a letter reporting the sale of the slave cargo on the ship *Ruby*, the Jamaican merchant John Cunningham wrote, "I sold 129 slaves. . . . There were 45 boys and girls . . . many not more than 8 or 9 years of age."[9] Over 30 percent of the captives sold from this ship were children.

Although it would be problematic to generalize, there are other records of sale that also make it clear that African children were available for sale in sizeable proportions in Jamaican ports. In 1793, on the slave ships *Rodney, Jupiter,* and *Barque Fanny,* for example, the proportion of children and adolescents sold in Jamaica were 30 percent, 42 percent, and 34 percent, respectively. Records of sale sometimes distinguished among adults, adolescents, and those considered below the age of adolescence. Adolescents were referred to as "men/boys" and "women/girls" while children were listed simply as "boys" and "girls." The very young were referred to as "child" or "infant at breast." Though it seems as though planters would have preferred not to purchase African children they deemed to be too young, they certainly did purchase them if they were sold at a low enough price. Sometimes children were purchased with the specific intention of teaching them a particular trade.[10]

There were also an increasing number of Jamaican-born enslaved children on the island during the late eighteenth and early nineteenth century. On older, more established plantations, where the slave populations were predominantly Jamaican born, there tended to be higher birth rates and lower death rates. Even before the end of the slave trade, in certain parts of Jamaica, there was a "trend towards demographic self-sufficiency."[11]

A demographic analysis of a small sample of slave communities makes it clear that children were very much part of the slave population. In 1770, on Pepper Penn, which was located in the parish of St. Elizabeth, approximately 28 percent of the slave population was listed as children. Similarly, in 1771 on Barton Isles Penn children accounted for 23.4 percent of the slave population. Between 1799 and 1818, on the Westmoreland sugar plantation Mesopotamia, children aged fourteen and under accounted for 29.1 percent of the slave population. In addition, Barry Higman's analysis of age structure on twelve estates in 1817 also shows that children accounted for a significant proportion of the slave population. In his study, he calculates that the percentage of persons under the age of eighteen ranged from 25.6 percent to 41.9 percent.[12]

The willingness to use child labor during this period, however, was by no means peculiar to Jamaica. Children were an important source of labor in Britain. Despite criticisms, which were essentially grounded in Enlightenment thinking, during the eighteenth and nineteenth century working-class children of Britain were treated with little sympathy. The onset of the Industrial Revolution meant that increasing numbers of children would spend their early years laboring under harsh conditions in textile trades and mills. Some were often sent to work in factories, by their parents, at the age of six or seven and made to work between twelve and sixteen hours each day. Others, particularly orphans and paupers, were sent to industrial areas and, in order to meet the labor demand, were forced into factory work by the state. Nonetheless, all working-class children who labored in factories were made to labor under "unremitting working routines" and in a "hostile environment." Although the scholarly emphasis on British child labor has foregrounded the experiences of children in factories, children working in mines and in agricultural areas also labored under harsh conditions during this period. Regardless of the type of work, children were seen as a cheap and easily exploitable source of labor.[13]

British child laborers lived in "an age accustomed to brutality." As a result, they were quite often victims of the "unrestrained vent" of "brutal and sadistic overseers." Children could be beaten for tardiness, for unsatisfactory performance, or because they were too exhausted to continue working. Not surprisingly, the beatings in the workplace were so harsh and brutal that they would sometimes leave scars. Rarely would parents complain, however, as they feared their jobs would be at risk. Nor were working-class children exempt from the brutal punishments sanctioned by the state. It was not uncommon for small children to be sentenced to death or transported for relatively minor crimes such as theft. As late as 1814, five children were sentenced to death. The youngest was eight years old and none of them was over fourteen.[14] Although it was not uncommon for such death sentences to be commuted, the mere fact that children could be given the death penalty, and other harsh sentences, for crimes such as theft certainly suggests that the courts were generally unsympathetic and insensitive to the plights of children in the late eighteenth and early nineteenth centuries.

Needless to say, in Jamaica both the conditions and type of labor that enslaved child laborers performed were also harsh and trying. Although the sugar plantation was an "agro-industrial complex," the labor of enslaved children on sugar plantations was generally restricted to the agricultural realm. Those working on plantations, including coffee plantations, were generally organized into three gangs. Children who were approximately between the ages of four and ten tended to work in what was referred to as the "third gang" (or fourth gang on larger estates) and performed tasks such as weeding and collecting food for hogs. Older children were made to work in the "second gang," which would require them to perform more strenuous types of field labor. Similarly, the children and adolescents working on livestock pens would be assigned tasks suitable to their size and age.[15]

But not all children were made to perform agricultural tasks. In 1762, when Thomas Thistlewood bought a young "Congo girl," who was estimated to be about nine or ten years old, he sent her to be apprenticed as a "sempstress." Similarly, at another slave sale several years later, a woman named Mrs. Cope went in search of a young girl who could also be trained as a "sempstress." Mrs. Cope intended to purchase a young slave of a very specific description. She wanted a girl whose ethnicity was Ebo, who was "about 12 years of age, with small feet, not bow-legged, nor teeth filed, small hands and long, taper fingers." Moreover, the racially hierarchical organization of Jamaican slave society ensured that enslaved children with some white ancestry were more likely to escape field labor and to be trained in positions that were considered relatively privileged. For young girls, these would be domestic positions and young boys would be geared towards either domestic positions or skilled labor.[16]

Given the continued influence of British ideology on Jamaican colonial thinking, it seems reasonable to suggest that colonial attitudes about the exploitation of child labor—albeit enslaved child labor—were part of a long-standing British tradition that utilized the labor of children. Despite imperial-colonial linkages, however, British use of child labor was not precisely replicated in the colonies. In fact, there were a number of fundamental differences.

Of course, the most obvious difference was that the vast majority of child laborers in Jamaica were enslaved and those of Britain were not. The slave status of Jamaican child laborers meant that they were not subjects of the British crown but, in fact, were legally defined as the *property of* subjects to the crown. Hence, the labor conditions of enslaved children in Jamaica were shaped by their legal status as colonial property. This legal reality had a significant impact on the lives of enslaved children. Most obviously, enslaved children had no rights to wages nor did their parents have any legal rights to the fruits of their labor. Enslaved adults could only benefit from the labor of their children, if it was sanctioned by their owner. Under slavery, the parent-child relationship would always be secondary to that of the slave owner and slave child. As a result, the interests of enslaved families were legally subordinate to the social and economic interests of the white planter class. Enslaved children were always at risk of being separated from their families and ultimately their fate would be determined by the economic interests of their owner. The experience of African children, however, was different from that of Jamaican-born children.

Enslaved children born in Jamaica generally stayed under the care of their mothers when very young. Mothers and their very young children tended to be sold together. As children got older the risk of their being separated from family members would increase. But escape from the Jamaican slave labor system was always an option, and here too young Jamaican-born children were more likely to stay under the protection of their mothers. Runaway advertisements often reported the escape of women who left with their children in tow. This was certainly the case of Sarah, for example, who ran away with her eleven-month-old infant. Similarly, "a small yellow wench" named Ancilla was reported to have absconded with her "young mulatto female child" from the Liguanea area.[17]

As Jamaican-born enslaved children got older, however, their escape from a life of slave labor was more likely to be independent of family members. A case in point is the reported escape of Caesar, "a Creole Negro Boy" who was estimated to be about eleven years old. There is evidence to suggest that children even younger than this attempted to escape. In 1781, William Tedder placed a notice in the *Royal Gazette* reporting that he had "found" a young boy whom he described as "creole" and was estimated to be about six or seven years of age.[18]

For those children who had been purchased in Africa and forcibly transported to Jamaica, however, the trauma of the separation from family members would have occurred long before their arrival on the island. The horror of their enslavement would only be heightened when they arrived in Jamaica and were inserted into an unfamiliar environment, where they were alone and many on the island could not speak their language. Unlike the child laborers of Britain and Jamaican-born slave children, African children would have little understanding about the cultural assumptions and social expectations of the world in which they were to labor.

Not surprisingly, both African children and adults used folk beliefs to explain the processes that led to their enslavement. In fact, the enslaved often linked the slave trade and slavery to cannibalism and witchcraft. According to Olaudah Equiano, who had been captured at the age of eleven, the "dread" of being eaten by whites was ever present throughout the middle passage. Even when the ship docked in the West Indies, the enslaved continued to believe that they would be eaten once they were taken on land. Equiano reported that not until some "old slaves," no doubt African born, were brought on board to pacify them was it understood that they were brought to labor and not to be eaten.[19]

Once young Africans realized that they were to participate in a system of labor, however, their initial understanding of the Jamaican slave labor system would be informed by their own experiences of African labor systems. Unfortunately, the history of childhood and child labor in Africa remains undeveloped in the scholarly literature. There can be little doubt, however, that young Africans brought to Jamaica would have their own peculiar social and cultural expectations of the new environment and these would be informed by their social circumstances in Africa. As Paul Lovejoy and David Trotman have recently argued, "enslaved Africans still interpreted what they confronted in [the Americas] in light of their previous experiences" in Africa. As these authors point out, however, the age and social standing of the enslaved are two factors, among others, that would also influence attitudes and reactions to enslavement in the Americas.[20] For that reason, different African children would have different expectations about working in the slave labor system of Jamaica.

There is evidence to suggest that African attitudes toward enslavement may have been influenced by socioeconomic background. Some sources suggest that the enslaved brought to Jamaica who were originally of high social ranking in Africa were particularly resistant to their newly assigned slave status. According to the slave trader Hugh Crow, the "Breeche"—a high-ranking social group among the Igbo—were more likely than "their countrymen" to resist enslavement. Once members of this high-status group were put on board slave ships, they would often encourage others to "shake off their bondage"—so much so that ship captains, who made their slave purchases at the Bight of Biafra, were generally averse to purchasing them. Crow's assessment of high-ranking Igbos supports Bryan Edwards's conclusion that Gold Coast Africans who were of a "'free condition in their native country' were 'the most desperate, to regain [their] freedom.'"[21] It is highly likely, then, that the responses and reactions of African youths to slavery in Jamaica were shaped, at least in part, by their socioeconomic standing in Africa.

For example, there can be little doubt that when she was brought to Jamaica the expectations of Afiba, a fifteen-year-old girl from the Gold Coast, were quite different from those of Adam, a fourteen-year-old brought to the island from West Central Africa. The former had lived her life as a slave in the Gold Coast long before being sold into the Atlantic slave trade by her master. The latter had been "stole[n]" by one of his "countrymen" even though he was reportedly the son of "a great warrior" who had often captured and sold others into slavery.[22] As these two cases make clear, enslaved African children were drawn from a range of socioeconomic contexts. Despite the difference of their backgrounds in Africa, both of these young Africans would have an understanding of African slavery that would be in sharp contrast to the racialized slave system of Jamaica. Moreover, any African notions about the obligations to and the expectations of children and youth would clash with colonial ideas of child labor circulating in Jamaica.

To even further complicate the situation, because Afiba and Adam were each drawn from different social and economic circumstances, it is very likely that their attitudes and reactions to a life of slave labor in Jamaica would have been shaped by their own peculiar life stories. Given that Adam's father was of a high social rank, it seems reasonable to assume that his response to a life of slavery in Jamaica would be informed by the notion that he was unfairly enslaved in Africa and so unfairly assigned slave status. For Afiba, her response and reaction to Jamaican slavery would quite likely stem from the disjuncture between her understanding of social obligations between masters and slaves in Africa and the reality of slave life in Jamaica. This is not to say that Afiba's slave status in Africa necessarily made her less resistant to her slave status in Jamaica. In fact, it is quite possible that both of these African youths were equally resistant to their enslavement in Jamaica—albeit for different reasons. For Afiba, acts of resistance would most likely be grounded in the sense of violation she felt when aspects of

Jamaican slavery did not meet her African-oriented expectations of master-slave relationships. For Adam, it would be an outright resistance to slave status. No doubt, the gender of these African youths also influenced their expectations of and responses to slavery in Jamaica. Afiba and Adam would not only have assumptions about the nature of master-slave interactions, but they would also have assumptions about how gender relationships operated within the context of master-slave dynamics.

Not surprisingly, for some of these young Africans the difference between their expectations and the reality of slave life and labor in Jamaica was too much to bear. For this reason, many young Africans would brave the unknown and unfamiliar. In 1779, a runaway advertisement announced the escape of a "Congo Negro Boy" named Fortune who was approximately thirteen years of age. Unfortunately, there is nothing to indicate specifically why Fortune decided to run away. Given that he could only speak "tolerable English" and was only "slightly acquainted" with Kingston, however, it is clear that any fear he might have of the unknown could not rival his frustration with the conditions of his enslavement. But Africans even younger than Fortune and less familiar with the island also opted to run away. This was the case of a young African, between ten and twelve years of age, who was originally from "the Coromantee country." His effort at escape was in vain as he was later found in Kingston. Nonetheless, the fact that he could speak no English and so would be unable to communicate in an unfamiliar environment did not act as a deterrent as he resisted a life where he would be made to labor under the Jamaican slave system.[23]

Of course the age of the African children influenced their ability both to resist and to adapt to colonial expectations of enslaved child labor. The younger the child, the more malleable he or she would be, so that younger children would be better able to acclimatize to the social and cultural assumptions of Jamaican slave society. This fact was not lost on contemporaries who noted that African children brought to the island would more easily adapt and eventually "acquire the speech and manners" of their environment.[24]

Conclusion

The rhetoric of childhood and slavery had long been intertwined in the eighteenth and nineteenth century. Jamaica's colonial relationship with

Britain meant that those opposed to the exploitation of child labor in Britain could easily draw from the imagery of slavery in the colonies to advance their cause.[25] Ironically, apologists for slavery would also use notions of childhood to justify their support of slavery systems. Africans and people of African descent were often deemed childlike and so, it was argued, required the wisdom and guidance of whites. The children of this supposedly childlike "race," however, had their own ideas about childhood and child labor.

There can be little question that there were different expectations about the obligations to and obligations of child laborers circulating in Jamaica. The use of child labor had a long history in Britain. It is not surprising, then, that the use of child labor in Jamaica would offend few sensibilities and that white Jamaican colonials would choose to capitalize on the labor of enslaved children. Colonial ideas about child labor were, in fact, a racialization of preexisting British notions and the use of child labor— albeit enslaved child labor—was an extension of a tradition that had a long history in Britain.

Of course, notions about child labor would take new form in the colonial context. They would be reshaped to suit the economic priorities of the white planter class. For this reason, the justifications for using the labor of enslaved children in Jamaica did not parallel the British defense of child labor. In Britain, justifications were class based, and the employment of children was often defended as a means to teach industry to paupers and orphans.[26]

In Jamaica, however, the defense of white colonial class interests was articulated in racist terms. The enslavement of children in Jamaica, like that of their parents, was justified because, according to colonial whites, they were racially inferior. Their supposed inferiority was manifested in a number of unredeeming traits. Colonial whites maintained that the enslaved were an inherently lazy, dishonest, and immoral racial group and that they could only be productive if guided by whites who would have the power of the law and the whip.

Needless to say, such colonial ideas would be in conflict with those of the enslaved. Children born in Africa, who were brought to the island, would have their own notions about the norms of childhood and youth. These notions would be influenced by their age, social status in Africa, and cultural understanding of the obligations to and the expectations of children and youth. In contrast, Jamaican-born children would only have their experiences on the island to inform their outlook and so would be better able to understand the social and cultural expectations of white colonials.

NOTES

1. See for example, David Eltis and Stanley Engerman, "Was the Slave Trade Dominated by Men?" *Journal of Interdisciplinary History* 1 (1992): 237–57, quote on 245. More recently, the publication of the Dubois Slave Trade Database has allowed scholars to sketch an even more nuanced demographic portrait of the slave trade. See David Eltis, Stephen D. Behrendt, David Richardson, and Herbert S. Klein, *The Trans-Atlantic Slave Trade: A Database on CD-ROM* (New York: Cambridge University Press, 1999).

2. For the Bight of Biafra, see table 1 in Nwokeji, "African Conceptions of Gender and the Slave Traffic," 67. For the Gold Coast, calculations are based on data taken from the ship records of sixty-seven voyages, which included data about the age and sex ratios of the enslaved purchased in this region between 1776 and 1800. For West Central Africa, calculations are based on a sample size of seventy-one voyages. Eltis et al., *Trans-Atlantic Slave Trade*. For data on the Jamaican-born enslaved see Higman, *Slave Population and Economy in Jamaica*, 76.

3. Petley, "Slavery, Emancipation, and the Creole World View of Jamaican Colonists, 1800–1834," 93–114.

4. King, *Stolen Childhood*; Schwartz, *Born in Bondage*.

5. Fox to Committee, April 1792, *Parliamentary Register or History of the Proceedings & Debates of the House of Commons* (London, 1793), vol. 34, 307.

6. See the description of the methodology used in Eltis et al., *Trans-Atlantic Slave Trade*.

7. Barry Higman, among others, has argued that planters had a consistent preference for adult males. Higman, *Slave Population and Economy in Jamaica*, 80.

8. Simon Taylor to Robert Taylor, December 3, 1798, TAYL/1, Letterbook B, Simon Taylor Papers, Institute of Commonwealth Studies (ICS), London [UK]; Hall, *In Miserable Slavery*, 119; Letter from George Turner to Duke, November 9, 1791, Tweedie Papers, File 4/45 # 66, ff. 33, Jamaica National Archives (JNA). Hereafter, please note that all correspondence from the Simon Taylor Papers was found at the ICS and all from the Tweedie Papers was found in the JNA.

9. Francis Grant to James Rogers, August 4, 1789, C107/9; Thomas & William Salmon & Co. to James Rogers, May 3, 1792, C107/9; Francis Grant to James Rogers, April 10, 1789, C107/9; John Cunningham to James Rogers, April 20, 1792, C107/6. Hereafter, please note that all correspondence from the C107 series was found in the Public Record Office (PRO) in London (UK).

10. "Record of Sale for Rodney," July 20, 1793, C107/59; "Record of Sale for 342 Slaves," July 3, 1793, C107/59; "Sale of Negroes on Barque Fanny," January 25, 1793, C107/59. See also "Sale of 72 Negroes (including a child)," February 21, 1791, C107/5; "Account Sales of 45 Slaves Including an Infant at the Breast," July 28, 1789, C107/6. For references to infants see C107/5, "Sale of 72 Negroes (includ. a Child) imported from Africa in the Schooner Flora," February 21, 1791. For reference to young Africans being purchased to be taught trades, see Hall, *In Miserable Slavery*, 126, 178.

11. Craton, "Jamaican Slave Mortality," 27.

12. Pepper Penn statistics calculated from "A List of Slaves on Pepper Penn taken 31st December 1770"; Barton Penn Statistics calculated from "A List of Slaves on Barton Isles Penn 1st Jan'y 1805," both in Papers of Caleb and Ezekial Dickinson, Dickinson Papers (Microfilm), Yale University; for Mesopotamia see table 2, Dunn, "A Tale of Two Plantations," 45; table 14, Higman, *Slave Population and Economy in Jamaica*, 95.

13. Walvin, *A Child's World*, 45–78; Cunningham, "The Employment and Unemployment of Children," 115–50.

14. Walvin, *A Child's World*, 58.

15. Mintz, *Sweetness and Power*; Higman, *Slave Population and Economy in Jamaica*, 18–26, 188–89.

16. Hall, *In Miserable Slavery*, 126, 178.

17. *Royal Gazette*, September 16–21, 1781.

18. *Royal Gazette*, July 21–28 and November 17–24, 1781.

19. Piersen, "White Cannibals, Black Martyrs," 147–59; Thornton, "Cannibals, Witches, and Slave Traders," 273–94; Olaudah Equiano, *Equiano's Travels: The Interesting Narrative of the Life of Olaudah Equiano or Gustavus Vassa, the African* (London: Heinemann, 1967), 31.

20. Lovejoy and Trotman, "Enslaved Africans and Their Expectations," 69–70.

21. Hugh Crow, *Memoirs of Captain Hugh Crow*, 199, cited in M. D. W. Jeffreys, "The Winged Solar Disk or Ibo ITΣI Facial Scarification," *Africa* 21.2 (1951): 74–75.

22. Edwards, *British Colonies in the West Indies*, vol. 2, 124–26.

23. *Jamaica Mercury & Kingston Weekly Advertiser*, September 11–18, 1779; *Royal Gazette*, December 8–15, 1781.

24. See for example, B. Higman, ed., *Characteristic Traits of the Creolian and African Negroes in Jamaica* (Mona, Jamaica: Caldwell Press, 1976), 9.

25. Walvin, *A Child's World*, 62–65.

26. Cunningham, "Employment and Unemployment of Children," 119.

"The Younger Sort Reverence the Elder"
A Pilgrim Describes Indian Childrearing

Prior to the late nineteenth century, Native Americans rarely recorded their childhood memories. As a result, most of what we know about colonial Indian childrearing comes from documents produced by European settlers. The following brief excerpts from a Pilgrim settler's account of the first two years of Plymouth colony offer hints at the ways in which Indians living in the Cape Cod area raised their children—albeit from the point of view of an English colonist. (Edward Winslow, Good Newes from New England: A True Relation of things very remarkable at the Plantation of Plimoth [London, 1624], 56, 58–59)

. . . They train up the most forward and likeliest boys from their childhood in great hardness, and make them abstain from dainty meat, observing divers orders prescribed, to the end that when they are of age the Devil may appear to them, causing them to drink the juice of Sentry and other bitter herbs till they cast, which they must disgorge into the platter, and drink again, and again, till at length through extraordinary oppressing of nature it will seem to be all blood, and this the boys will do with eagerness at the first, and so continue till by reason of faintness they can scarce stand on their legs, and then must go forth into the cold: also they beat their shins with sticks, and cause them to run through bushes, stumps, and brambles, to make them hardy and acceptable to the Devil, that in time he may appear unto them. . . .

When they bury the dead they sow up the corps in a mat and so put it in the earth. If the party be a Sachem they cover him with many curious mats, and bury all his riches with him, and enclose the grave with a pale. If it be a child the father will also put his own most special jewels and ornaments in the earth with it, also will cut his hair and disfigure himself very much in token of sorrow. If it be the man or woman of the house, they will pull down the mattes and leave the frame standing, and bury them in or near the same, and either remove their dwelling or give over house-keeping. . . .

The younger sort reverence the elder, and do all mean offices whilst they are together, although they be strangers. Boys and girls may not wear their hair like men and women, but are distinguished thereby. A man is not accounted a man till he do some notable act, or show forth such courage and resolution as becometh his place. The men take much tobacco, but for boys so to do they account it odious.

All their names are significant and variable, for when they come to the state of men and women, they alter them according to their deeds or dispositions.

"I Have Often Been Overcome
While Thinking on It"
A Slave Boy's Life

One of only a handful of first-person accounts written by slaves, A Narrative
of the Life of Venture *recounts a young boy's capture by slave traders in
Africa, his transportation to America, and his life as a slave.* (Venture Smith,
*A Narrative of the Life and Adventures of Venture, a Native of Africa, but
Resident above Sixty Years in the United States of America, Related by Him-
self* [New London, Conn., 1798])

CHAPTER 1: *Containing an account of his life, from his birth to
the time of his leaving his native country.*

I was born at Dukandarra, in Guinea, about the year 1729. My father's
name was Saungm Furro, Prince of the Tribe of Dukandarra. My father
had three wives. Polygamy was not uncommon in that country, especially
among the rich, as every man was allowed to keep as many wives as he
could maintain. By his first wife he had three children. The eldest of them
was myself, named by my father Broteer. The other two were named Cun-
dazo and Soozaduka. My father had two children by his second wife, and
one by his third. I descended from a very large, tall and stout race of
beings, much larger than the generality of people in other parts of the
globe, being commonly considerably above six feet in height, and in every
way well proportioned. . . .

. . . A message was brought . . . to my father, that . . . a numerous army,
from a nation not far distant, furnished with musical instruments, and all
kinds of arms then in use [had been] instigated by some white nation who
equipped and sent them to subdue and possess the country, [was invading

a nearby nation] . . . . This nation had made no preparation for war, having been for a long time in profound peace that they could not defend themselves against such a formidable train of invaders, and must therefore necessarily evacuate their lands to the fierce enemy, and fly to the protection of some chief; and that if he would permit them they should come under his rule and protection when they had to retreat from their own possessions. He was a kind and merciful prince, and therefore consented to these proposals. . . .

He gave them every privilege and all the protection his government could afford. But they had not been there longer than four days before news came to them that the invaders had laid waste their country, and were coming speedily to destroy them in my father's territories. This affrighted them, and therefore they immediately pushed off to the southward, into the unknown countries there, and were never more heard of.

Two days after their retreat, the report turned out to be but too true. A detachment of the enemy came to my father and informed him, that the whole army was encamped not far out of his dominions, and would invade the territory and deprive his people of their liberties and rights, if he did not comply with the following terms. These were to pay them a large sum of money, three hundred fat cattle, and a great number of goats, sheep, asses, &c.

My father told the messenger that he would comply rather than that his subjects should be deprived of their rights and privileges, which he was not then in circumstances to defend from so sudden an invasion. Upon turning out those articles, the enemy pledged their faith and honor that they would not attack him. On these he relied and therefore thought it unnecessary to be on his guard against the enemy. But their pledges of faith and honor proved no better than those of other unprincipled hostile nations; for a few days after a certain relation of the king came and informed him, that the enemy who sent terms of accommodation to him, and received tribute to their satisfaction, yet meditated an attack on his subjects by surprise, and that probably they would commence their attack in less than one day, and concluded with advising him, as he was not prepared for war, to order a speedy retreat of his family and subjects. He complied with this advice.

The same night which was fixed upon to retreat, my father and his family set off about break of day. The king and his two younger wives went in one company, and my mother and her children in another. We left our dwellings in succession, and my father's company went on first. We directed our course for a large shrub plain, some distance off, where we intended to conceal ourselves from the approaching enemy, until we could refresh and rest ourselves a little. But we presently found that our retreat was not secure. For having struck up a little fire for purposes of cooking victuals, the enemy who happened to be encamped a little distance off, had sent out a scouting party which discovered us by the smoke of the fire, just as we were extinguishing it and about to eat. As soon as we had finished eating, my father discovered the party, and immediately began to discharge arrows at them. This was what I first saw, and it alarmed both me and the women, who being unable to make any resistance, immediately betook ourselves to the tall thick reeds not far off, and left the old king to fight alone. For some time, I beheld him from the reeds defending himself with great courage and firmness, till at last he was obliged to surrender himself into their hands.

Then they came to us in the reeds, and the very first salute I had from them was a violent blow on the head with the fore part of a gun, and at the same time a grasp round the neck. I then had a rope put about my neck, as had all the women in the thicket with me, and were immediately led to my father, who was likewise pinioned and haltered for leading. In this condition we were all led to the camp. The women and myself being pretty submissive, had tolerable treatment from the enemy, while my father was closely interrogated respecting his money which they knew he must have. But as he gave them no account of it, he was instantly cut and pounded on his body with great inhumanity, that he might be induced by the torture he suffered to make the discovery. All this availed not the least to make him give up his money, but he despised all the tortures which they inflicted, until the continued exercise and increase of torment, obliged him to sink and expire. He thus died without informing his enemies of the place where his money lay. I saw him while he was thus tortured to death. The shocking scene is to this day fresh in my mind, and I have often been overcome while thinking on it. . . .

The invaders then pinioned the prisoners of all ages and sexes indiscriminately, took their flocks and all their effects, and moved on their way towards the sea. On the march the prisoners were treated with clemency, on account of their being submissive and humble. Having come to the next tribe, the enemy laid siege and immediately took men, women, children, flocks, and all their valuable effects. They then went on to the next district which was contiguous with the sea, called in Africa, Anamaboo. The enemy's provisions were then almost spent, as well as their strength.

The inhabitants knowing what kind of conduct they had pursued, and what were their present intentions, improved the favorable opportunity, attacked them, and took enemy, prisoners, flocks and all their effects. I was then taken a second time. All of us were then put into the castle, and kept for market. On a certain time I and other prisoners were put on board a canoe, under our master, and rowed away to a vessel belonging to Rhode Island, commanded by capt. Collingwood, and the mate Thomas Mumford. While we were going to the vessel, our master told us all to appear to the best possible advantage for sale. I was bought on board by one Robertson Mumford, steward of said vessel, for four gallons of rum, and a piece of calico, and called VENTURE, on account of his having purchased me with his own private venture. Thus I came by my name. All the slaves that were bought for that vessel's cargo, were two hundred and sixty.

CHAPTER II: *Containing an account of his life, from the time of his leaving Africa, to that of his becoming free.*

After all the business was ended on the coast of Africa, the ship sailed from thence to Barbadoes. After an ordinary passage, except great mortality from small pox, which broke out on board, we arrived at the island of Barbadoes: but when we reached it, there were found out of the two hundred and sixty that sailed from Africa, not more than two hundred alive. These were all sold, except for myself and three more, to the planters there.

The vessel then sailed for Rhode Island, and arrived there after a comfortable passage. Here my master sent me to live with one of his sisters, until he could carry me to Fisher's Island, the place of his residence. I had then completed my eighth year. After staying with his sister some time I was taken to my master's place to live.

When we arrived at Narragansett, my master went ashore in order to return a part of the way by land, and gave me the charge of the keys of his trunks on board the vessel, and charged me not to deliver them up to any body, not even to his father without his orders. To his directions I promised faithfully to conform. When I arrived with my master's articles at his house, my master's father asked me for his son's keys, as he wanted to see what his trunks contained. I told him that my master intrusted me with the care of them until he should return, and that I had given him my word to be faithful to the trust, and could not therefore give him or any other person the keys without my master's directions. He insisted that I should deliver him the keys, threatening to punish me if I did not. But I let him know that he should not have them say what he would. He then laid aside trying to get them. But notwithstanding he appeared to give up trying to obtain them from me, yet I mistrusted that he would take some time when I was off my guard, either in the day time or at night to get them, therefore I slung them around my neck, and in the day concealed them in my bosom, and at night I always lay with them under me, that no person might take them from me without being apprized of it. Thus I kept the keys from every body until my master came home. When he returned he asked where VENTURE was. As I was then within hearing, I came, said, here sir, at your service. He asked me for his keys, and I immediately took them off my neck and reached them out to him. He took them, stroked my hair, and commended me, saying in presence of his father that his young VENTURE was so faithful that he would never have been able to have taken the keys from him but by violence; that he should not fear to trust him with his whole fortune, for that he had been in his native place so habituated to keeping his word, that he would sacrifice even his life to maintain it.

The first of the time of living at my master's own place, I was pretty much employed in the house at carding wool and other household business. In this situation I continued for some years, after which my master put me to work out of doors. After many proofs of my faithfulness and honesty, my master began to put great confidence in me. My behavior to him had as yet been submissive and obedient. I then began to have hard tasks imposed on me. Some of these were to pound four bushels of ears of corn every night in a barrel for the poultry, or be rigorously punished. At other seasons of the year I had to card wool until a very late hour. These tasks I had to perform when I was about nine years old. Some time after I had another difficulty and oppression which was greater than any I had ever experienced since I came into this country. This was to serve two masters. James Mumford, my master's son, when his father had gone from home in the morning, and given me a stint to perform that day, would order me to do *this* and *that* business different from what my master directed me. One day in particular, the authority which my master's son had set up, had like to have produced melancholy effects. For my master having set me off my business to perform that day and then left me to perform it, his son came up to me in the course of the day, big with authority, and commanded me very arrogantly to quit my present business and go directly about what he should order me. I replied to him that my master had given me so much to perform that day, and that I must therefore faithfully complete it in that time. He then broke out in a great rage, snatched a pitchfork and went to lay me over the head therewith; but I as soon got another and defended myself with it, or otherwise he might have murdered me in his outrage. He immediately called some people who were hearing at work for him, and ordered them to take his hair rope and come and bind me with it. They all tried to bind me but in vain, tho' there were three assistants in number. My upstart master then desisted, put his pocket handkerchief before his eyes and went home with a design to tell his mother of the struggle with young VENTURE. He told her that their young VENTURE had become so stubborn that he could not controul him, and asked her what he should do with him. In the mean time I recovered my temper, voluntarily caused myself to be bound by the same men who tried in vain before, and carried before my young master, that he might do what he pleased with me. He took me to a gallows made for the purpose of hanging cattle on, and suspended me on it. Afterwards he ordered one of his hands to go to the peach orchard and cut him three dozens of whips to punish me with. These were brought to him, and that was all that was done with them, as I was released and went to work after hanging on the gallows about an hour.

After I lived with my master thirteen years, being then about twenty-two years old, I married Meg, a slave of his who was about my age. My master owned a certain Irishman, named Heddy, who about that time formed a plan of secretly leaving his master. After he had long had this plan in meditation he suggested it to me. At first I cast a deaf ear on it, and rebuked Heddy for harboring in his mind such a rash undertaking. But after he had persuaded and much enchanted me with the prospect of gaining my freedom with such a method, I at length agreed to accompany him. Heddy next inveigled two of his fellow servants to accompany us. The place to which we designed to go was the Mississippi. Our next business was to lay in a sufficient store of provisions for our voyage. We privately collected out of our master's store, six great old cheeses, two firkins of butter, and one whole batch of new bread. When we had gathered all our own clothes and some more, we took them all about midnight, and went to the water side. We stole our master's boat, embarked, then directed our course for the Mississippi river.

We mutually confederated not to betray or desert one another on pain of death. We first steered our course for Montauk point, the east end of Long-Island. After our arrival there we landed, and Heddy and I made an incursion into the island after fresh water, while our two comrades were left at a little distance from the boat, employed at cooking. When Heddy and I had sought some time for water, he returned to our companions, and I continued on looking for my object. When Heddy had performed his business with our companions, who were engaged in cooking, he went directly to the boat, stole all the clothes in it, and then travelled away for East-Hampton, as I was informed. I returned to my fellows not long after. They informed me that our clothes were stolen, but could not determine who was the thief, yet they suspected Heddy as he was missing. After reproving my two comrades for not taking care of our things which were in the boat, I advertised Heddy and sent two men in search of him. They pursued and overtook him at Southampton and returned him to the boat. I then thought it might afford some chance for my freedom, or at least a palliation for my running away, to return Heddy immediately to his master, and inform him that I was induced to go away by Heddy's address. Accordingly I set off with him and the rest of my companions for our master's, and arrived there without any difficulty. I informed my master that Heddy was the ringleader of our revolt, and that he had used us ill. He immediately put Heddy into custody, and myself and companions were well received and went to work as usual.

Not a long time passed after that, before Heddy was sent by my master to New-London gaol. At the close of that year I was sold to a Thomas Stanton, and had to be separated from my wife and one daughter, who was about one month old. He resided at Stonington-point. To this place I brought with me from my last master's, two johannes, three old Spanish dollars, and two thousand of coppers, besides five pounds of my wife's money. This money I got by cleaning gentlemen's shoes and drawing boots, by catching musk-rats and minks, raising potatoes and carrots, &c. and by fishing in the night, and at odd spells.

All this money amounting to near twenty-one pounds York currency, my master's brother, Robert Stanton, hired of me, for which he gave me his note. About one year and a half after that time, my master purchased my wife and her child, for seven hundred pounds old tenor. One time my master sent me two miles after a barrel of molasses, and ordered me to carry it on my shoulders. I made out to carry it all the way to my master's house. When I lived with Captain George Mumford, only to try my strength, I took up on my knees a tierce of salt containing seven bushels, and carried it two or three rods. Of this fact there are several eye witnesses now living.

Towards the close of the time that I resided with this master, I had a falling out with my mistress. This happened one time when my master was gone to Long-Island a gunning. At first the quarrel began between my wife and her mistress. I was then at work in the barn, and hearing a racket in the house, induced me to run there and see what had broken out. When I entered the house, I found my mistress in a violent passion with my wife, for what she informed me was a mere trifle; such a small affair that I forbear to put my mistress to the shame of having it known. I earnestly requested my wife to beg pardon of her mistress for the sake of peace even if she had given no just occasion for offence. But whilst I was thus saying my mistress turned the blows which she was repeating on my wife to me. She took down her horse-whip, and while she was glutting her fury with it, I reached out my great black hand, raised it up and received the blows of the whip on it which were designed for my head. Then I immediately committed the whip to the devouring fire.

When my master returned from the island, his wife told him of the affair, but for the present he seemed to take no notice of it, and mentioned not a word of it to me. Some days after his return, in the morning as I was putting on a log in the fire-place, not suspecting harm from any one, I received a most violent stroke on the crown of my head with a club two feet long and as large around as a chair-post. This blow very badly wounded my head, and the scar of it remains to this day. The first blow made me have my wits about me as you may suppose, for as soon as he went to renew it, I snatched the club out of his hands and dragged him out of the door. He then sent for his brother to come and assist him, but I presently left my master, took the club he wounded me with, carried it to a neighboring Justice of the Peace, and complained of my master. He finally advised me to return to my master, and live contented with him until he abused me again, and then complain. I consented to do accordingly. But before I set out for my master's, up he come and his brother Robert after me. The Justice improved this convenient opportunity to caution my master. He asked him for what he treated his slave thus hastily and unjustly, and told him what would be the consequence if he continued the same treatment towards me. After the Justice had ended his discourse with my master, he and his brother set out with me for home, one before and the other behind me. When they had come to a bye place, they both dismounted their respective horses, and fell to beating me with great violence. I became enraged at this and immediately turned them both under me, laid one of them across the other, and stamped both with my feet what I would.

This occasioned my master's brother to advise him to put me off. A short time after this I was taken by a constable and two men. They carried me to a black-smith's shop and had me hand-cuffed. When I returned home my mistress enquired much of her waiters, whether VENTURE was hand-cuffed. When she was informed that I was, she appeared to be very contented and was much transported with the news. In the midst of all this content and joy, I presented myself before my mistress, shewed her my hand-cuffs, and gave her thanks for my gold rings. For this my master commanded a negro of his to fetch him a large ox chain. This my master locked on my legs with two padlocks. I continued to wear the chain peaceably for two or three days, when my master asked me with contemptuous hard names whether I had not better be freed from my chains and go to work. I answered him, No. Well then, said he, I will send you to the West-Indies or banish you, for I am resolved not to keep you. I answered him I crossed the waters to come here, and I am willing to cross them to return.

For a day or two after this not any one said much to me, until one Hempsted Miner, of Stonington, asked me if I would live with him. I answered him that I would. He then requested me to make myself discontented and to appear as unreconciled to my master as I could before that he bargained with him for me; and that in return he would give me a good chance to gain my freedom when I came to live with him. I did as he requested me. Not long after Hempsted Miner purchased me of my master for fifty-six pounds lawful. He took the chain and padlocks off me immediately after.

It may here be remembered, that I related a few pages back, that I hired out a sum of money to Mr. Robert Stanton, and took his note for it. In the fray between my master Stanton and myself, he broke open my chest containing his brother's note to me, and destroyed it. Immediately after my present master bought me, he determined to sell me at Hartford. As soon as I became apprized of it, I bethought myself that I would secure a certain sum of money which lay by me, safer than to hire it out to Stanton. Accordingly I buried it in the earth, a little distance from Thomas Stanton's, in the road over which he passed daily. A short time after my master carried me to Hartford, and first proposed to sell me to one William Hooker of that place. Hooker asked whether I would go to the German Flats with him. I answered, No. He said I should, if not by fair means I should by foul. If you will go by no other measures, I will tie you down in my sleigh. I replied to him, that if he carried me in that manner, no person would purchase me, for it would be thought that he had a murderer for sale. After this he tried no more, and said he would not have me as a gift.

My master next offered me to Daniel Edwards, Esq. of Hartford, for sale. But not purchasing me, my master pawned me to him for ten pounds, and returned to Stonington. After some trial of my honesty, Mr. Edwards placed considerable trust and confidence in me. He put me to serve as his cup-bearer and waiter. When there was company at his house, he would send me into his cellar and other parts of his house to fetch wine and other articles occasionally for them. When I had been with him for some time, he asked me why my master wished to part with such an honest negro, and why he did not keep me himself. I replied that I could not give him the reason, unless it was to convert me into cash, and speculate with me as with other commodities. I hope he can never justly say it was on account of my ill conduct that he did not keep me himself. Mr Edwards told me that he should be very willing to keep me himself, and that he would never let me go from him to live, if it was not unreasonable and inconvenient for me to be parted from my wife and children; therefore he would furnish me with a horse to return to Stonington, if I had a mind for it. As Miner did not appear to redeem me I went, and called at my old master Stanton's first to see my wife, who was then owned by him. As my old master appeared much ruffled at my being there, I left my wife before I had spent considerable time with her, and went to Colonel O. Smith's. Miner had not as yet wholly settled with Stanton for me, and had before my return from Hartford given Col. Smith a bill of sale for me. These men once met to determine which of them should hold me, and upon my expressing a desire to be owned by Col. Smith, and upon my master's settling the remainder of the money which was due Stanton for me, it was agreed that I should live with Col. Smith. This was the third time of my being sold, and I was then thirty-one years old. As I never had an opportunity of redeeming myself whilst I was owned by Miner, though he promised to give me a chance, I was then very ambitious of obtaining it. I asked my master one time if he would consent to have me purchase my freedom. He replied that he would. I was then very happy, knowing that I was at that time able to pay part of the purchase money, by means of the money which I some time since buried. This I took out of the earth and tendered to my master, having previously engaged a free negro man to take his security for it, as I was the property of my master, and therefore could not safely take his obligation myself. What was wanted in redeeming myself, my master agreed to wait on me for, until I could procure it for him. I still continued to work for Col. Smith. There was continually some interest accruing on my master's note to my friend the free negro man above named, which I received, and with some besides which I got by fishing, I laid out in land adjoining my old master Stanton's. By cultivating this land with the greatest diligence and economy, at times when my master did not require my labor, in two years I laid up ten pounds. This my friend tendered to my master for myself, and received his note for it.

Being encouraged by the success which I had met in redeeming myself, I again solicited my master for a further chance of completing it. The chance for which I solicited him was that of going out to work the ensuing winter. He agreed to this on condition that I would give him one quarter of my earnings. On these terms I worked the following winter, and earned four pounds sixteen shillings, one quarter of which went to my master for the privilege, and the rest was paid him on my own account. This added to the other payments made up forty four pounds, eight shillings, which I had paid on my own account. I was then about thirty five years old.

The next summer I again desired he would give me a chance of going out to work. But he refused and answered that he must have my labor this summer, as he did not have it the past winter. I replied that I considered it as hard that I could not have a chance to work out when the season became advantageous, and that I must only be permitted to hire myself out in the poorest season of the year. He asked me after this what I would give for the privilege per month. I replied that I would leave it wholly with his own generosity to determine what I should return him a month. Well then, said he, if so two pounds a month. I answered him that if that was the least he would take I would be contented.

Accordingly, I hired myself out at Fisher's Island, and earned twenty pounds; thirteen pounds six shillings of which my master drew for the privilege, and the remainder I paid him for my freedom. This made fifty-one pounds two shillings which I paid him. In October following I went and wrought six months at Long Island. In that six months' time I cut and corded four hundred cords of wood, besides threshing out seventy-five bushels of grain, and received of my wages down only twenty pounds, which left remaining a larger sum. Whilst I was out that time, I took upon my wages only one pair of shoes. At night I lay upon the hearth, with one coverlet over and another under me. I returned to my master and gave him what I received on my six months labor. This left only thirteen pounds eighteen shillings to make up the full sum for my redemption. My master liberated me, saying I might pay what was behind if I could ever make it convenient, otherwise it would be well. The amount of the money which I had paid my master towards redeeming my time, was seventy-one pounds two shillings. The reason of my master for asking such an unreasonable price, was he said, to secure himself in case I should ever come to want. Being thirty-six years old, I left Col. Smith once for all. I had already been sold three different times, made considerable money with seemingly nothing to derive it from, been cheated out of a large sum of money, lost much by misfortunes, and paid an enormous sum for my freedom.

Part II

Family and Society

When Philip Vickers Fithian, a Princeton student who, needing money, consented to work for a year or two in the South as a plantation tutor, arrived at Robert Carter's plantation on the eve of the American Revolution, he became part of the household of one of the elite families in colonial Virginia. His delightful letters and journal entries described a family of children ranging in age from eighteen to seven—not counting the baby, Sarah, and John, age four—with a wide range of personalities and attributes, which he introduces in one of his first journal entries:

Ben, the eldest: "a youth of genius."
Bob, the other Brother: "extremely volatile & unsettled in his temper."
Harry, the Nephew: "rather stoical, sullen, or saturnine."
Miss Priscilla, the eldest Daughter: "upon the whole in the first Class of the female Sex."
Fanny: "the Flower in the Family."
Betsy: "young, quiet, and obedient."
Harriot: "bold, fearless, noisy and lawless."

Although this may read like the cast description for a modern teen-centered television drama, the Carter family reflected the behaviors and expectations of colonial families. During the year Fithian spent with the Carters, he witnessed and experienced the full range of family dynamics, from warm and charming to angry and dysfunctional.

A similar spread of family styles appears in the essays in this section, from the warm and practical parent-child relationships formed in the elite families of South Carolina to the sometimes complicated associations among brothers and sisters to the sad cases of child abuse at the hands of parents and employers in New Amsterdam. The pieces are complemented by an extended excerpt from Fithian's journal and a sampling from the letters of the precocious and dutiful Eliza Lucas; both indicate a range of emotional and material relationships peculiar to the great plantation families of the colonial South. However, these relationships were not simply colonists' attempts to incorporate Old World assumptions and traditions into their colonial lives. They also reveal the ways in which the stresses and opportunities of the New World forced colonists to rethink age-old family customs and habits.

Chapter 4

Sibling Relations in Early American Childhoods
A Cross-Cultural Analysis

C. Dallett Hemphill

Young Ben Franklin was sure the situation was unjust. While "still a boy" and bound by indenture to learn printing from his older brother James, he could not reconcile James's assertion of superiority with his own sense of what was proper between siblings: "Though a brother, he considered himself as my master, and me as his apprentice, and accordingly, expected the same services from me as he would from another, while I thought he demean'd me too much in some he requir'd of me, who from a brother expected more indulgence." Apparently Ben was not alone in his thinking, as, he continued, "Our disputes were often brought before our father, and I fancy I was either generally in the right, or else a better pleader, because the judgment was generally in my favor. But my brother was passionate, and had often beaten me, which I took extreamly amiss." Eventually, the situation not improving, Ben left for Philadelphia.[1]

Franklin's sense that relations between brothers should not resemble those between master and servant raises the question of how sibling ties were regarded and experienced by early Americans. Asking this question presents several opportunities. A focus on siblings can widen our view of childhood beyond the parent-child relations that have been historians' traditional focus. It also presents a new avenue for cultural comparison in the context of the colonial period, when previously separate Europeans, Indians, and Africans began to live side by side on the eastern seaboard of North America. Scholars have long considered the similarities and differences among these three premodern cultures, including such related topics as kin-reckoning, household structure, childrearing, and the gender division of labor. But the focus has been on marriage and parenting, not sibling relations, and this has been a wasted opportunity since all humans share their longest lasting family ties with siblings. Finally, comparing sibling ties in these three colonial cultures allows for a fresh approach to the relationship between family and society, an issue over which early modern historians have reached a stalemate. The pioneering studies of European and early American families described them as microcosms of the larger society, but scholars have recently questioned whether families really did evolve in tandem with politics, religion, and the economy.[2] A focus on colonial siblings suggests a mediating position by showing how this family relationship provided a counterbalance to larger relations of power. The way it did so underscores important differences among the three colonial societies; at the same time, comparison reveals that children in all three cultures shared a relationship that was both loving and fragile.

Europeans, Indians, and Africans in colonial America attributed different degrees of cultural importance to the sibling relationship. Paradoxically, while we have much more evidence of European life, we have more evidence of the importance of sibling relations in both Native American and African American cultures. In both cases, the terms "brother" and "sister" were used to describe a number of relationships beyond those of children who shared parents, while European Americans rarely mentioned sibling relations even in their descriptions of nuclear family life. New England Algonquians, for example, called first cousins by sibling terms. Both Native American and African American groups also resorted to fictive sibling relations when the real thing was lacking. The Iroquois adopted brothers and sisters from among captives to replace those who had been lost in war. African Americans taught their children to address all adults of the slave community as aunt and uncle, a practice probably rooted in a pragmatic attempt to invoke the obligations of adults to care for siblings' children in the event of parental death or separation.[3]

In contrast, early modern Europeans thought of families as comprised of husbands and wives, parents and children, and masters and servants, at least judging from the sermons and religious tracts that described ideal family life. Brothers and sisters were there, of course, but they do not appear in contemporary prescriptions. Even child-rearing advice was written as if parents raised their children one at a time. While historians have not confined themselves to these contemporary discussions of the family in their studies—they have also used diaries, court records, letters, and other sources of information on actual family life—the mindset of their seventeenth- and eighteenth-century subjects has somehow confined their questions. As a result, siblings are virtually absent from the many modern studies of early European American families. To be sure, actual brothers and sisters could be extremely important to individuals in all three of these societies, but it is significant that Africans and Native Americans found sib-ship a metaphor for other important relations while Europeans hardly acknowledged its importance within the nuclear family.[4]

The primary reason for this difference among European, Native, and African Americans was probably a difference in worldview rooted in other social structures. The few modern studies of sibling relations, mostly produced by psychologists focusing on twentieth-century families, describe them as inherently more "lateral" or "horizontal" than the more "vertical" husband-wife or, especially, parent-child relationships.[5] The larger paradigm for both familial and social relations in early Anglo-America was hierarchical, and thus siblings did not fit, while the clearly though differently unequal marriage and parent-child relations did. Ben Franklin's strong feeling that an older brother should not treat a younger brother like a servant is an illustration of this lack of fit between sibling relations and the other hierarchies of his culture. Without wishing to romanticize or overgeneralize (as there was a good deal of cultural variation within all three colonial groups), it is fair to say that Eastern Woodlands Native Americans and the West African societies from whence most colonial African Americans were taken tended to be more "horizontal" or egalitarian in their families and polities. Kin ties, and especially sibling ties, were a paramount means of organizing relationships and households among both groups. We can thus see a fit between the greater egalitarianism of these societies and their more lateral conception of kin ties, a fit that allowed and predisposed these groups to make more of the sibling relation than did Europeans. The attempt to address treaty partners as equals by addressing them as brothers, for example, was so marked among such groups as the Iroquois that Europeans felt compelled to adopt this custom of address when dealing with Indians.[6]

As implied by some of the examples already described, a big clue to the relative cultural importance of sibling relations lies in language. Scholars have long noted that humans tend to have many terms for things of importance in their society—the proverbial multiplicity of Eskimo words for snow. New England Algonquians had such a plethora of terms for sibling relations, which varied for the age and sex of one sibling relative to another. This particular clue reminds us not to overstress the egalitarianism of this relation, as varied inflection according to age and gender suggests at least differentiation along these lines, if not inequality. Of course men dominated in this society, as in others. But gender inequality varies greatly from group to group. Among New England Algonquians, for example, the status of sister was enhanced. The same was true of the matrilineal Iroquois, among whom brothers formed especially strong ties with their sisters' children.[7] In any case, the elaborate language for siblings among New England tribes fits with other evidence that Native American groups regarded the sibling relationship as important.

The cultural importance of sibling ties in these societies did not correlate with relative numbers of siblings. Native American and African American families were generally smaller than European American families. Through later weaning and abstinence during nursing, Native American women gave birth at three- or four-year intervals rather than the two-year average among Europeans. European reporters from New England to Pennsylvania and as far west as Ohio remarked on the resulting smaller Indian family sizes of four to six children on average. Moreover, infant mortality rates were high among Native Americans, a reality resulting from the larger demographic catastrophe whereby Indian populations were steadily decimated by imported European diseases. In healthy circumstances, African American women could bear the most children of all three groups—as many as eight or nine—because they started childbearing earliest. The difficulties of family formation were such, however, that low birth rates prevailed in the Chesapeake until the 1720s and until the end of the colonial period in the North and lower South. Slave family size was further reduced by high infant mortality owing to the hard conditions of slavery. Completed European families were the largest, then, averaging between seven and eight children in New England through the colonial era. South of New England, especially among the non-English, in urbanizing areas, and in the Chesapeake, families were smaller at first, but caught up by the mid-eighteenth century. Child mortality was a more modest threat to European American than to African American or Indian families, but it was a real one, especially in the seventeenth-century South. Things improved over the eighteenth century, and scholars have recently suggested that only one baby in six died in early New England. This best case scenario still meant that, on average, each family would lose one child.[8] Owing to these birth and mortality rates, children in all three cultures grew up with a smaller number of brothers and sisters than we might expect from these preindustrial societies, and most children, even the Europeans of relatively healthy New England, experienced the death of a sibling. Yet throughout the colonial period Europeans were likely to grow up with more brothers and sisters than their African and Indian neighbors. Their relative lack of acknowledgment of the sibling relationship did not owe, then, to demographics, but to culture.

The roles sibling relations played in colonial cultures are further illuminated by the ways these three peoples treated differences between siblings. European observers frequently remarked on the gender-differentiated play of Indian brothers and sisters, based on their future adult roles. That is, young Indian boys often hunted or played at war, while their sisters mimicked their mothers' agricultural and domestic work. Gabriel Sagard's description of Huron children was typical: "Just as the little boys have their special training and teach one another to shoot with the bow as soon as they learn to walk, so also the little girls, whenever they begin to put one foot in front of the other, have a little stick put into their hands to train them, and teach them early to pound corn." Given the equally clear (though different) gender division of labor among adult Anglo-Americans, one might expect like differences in play among their children, but European descriptions give more emphasis to Indian gender-segregated play. The implication is that European American brothers and sisters played together, especially during their first six years, when they were clothed alike in the gowns of infancy. When boys donned their first breeches at age seven they may have begun to escape the company of their mothers and sisters. Some scholars have suggested that English boys were allowed more freedom to play outdoors than were girls. Soon we get glimpses of young girls training in housewifery alongside their mothers, while it appears that boys began to join their fathers in fieldwork after the age of ten. But their early play may have been less divergent than that of young Indian brothers and sisters.[9]

Note the overall contrast here—while Europeans gave less cultural acknowledgment to the relatively egalitarian sibling tie, their starker and generally unquestioned patriarchal worldview may have made them less concerned with reinforcing gender differences at a young age. Indian families, in contrast, may have stressed gender difference from infancy to balance the more egalitarian kin ties of their culture. We can only speculate about this issue as regards African Americans. It is possible that the play of enslaved African American brothers and sisters was shared, given the relative murkiness of the gender division of labor among male and female adult field hands. On the other hand, antebellum historians have shown that adult slaves reinforced gender differences where they could, so maybe their young colonial ancestors did the same.[10]

Brothers and sisters differ in age as well as gender, and it appears that the cultural balancing pattern we have seen was repeated here, too, at least among Europeans (evidence for both Indian and African groups is too scant to permit comparison on this issue). Given their hierarchical worldview, we might expect European colonists to have wanted younger brothers and sisters to defer to older siblings, but there is no evidence of this. Although family treatises revolved around the concept of deference to elders, elders meant parents and masters. The concept was not elaborated to include older brothers and sisters. Some scholars have assumed that older siblings exercised authority over younger siblings in a caretaking capacity. This would seem logical given age differences within families. (Women gave birth over their entire natural childbearing span, so there could be a twenty-year age difference between the eldest and the youngest.) But there is little mention of this in extant sources.[11]

A survey of fifty eighteenth-century family portraits provides corroborating evidence of a lack of adult emphasis on age and gender difference among elite European American brothers and sisters. This information is useful as silent commentary on sibling relations in a society that did not record many ideas about them. While boys and girls older than seven were dressed differently, one looks in vain for pronounced hierarchy in the placement, postures, or gaze of siblings of different ages. In particular, artists and patrons did not seem all that concerned with shoring up a higher status for older children.[12] The relative egalitarianism of sibling relations seemed to coexist with the hierarchy of other family relations. This fits with another important piece of evidence, the colonists' rejection of the English legal tradition of primogeniture. While the lack of land in England had engendered a tradition of leaving most of the family land to the eldest son, in the land-rich new world, European colonists treated their sons and daughters more equally. Again, they allowed the essential egalitarianism of the sibling bond to mitigate the otherwise hierarchical experience of family and society. Colonial parents sometimes declared outright that they wished to express their equal love for their children through their portions.[13]

The cultural construction of sib-ship in these three societies suggests that siblings presented the family with an egalitarian relationship that was more easily acknowledged in the more generally egalitarian Native American and African American cultures, but that nevertheless served to attenuate the experience of inequality within European families. By the same token, patterns of gender differentiation among siblings may have provided an order in Indian society that was not necessary among the more clearly patriarchal Europeans.

Scholars have based their argument that the sibling relationship is inherently egalitarian on modern research that shows that brothers and sisters share a great deal of experience despite differences in gender and age. It is difficult to recover the quality of colonial sibling relations across the centuries, but we can ask whether conditions were adequate to sustain such sharing. Birth spacing and infant mortality could cause age gaps between brothers and sisters in all three colonial societies, and parental death and remarriage could add to the gaps. Brothers and sisters were not greatly separated, however, as they are today, by age-graded institutions and experiences. In all three colonial cultures, we can assume that surviving siblings spent a good deal of time together as young children. Most dwellings were small in the early colonial era—often one room—so brothers and sisters ate, played, and slept together. Siblings often got smallpox or measles together, which confirms that they shared the same space, if not the same bed. Pious European families gathered for family prayer and sat down to dine together. Some New England siblings were even possessed by witches together. In all three societies, serious work was not required of young children, so they probably spent most of their time in play. (Those few—mostly New England—children who went to school shared one-room schoolhouses with their siblings.) If the family lived on a semi-isolated farmstead, as was the case for many European Americans, brothers and sisters would constitute a child's main playmates. Those who dwelled in European towns, Indian villages, or African slave quarters would have played with siblings among a wider group of neighboring children.[14]

Most European, African, and Indian brothers and sisters must have seen a good deal of each other, then, at least until adolescence. But there were exceptions. After King Phillip's War in the 1670s, many New England Indian children ended up as servants in English households, often at very young ages, and generally separated from siblings. English children could also be thus "bound out" if orphaned or from families too poor to properly care for them. And when local authorities in New England, New York, and the Chesapeake placed impoverished orphans in new households, they made little effort to keep siblings together. Young English brothers and sisters of all classes also experienced temporary separations. Infants could be sent to grandparents to be weaned or in hopes that a change of climate would cure them of illness. Some were temporarily separated by the process of emigration.[15]

Even if they were never separated in early childhood, many colonial siblings were parted at puberty. Like their English counterparts, European colonists often put their adolescents out to other households—for formal apprenticeships, to pursue education, or simply to provide household or farm help. While early New Englanders appear to have been the biggest separators of teens from their siblings, some elite New York and Chesapeake families did the same. (William Penn advised his fellow Quakers to adopt a middling position—to separate siblings, but not for long.) Sometimes siblings were placed with older siblings, thereby mitigating the sibling separation, although young Ben Franklin preferred other masters to his brother. In both the North and the South, extended stays with older sisters were a common means of securing appropriate female education for younger sisters, as well as domestic help for the elder. But there is no evidence that placing siblings with siblings was a preferred or even frequent arrangement.[16]

Enslaved African American adolescents were also often separated from their brothers and sisters, but their parents had even less to say about the removal of their children than impoverished European or Indian parents. While some masters recognized and honored the sibling bond by keeping siblings together, the clear preference for buying and selling teen-aged slaves necessitated sibling separation. Teenagers were vulnerable precisely because there was a greater reluctance to separate husbands and wives and mothers from young children. Thus the sibling relationship was the slave family tie most likely to be severed. Moreover, there is a tragic irony in the relationship between white and black siblings: because most slave sales happened in order to settle estates, the more inheriting white siblings there were in a slave-owning family, the more likely it was that black siblings would be divided up and thus separated from each other. Despite their frequency, there is ample evidence that these forced separations between African American brothers and sisters were traumatic.[17]

The placing out or sale of siblings added to the age gaps caused by long childbearing careers and sibling death to reduce the number of brothers and sisters living together at one time. Once again, the evidence is richest for affluent European Americans, but this just reminds us that the reduction of sibling groups occurred even among the materially best off. Boston minister Benjamin Colman and his wife lost two babies, for example, and then came their daughter Jane, who was an only child for her first seven years. Perhaps Colman did not address sibling relations in his many sermons on the family because, although he had several children, he was not long surrounded by siblings. To cite another example, while Samuel Sewall fathered fourteen children, deaths, separations, and age gaps meant that he often had just three at home with him. This pattern of a small number of siblings at home at one time receives striking confirmation in family portraits. Half of the sample of fifty portraits depict just two siblings, another quarter just three or four. Only a few late-eighteenth-century examples show larger families. Portraits, then, were more a snapshot of a coresident family at one point in time than a record of all children born to a family. Since two-thirds of the portraits depict young children, portraits either showed young families or young siblings after older siblings had left home.[18]

Thus among young Indians, Africans, and Europeans alike, childbearing patterns, mortality, and separations could easily disrupt sibling relationships. It is difficult to know how these disruptions affected the emotional tenor of relationships between young brothers and sisters, but the little evidence we have suggests that siblings in all three cultures could have loving relations despite the challenges. It is striking that some of the strongest images of sibling affection emerge from the scantiest pool of evidence: sources on African American life. Strong sibling ties were in keeping with West African traditions, and some eighteenth-century slaves reported warm sibling relations in their African childhoods. One scholar found at least three pairs of African-born brothers running away together in eighteenth-century Virginia, and American-born slave brothers kept up the habit. Masters often suspected that escaped slaves had either run with or to siblings. These are indications that the sibling bond was strong in adulthood; we also have bits of evidence of strong ties among younger sibs. Some slaves wrote of the great sorrow they felt in childhood at the whippings or deaths of their siblings. Boyrereau Brinch described a six-year-old boy pleading for a slave driver to stop whipping his older sister in a way station on Barbadoes, and then crying himself to sleep on her dead body. James Carter of Virginia remembered searching in agony along a riverbank for the remains of his brother Henry, brutally murdered by their master. A cross-cultural source suggests that Native Americans also had an ethic of strong sibling ties: captivity narratives show members of different Indian groups fiercely devoted to the fictive siblings they adopted from among European child captives. Mary Jemison, adopted in place of a deceased brother by Seneca Indians in the 1750s, recalled that her Indian brothers and sisters positively doted on her. When the European community tried to ransom her back, they refused to part with her. Extant evidence also permits occasional glimpses of strong affection between young European American sibs. Tace Bradford of Philadelphia wished her fourteen-year-old brother Tom could come home from Princeton so that she could "have the pleasure of a Lovd Brothers company." She claimed that "I would rather be miserable all my life than you should be so one day," and to be his "loving and affectionate sister till Death."[18] Ben Franklin recalled happy early years with his siblings, especially his sister Jane, but we must remember that he, too, was gone by his late teens. Indeed, in all three cultures, the glimpses we get of strong emotional ties between young siblings are also glimpses of siblings torn apart—whether enslaved Africans attempting to reunite with siblings, Indians trying to replace lost siblings with European captives, or Europeans separated in their teens.[19]

Ben and Jane Franklin's intense feelings for each other are clearest in middle age: "you wonce told me my Dear Brother that as our Numbers of Bretheren & Sisters Lessened the Affections of those of us that Remain should Increes to Each other." Ben and Jane sat down to dinner as children with nine other siblings, but in their fifties, they had only each other remaining, and they were very close. Adult sibling relations are beyond the province of this essay—suffice it to say that there is a great deal of evidence of strong and supportive relations among adult siblings in all three cultures of colonial America. Given childhood experience, these are best described as the relations of survivors—whether of African slavery, Indian demographic catastrophe, or the admittedly less onerous but still undeniable challenge of surviving to adulthood in Anglo-America. While their different worldviews led them to make different cultural uses of the idea of sibling relations and their different material realities led to different completed family sizes, for all three peoples sibling bonds in childhood were at once close and vulnerable to disruption. The close ties of adult siblings suggest that vulnerability only made the survivors value each other all the more.[20]

NOTES

1. Benjamin Franklin, *Autobiography,* an Electronic Edition, EADA http://www.mith2.umd.edu/eada, 20–35.

2. Aries, *Centuries of Childhood;* Stone, *The Family, Sex, and Marriage in England;* Morgan, *The Puritan Family;* Demos, *A Little Commonwealth;* Ozment, *Ancestors;* Pollock, *Forgotten Children.*

3. Kathleen Bragdon, *Native Peoples of Southern New England* (Norman: University of Oklahoma Press, 1996), 164; Daniel K. Richter, *The Ordeal of the Longhouse: The Peoples of the Iroquois League in the Era of European Colonization* (Chapel Hill: University of North Carolina Press, 1982), 66–74; Morgan, *Slave Counterpoint,* 553.

4. Typical family treatises are Cotton Mather, *A Family Well Ordered* (Boston: B. Green for Michael Perry, 1699); Benjamin Colman's *The Well-Ordered Family* (Boston: B. Green for N. Buttolph, 1712); and William Penn's *Some Fruits of Solitude* (Newport, RI: James Franklin, 1749). All are available in multiple editions in *Early American Imprints,* Series I, *Evans.* See also Morgan, *Puritan Family,* 150; Demos, *Little Commonwealth;* Frost, *The Quaker Family;* Donald P. Irish, "Sibling Interaction: A Neglected Aspect in Family Life Research," *Social Forces* 42 (1964): 279–88. The big exception to the neglect of sibling relations in early American family history is Lorri Glover's study of the South Carolina elite, *All Our Relations.*

5. Glover, *All Our Relations,* 31, 39, 46–47, 170 n.29, 172, n.46.

6. Plane, *Colonial Intimacies,* 5, 20; Morgan, *Slave Counterpoint,* 553; Gutman, *The Black Family in Slavery and Freedom,* 200–201; Richter, *Ordeal of the Longhouse,* 41.

7. Bragdon, *Native Peoples,* 162, 164, 165, 181; Richter, *Ordeal of the Longhouse,* 20.

8. Axtell, *The Indian Peoples of Eastern America,* 4, 15, 22, 24; Main, *Peoples of a Spacious Land,* 104–5, 112–15, 124, 165; Plane, *Colonial Intimacies,* 109–10; Morgan, *Slave Counterpoint,* 81, 87–90; Ira Berlin, *Generations of Captivity: A History of African-American Slaves* (Cambridge, MA: Harvard University Press, 2003), 72–73, 83–84; Demos, "Developmental Perspectives on the History of Childhood," 88; Glover, *All Our Relations,* 26, 27; Scott, "Sisters, Wives, and Mothers," 40; Robert Gross, *The Minutemen and Their World* (New York: Hill and Wang, 1976), 77; Maria Van Rensselaer, *Correspondence of Maria van Rensselaer, 1669–1689,* ed. A. J. F. van Laer (Albany: State University of New York Press, 1935), 3; Stephanie G. Wolf, *Urban Village: Population, Community, and Family Structure in Germantown, Pennsylvania, 1683–1800* (Princeton, NJ: Princeton University Press, 1976), 39–40, 269, 279, 280; Lorena Walsh, "Till Death Do Us Part," in Graff, *Growing Up in America,* 111, 125; Smith, *Inside the Great House,* 26, 27; Peter G. Slater, "'From the Cradle to the Coffin'"; Graham, *Puritan Family Life,* 18, 20, 47, 48, 104–5;

Bremner, *Children and Youth in America,* vol. 1, 45–48; Silverman, *Cotton Mather,* 38, 173, 272–73.

9. Axtell, *Indian Peoples,* 31, 33, 35, 36 (Sagard), 41, 42; Smith, *Inside the Great House,* 59; Graham, *Puritan Family Life,* 97; Main, *Peoples of a Spacious Land,* 138–39, 144–45, 152; John Winthrop, *The Journal of John Winthrop,* abridged ed. by Richard Dunn and Laetitia Yeandle (Cambridge, MA: Harvard University Press, 1996), 54.

10. Eugene Genovese, *Roll Jordan Roll: The World the Slaves Made* (New York: Random House, 1974).

11. Morgan, *Puritan Family,* 28; Main, *Peoples of a Spacious Land,* 104, 107, 124–25, 144, 153, 165; Glover, *All Our Relations,* 28; Graham, *Puritan Family Life,* 20, 104–5; Wolf, *Urban Village,* 263–64.

12. C. Dallett Hemphill, "Representing Siblings in Early American Paintings" unpub'd. paper for workshop on "Object Relations in Early North America," Huntington Library, May 2004.

13. Main, *Peoples of a Spacious Land,* 78–79; Glover, *All Our Relations,* 10–12; Levy, *Quakers and the American Family,* 181–82, 188; Narrett, *Inheritance and Family Life in Colonial New York City,* 8, 54, 114, 128–52; Wolf, *Urban Village,* 71, 322; Shammas et al., *Inheritance in America,* 32–34, 55–57, 62, 67.

14. Demos, "Developmental," 88; Gross, *Minutemen and Their World,* 83; Main, *Peoples of a Spacious Land,* 118, 123, 153, 155; Silverman, *Cotton Mather,* 266; Wolf, *Urban Village,* 280; Walsh "Till Death Do Us Part," 120.

15. Plane, *Colonial Intimacies,* 101–2, 216 n.23; Bremner, *Children and Youth in America,* vol. 1, 56–57, 62, 68–71, 119–20; Samuel Sewall, *The Diary of Samuel Sewall, 1674–1729,* ed. M. Halsey Thomas (New York: Farrar, Straus and Giroux, 1973), 46, 116; Winthrop, *Journal,* p. 41.

16. Morgan, *Puritan Family,* 75–77, 109; Graham, *Puritan Family Life,* 112, 122–25, 132–33, 141–66, 223; Main, *Peoples of a Spacious Land,* 148–51; Van Rensselaer, *Correspondence,* 5, 112; Frost, *Quaker Family,* 144; Esther Edwards Burr, *The Journal of Esther Edwards Burr, 1754–1757,* ed. Carol Karlsen and Laurie Crumpacker (New Haven, CT: Yale University Press, 1984), 27, 119, 291; Glover, *All Our Relations,* 35; Demos, *Little Commonwealth,* 120–22; Franklin, *Autobiography,* 30–34.

17. Morgan, *Slave Counterpoint,* 70–73, 512, 514, 518, 521, 523; Narrett, *Inheritance and Family Life,* 188–91; Bremner, *Children and Youth in America,* 68–69.

18. Ebenezer Turrell, *Memoirs of the Life and Death of the Pious Mrs. Jane Turrell* (Boston, 1735), 60–61, in Perry Miller and Thomas Johnson, *The Puritans: A Sourcebook of Their Writings,* vol. 2 (New York: Harper, 1938), 541; Sewall, *Diary,* 314.

19. Boyrereau Brinch, *The Blind African Slave; or, Memoirs of Boyrereau Brinch, Nick-named Jeffrey Brace,* ed. Benjamin F. Prentiss (St. Albans, VT: Harry Whitney, 1810), 20, 69, 74, 95, 97–103; James Albert, *A Narrative of the Most Remarkable Particulars in the Life of James Albert Ukawsaw Gronniosaw, an African*

Prince (Bath, 1770), 10–11, 19; Morgan, *Slave Counterpoint*, 392, 449, 464–65, 548–49; Bremner, *Children and Youth in America*, 15; Gutman, *Black Family in Slavery and Freedom*, 201; James E. Seaver, *A Narrative of the Life of Mrs. Mary Jemison* (Norman: University of Oklahoma Press, 1992), 78, 80–93; Tace Bradford to Tom Bradford, August 20, 1760, Folder 1, Correspondence, 1747–1795, Bradford Family Papers, Historical Society of Pennsylvania.

20. Silverman, *Cotton Mather*, 39; Bremner, *Children and Youth in America*, 136–37; Kenneth Minkema, "Hannah and Her Sisters: Sisterhood, Courtship, and Marriage in the Edwards Family in the Early Eighteenth Century," *New England Historical and Genealogical Register* 146 (January 1992): 43; Frost, *Quaker Family*, 126; Carl Van Doren, ed., *The Letters of Benjamin Franklin and Jane Mecom* (Princeton, NJ: University of Princeton Press, 1950), 93; Franklin, *Autobiography*, 10.

Chapter 5

"I Shall Beat You, So That the Devil Shall Laugh at It"

Children, Violence, and the Courts in New Amsterdam

Mariah Adin

Geertje, coming forward alone, was asked, how it happened, that there was a noise last evening at her house and that the doors were open? Answering, denies it; saying, that they were all abed at nine o'clock. The Burgomaster Allard Anthony says, he himself heard it, and that he and his wife passed there at half past ten; whereupon she answered, that she beat her children for coming so late home.[1]

While the history of children is a fairly understudied topic to begin with, the history of children and violence in colonial America has been relatively neglected by the historiography. Most studies of children and their treatment have been part of a larger discourse on either child-rearing practices, general violence in the family, or the more readily examined cases of infanticide. But short of murder, other avenues of violence and neglect committed against children in the early modern community have not yet been particularly singled out for specific study.[2]

This lacuna may be largely due to a peculiar blind spot in the dialectic surrounding the study of children, and particularly abused children. Children have been conceptualized as constant, existing in a static state of dependency—an idea that fits neatly into the prevailing patriarchal "little commonwealth" paradigm, which emphasizes the idealized power relationships between adult-child/master-slave/male-female. A holdover from the Enlightenment, the concept *child* (the word itself signifying a lack of reason, hence the *childish* behavior of seemingly irrational adults) is tinged with dependency, lack of reason, and, above all, need for protection. It describes a category of people who are not seen as participants, only spectators, in the systems of power swirling around them.[3]

Let us pause for a moment to reconsider how we visualize relationships between people and the systems they participate in. Picture, for a moment, that you hold in your hand a crystal. Now, hold that crystal up to the light. Perhaps you see the light reflected through it as red. But move your head to the side, just a little, and you may see that it is refracting green. Now pretend that the crystal is the legal system. Depending on where you are in relation to that system you may see a different color, yet both are legitimate. This is a *dichroistic power structure,* where power may be experienced legitimately by various people in slightly different ways depending upon their relationship to it. This conceptualization of power relations allows us to place those who often appear powerless, like children, at the very center of the system, instead of constantly positioning them peripherally to it. Too often, we consider children to simply be "in the dark"— unable to experience any "color" at all—when in truth, they may simply be seeing green instead of red.

This misperception of childhood is pervasively tenacious, as the state of dependency termed "childhood" is dismissed as a state that is mutable through time, and there is no acknowledgment that life stages, like all other categories, are artificial constructions that have been culturally imposed. While it is no longer possible to conceive of nonfluctuating and noncontested authority in the dynamics between men and women, or masters and slaves, the oversimplified dependent/depended-upon dichotomy does not sufficiently identify the relationship between adult and child. During this period, the labor of children was crucial for the survival of families and communities. Beyond this, children were responsible for the care of sick or aging parents, younger siblings, and the upholding (or destruction) of a family's status and reputation in the eyes of the community. Whenever people are needed, they hold a potential to negotiate, even if this potential is not institutionally recognized.[4]

This is not to say, however, that children are merely "little adults." The place of children within colonial society was one of a middling and constantly fluctuating space. Imagined legally as dependent, but in fact functionally independent, the idea of *child* was one of constant contestation and negotiation. Children, parents, community, magistrates—all sought to limit, define, and shape this slippery concept.

This article, then, seeks to investigate the ways in which the people of New Amsterdam sought to mold, stretch, and transfigure the boundary of *child*. Focusing on court cases involving the mistreatment of children, this article seeks to elucidate this middling space of contestation, finding the limits of the law, the desires of the community, and the resistance of children to violence and neglect. More importantly, this article attempts to examine the relationship between seemingly disenfranchised people and power—specifically, the way children were participants in the viewing, disseminating, and internalization of the power systems around them. While this article only examines a limited subset of cases, its main purpose is to find a useful lens of evaluation that will assist in the synthesis of the larger context of adult-child relationships in this period.

Like most other colonizers, the Dutch transported more than just cargo and people on their ships. The Dutch arrived in New Netherland with an extensive legal tradition, one based on the precepts of Roman law. This legal system differed drastically in its form from that of the surrounding English colonies, as it did not consist of codified groups of laws but was rather a vague expression of suggested societal norms. This was an advantageous system to have for export, as its lack of firm codification made it quite adjustable to new situations arising from the colonial experience. Because there were no firmly enacted legal statutes, magistrates were free to adjudicate each case on its own merit and to rule in whatever way best served both individual and communal justice within their specific community.

Within this vaguely defined system, how did Dutch law try to conceptualize *child*? Or, more importantly, what did the legal definition of the child indicate concerning children's participation in the legal process? The age of full majority in Holland, for both sexes, was tentatively set at the very late age of twenty-five years. Children below that age were described by the statutes as existing in a natural relationship of submission to parents or legal guardians. The words "*kinderen*" (children), "*minder-jarige*" (minor), and "*onbejaerde*" (underage) are used interchangeably throughout the codes. However, the law remained flexible as to how this standard should be applied, with an acknowledgment that it be considered applicable "if not in all, at all events in the majority of cases." Oftentimes, the suggested age of majority did, indeed, fluctuate from town to town, and magistrates were allowed to accelerate or retard the limit as they saw fit.[5]

Children were considered emancipated under the law either through marriage—which could be contracted by parents or guardians as young as fourteen for boys and twelve for girls (although children were not expected to contract their own marriages until the age of twenty-five and twenty, respectively)—or when they were tacitly permitted to have a home of their own and conduct business. Those considered minors by age or circumstance had no power to bind themselves contractually, with the exception of cases of delict. Instead, all contracts were entered into by children's parents or guardians on their behalf. This practice included minors who were orphans and placed under the protection of community members required to act in loco parentis in all legal matters, although not expected to fulfill any substantive role in the orphan's life. Essentially, children were legally bound to parents or guardians, who then held the right to transfer that dependency to masters, mistresses, or spouses.[6]

However, this right was not exclusive, and an important and intriguing exception is children's ability to contract themselves in criminal cases. Roman-Dutch law seemingly conceptualized criminal acts as creating a contract between the commissioning party and the victim. The contract called for compensation (typically in the form of money or service) in payment for the misdeed. A child who committed such an act was perceived as possessing the ability to enter into such a contract, and could be held personally responsible for his or her actions. Conversely, however, the injuries inflicted on a dependent would be brought to court by the party responsible for them—such as a master, guardian, or parent; or the right could be appropriated by the local *Schout* (sheriff).[7]

This is why, on November 25, 1659, Andries Clazen came to court on behalf of his "little daughter," charging that Jan Everzen Bout had "cut two holes with the tongs" in the child's head. The girl had only been in service to the defendant for three weeks, although Jan claimed that during that time she was a "stiffnecked thing and will not listen to what is said of her" and that he only threw the tongs "thro' hastiness" but without intent to injure the child. The *Schout*, as guardian of the peace, demanded that Bout pay a fine, as well as damages for pain and surgeon's fees. A statement from the surgeon, Hans Kierstede, was thereby requested, in order to ascertain the extent of the child's injuries—her father claiming she had "la[in] abed some days."

On the next court date, December 16, the child was ordered to appear and exhibit the wound, as well as testify to what had transpired. While the court did not record precisely what the child said (there is only the minimal statement: "The little girl declared to the Court the reason, why it happened") the court determined upon hearing "the declaration of the little daughter" as well as "having seen the wound" that Jan Bout was responsible for the surgeon's fees, twenty guilders "for the injury," and a ten guilder fine to the court.[8]

This case may be illustrative of several relationships between children and the judiciary system, or, to continue the crystal metaphor, of several colors refracted. Firstly, we see that the incident has occurred within the bounds of indentureship. Necessarily, this would have been accomplished through a contract signed by Andries Clazen and Jan Bout, in which the father essentially transferred the child's dependency from himself to an outside guardian. Coming into court to demand restitution on behalf of his daughter, he is also, de facto, reclaiming his position of dominance over the child's life and labor. This is a passive, and common, treatment of the child in the case—as an object situated in a power struggle between two dueling adult desires.

The dichroic quickly becomes trichroic when the *Schout* trumps the power of the father with the power of the state. His demand that the court levy a fine transforms the case from a civil matter to a criminal one. Simultaneously truncating the power of the father, and redefining the situation as one of public and communal concern, he is also championing the contract created between the child and the abuser. He argues that the contract should be upheld and fulfilled in the form of "payment of surgeon's fees and the pain." When the court agrees with the *Schout,* they too, are recognizing the contract between the child and the abuser.

Perhaps this is why the court held off on making its decision until after hearing the testimony of the little girl. It would have been possible to adjudicate the case solely on the basis of the surgeon's findings and the testimony of the child's father—certainly Jan had already admitted to the crime—but the magistrates felt compelled to hear the testimony of the child before making its decision. As the aggrieved party, the child is recognized as the holder of the contract, and thereby, her participation in the proceeding becomes necessary.

This case also exemplifies how children's testimony was considered in the New Amsterdam courtroom. Although Jan testified that the incident was accidental, and on the second court date his wife appeared to confirm his testimony, claiming "her husband flung the tongs at the child's head, but not with the intent to hurt her, and that it was of very little consequence," the court still believed the child's testimony over both the adults'.

The wound and the surgeon's statement, although proving the extent of the injuries, would not have been sufficient for the magistrates to necessarily find Jan Bout guilty of criminal misconduct—a finding that the ten guilder fine belies. They would have proven only that the child was struck with the tongs, but feasibly in an accidental manner. It is only the testimony of the child, which does not survive in the records, that pushes the court to declare the actions criminal in nature.

There is also another space of contestation and control in this story: the testimony of Jan Bout that the little girl was a "stiffnecked thing and will not listen to what is said to her." While we have no way of ascertaining the veracity of this statement, it is well within the realm of probability that tempers flared due to a perception of the little girl not properly adhering to her hierarchal place. Since the indenture agreement was made on her behalf by her father, it is quite possible that the child did not agree to being placed in servitude. Being "stiffnecked" and not obeying orders would have been one possible way for the child to express her discontent at the situation. Modern psychiatric studies have indicated that instances of physical abuse are often related to the care-giver's perceived lack of control and simultaneous belief that the child has command of the situation. Often, this perception is exacerbated by children reacting in a way that is unexpected by the adult. The children themselves, discerning the adult's perceived loss of situational control, may often try to maintain the power imbalance by becoming verbally or nonverbally unresponsive. The little girl's unresponsiveness to the adults, in the form of her disobedience, may have been a crucial power ploy engaged in upon her comprehension of the adults' relatively weak position.[9]

This case exemplifies several coetaneous relationships to power and the judiciary system. There is the contestation between adults as to the ownership, and protection, of the child. Father-master-community (in the form of the *Schout*) all make claims to their legitimacy for control. Existing concurrently is the child-judiciary-master triangle, in which the court recognizes the contract between the little girl and her master created by his abuse, and relies on her testimony in their decision to uphold that contract. Lastly, there is child-father-master, in which the three battle for the usurpation of dominance—the little girl resisting through unresponsive behavior, the master exerting dominance through violence, and the father prevailing by appealing to the community and judicial authority.

How do these dynamics change when the abuser is also the parent? On February 27, 1663, Lambert Huybersen Mol and his son, Huybert, were arrested in violation of the ordinance outlawing fighting. The *Schout*, Pieter Tonneman, demanded a 150-guilder fine from Lambert as "the deft. has been fighting with his son and drew a knife on him." Lambert, for his part, denied having drawn a knife on the child, but did admit "having given him a blow," flatly excusing his actions by stating "a father may well strike his child." This response is not terribly surprising, as apparently Lambert ran with a fairly rough crowd—on December 12, 1665, about two years after Lambert and Huybert had been arrested for fighting, Lambert's friend and drinking companion Gerrit Mannaet was arrested for a drunken escapade consisting of fighting with Lambert, and then going home and striking his own child on the chest with a knife.[10]

But in Lambert and Huybert's case, the community, again in the form of the sheriff, intervened to uphold communal values. While Lambert claimed his parental right to discipline his child, the community decided his actions were excessive and inappropriate. Interestingly, however, his son, Huybert, was also arrested for partaking in the fight. The court and community recognized the child's participation in the event, and felt the boy was culpable.

This case reveals a further aspect concerning the position of children in relation to violence in the legal discourse. As mentioned earlier, the words "*kinderen*" (children), "*minder-jarige*" (minor), and "*onbejaerde*" (under-age) are used interchangeably throughout the codes, and not accidentally. Further complicating the structure is the use of the term "*wezen*," which functions both as the plural form of "*wees*" (meaning "orphan") and as "person." The usage of the word "*wezen*" may indicate a conceptual continuity between a child without natural adult supervision and recognized personhood. But all the terms signify a spectrum of childhood that is tied primarily to legal prescriptions of age—legal prescriptions that were entirely flexible and enforced at magisterial discretion. Although children were conceptualized as *wezen* (person), albeit as a specific *type* of person (an *onbejaerde*—underage person, or *minder-jarige*—minor person), they were still held to what were considered the "natural laws" of humanity. While jurisprudence could be fashioned so that children were prevented from participating in specific, legally recognized financial transactions, they could not be held exempt under the law from the situations they *did* participate in. This signifies a tacit acknowledgment on behalf of the court that children did, indeed, possess enough free will to make a choice. On the basis of this reasoning, it would have been unnecessary and superfluous in New Amsterdam to have specific legal codes that protected children —children, as people, were allowed the same protections as everyone else, and, conversely, would be held to the same standards. Just as the adult servant, Lorens Holst, was able to accuse his master and mistress of ill treatment, so could the little boy of Abraham Pieterzen charge that his master threatened him, "I shall beat you, so that the Devil shall laugh at it."[11]

However, this *nondependent* view of children did have certain limitations, and was not held exclusively. The best example of the deliberation concerning the culpability of children by the courts is found in an anomalous case concerning the sodomy of a ten-year-old slave named Manuel Congo.[12]

On the 25th of June 1646, it was brought to the attention of the court that Manuel had been sodomized by a fellow slave named Jan Creoly while on the island of Curacao. The crime was reported to the magistrates of New Amsterdam by fellow slaves, and although we cannot be certain of the dynamics that underlay the reporting of this crime (was Jan an outsider, perhaps? disliked by the community, and therefore less likely to be protected by it?), it is worth noting that the investigation was initiated from within the slave community. Perhaps the slaves simply considered the abhorrent nature of the crime as nullifying normal communally preservationist protocols that kept outsiders at bay and incidents within the community unreported to local authorities.

Either way, the investigation led to the arrest of Jan, who was then examined "in the presence of the aforesaid boy." Manuel quickly confessed to the deed "without being threatened in any way," which subsequently led to Jan, "without torture and while free from irons," confessing that he had, in fact, "committed sodomy with the aforesaid boy" while on the island of Curacao. He was subsequently condemned to be "brought to the place of justice to be strangled there to death and his body burned to ashes, as an example to others"—the harshest punishment in the New Amsterdam records during this period.

But what to do with Manuel? The magistrates had to deliberate. According to tradition, "a person with whom sodomy has been committed deserves to be put to death," and during this period of Dutch culture, sodomy was perceived as the most communally destroying crime committable. In 1732, for example, the theater of Amsterdam was closed to appease a god believed to be punishing the prevalence of sodomy in the Netherlands with a plague of worms, eating away the foundations of the dikes.[13]

This, however, does not make it particularly less striking that in their deliberation of this case, the magistrates cite the Bible—a stylistic choice that is unique to these court records:

> ... on account of which sins God Almighty overthrew Sodom and Gamorrah [*sic*] of the plain and exterminated the inhabitants from the earth. ...
> God says: "For whosoever shall commit any of these abominations, even the souls that commit them shall be cut off from among their people."

This reference to the Bible, and the wrath of God, stands out quite starkly from the typical expression of community decency that other cases expounded. Crimes such as theft, manslaughter, or the rarely prosecuted adultery were not couched in religious terms but simply acknowledged as operating counter to the shared standards of morality professed by the community. Nor were they punished even remotely as harshly. People in New Amsterdam, committing serious crimes, would most likely find themselves severely fined or banished. The magistrates, however, did not feel the normal punishment to be sufficient for a crime that "on account of its heinousness may not be tolerated or suffered, in order that the wrath of God may not descend upon us as it did upon Sodom," and that had been committed by a man who "is not worthy to associate with mankind." Thereby, "invok[ing] the name of God so as to pass a just judgment and wishing to do justice" (also a unique invocation to the records), it was necessary to condemn Jan to a gruesome death, "as an example to others."

This brings us back to the question of what to do with Manuel. As we have already seen, children were viewed as functioning and participating members of society. Just as their testimony could be relied upon, or delict contracts between them and abusers recognized, they were also considered participants in criminal activities. But what to do, when the punishment for the crime was capital? Should a ten-year-old boy be condemned to strangulation, his body burned, in order to protect the better interests of the community? The magistrates and the director general of the colony (at this time, Willem Kieft) were reluctant to take this final step. In an almost apologetic tone, they rationalized their ruling for a lesser punishment for the child:

> ... he [Manuel] confesses that the same was committed by force and violence, as those who were present declared and which in view of the abomination is not described here, the said Creoly having likewise confessed that

he committed the crime by force, without the consent of the boy. And although according to law a person with whom sodomy has been committed deserves to be put to death, yet, in view of the innocense and youth of the boy, we have ordered that he be brought to the place where Jan Creoly shall be executed and that he be tied to a post, with wood piled around him, and be made to view the execution and be beaten with rods.

Manuel could not be entirely spared—to do so would be to go against the rulings of God, the protection of the community, and the fundamental view that children were active participants in cases of delict. However, the consideration of "the innocense and youth of the boy" once again highlights the middling and polymorphous stratum children inhabited. It is not likely, had the evidence of forced rape been less conclusive, that Manuel's "innocense and youth" would have spared him from a worse fate. However, in the bench's desire to justify its ruling, it chose to reference a cultural touchstone in which youth could denote a form of innocence— even if only of a partial kind.

While this case is indeed anomalous, it is sometimes within the extraordinary that a clearer boundary of societal mores can be perceived, and then translated back onto other instances that seemingly defy explanation. When, for example, two years later, Willem Gilfoordt's punishment for molesting the ten-year-old Maria Barentsz may have been mitigated by the magistrates because "of the fact that it has appeared to the director and council that shortly after the said crime one Willem Gerritsz Wesselsz with the will and consent of the said Maria Barentsz has had conversation with her," the lighter sentence was not due to a gendered structural flaw that ignored violent sexual acts. Rather, it resulted from the courts taking very seriously both the testimony of the child, and her ability to consent to participate in these events. If she claimed, as she did, that the sex with Wesselsz was consensual, the courts did not feel they could contradict her testimony. It is, in fact, because the child's testimony was both highly regarded and believed that her rapist was punished with a flogging and banishment, and her partner with sawing lumber for the company for a year. Although the court recognized that what transpired between Wesselsz and Barents was not rape, that consent was given without the permission of her parents necessitated a punishment for what today would be considered statutory rape.[14]

In many ways, this case illuminates a familiar problem in the relationship between children and the legal system. Much as historian Holly

Brewer has found in her work concerning children and testimony in the English colonies, rational thinking creates exclusive categories. And exclusive categories are then unable to acknowledge two contradictory but simultaneous ideas. A child may be viewed as a contributing member of the community, whose testimony can be acknowledged as coming from a rational, and therefore trustworthy, place, but who, conversely, can be held responsible for his or her participation in the events that happen to or around him or her. Or, children may be seen as wholly dependent, lacking reason, and while the ability to be an active participant in the things around them may be conceptually severely limited, they may enjoy an umbrella of special protections and exemptions. This duality continues in current legal literature, as psychologists, jurists, and the public debate the legitimacy of children's testimony, and it was certainly prevalent in English legal debates of the eighteenth century. However, in the seventeenth century, and certainly for the seventeenth-century Dutch community of New Amsterdam, children were *wezen* (people)—protected by the same laws and held to the same standards of conduct as all other persons.[15]

So what, then, does this imply concerning the early modern conceptualization of childhood? For the Dutch of New Amsterdam, childhood was a temporary, and fluctuating, state of economic dependency. It was not particularly different from the varying, polymorphous states of dependency within the "adult" world—between persons and the state, persons and the Dutch West India Company, husbands and wives, masters and servants, or people who became obligated to each other in cases of delict or by financial contract. In fact, Roman-Dutch law itself is centered on trying to define these varying degrees of obligation.

Because children were considered people, with interests to be protected, their testimony was valued in the courtroom. The accusations they brought against parents, masters, mistresses, or other community members were seriously considered and pursued by the courts. When, in June of 1659, the "little son of Nicolaas Velthuysen" complained to a family friend, Isaack de Forest, that his drunkard step-father was squandering the money left by his recently deceased mother, Janneke Willems, that had been earmarked for the child's care and maintenance, de Forest immediately went to the court of the Orphan Masters, and the court fiercely pursued the case over the next five months, until finally Nicolaas submitted to the inheritance being placed in the hands of guardians. Even though, as prescribed by the statutes, children could not instigate cases on their own behalf, they could, and did, find willing parents, community members, or even the state (in the form of the local *Schout*) who were willing to initiate the proceedings for them.[16]

Although this article has closely examined a very small handful of cases (indeed, the number of cases on the record involving children comprise only a small fraction of the litigation in New Amsterdam, less than 1 percent of the total cases for this period), these cases exemplify a specific dialectical paradigm in the rationality of *childhood*. Children were recognized by courts and community as having a similar access to power as their adult counterparts, a theorization that could be used to their advantage—in the upholding of delict contracts, the reliance on their testimony, and the willingness of the community and state to bring their complaints before the bench—or to their disadvantage, in their arrests for participating in delict, and their punishment for those perceived indiscretions. Children were not considered as existing in a static state of dependency that required special protections and exceptions under the law. However, to claim them as merely "miniature adults" would also be overly simplistic. Adults, too, did not exist in stable, equilibrious spaces of nondependency, and just as relationships and obligations between adults were multiform and not unilateral, so, too, the relationships between children and the community around them.

In violent or abusive situations, either financial or physical, the children of New Amsterdam were not passive victims. They actively participated in the events, and actively pursued injustices—either through forms of coded resistance or by finding avenues into the courtroom. A study of violence against children, therefore, cannot be merely the examination of what was or was not done by the state or the community to protect or prevent these situations, but must also be a study of how the children participated in all levels of the dialogue, how their activity was perceived, supported, or rejected by the community, and how this demonstrates the ways children interacted with the dichroistic power structures around them. Through the examination of these dialogues, we may come to a further understanding of how stages of metamorphosis were conceptualized, understood, and created within this community.

NOTES

1. Case of Geertje Teunis vs. Leentje Dirckx, from Berthold Fernow, ed., *Records of New Amsterdam*, 7 vols. (reprint Baltimore: Genealogical Publishing, 1976), vol. 4, 12.

2. For a comprehensive bibliographic essay concerning children in the colonial period see Holly Brewer, "Children and Parents," in David Vickers, ed., *A Companion to Colonial America* (Malden: Blackwell Publishers, 2003). For discussions of children and authority, see Fliegelman, *Prodigals and Pilgrims*; Brewer, *By Birth or Consent*. For children and violence, see Hoffer and Hull, *Murdering Mothers*; Pleck, *Domestic Tyranny*; Radbill, "Children in a World of Violence," in Ray Helfer and Ruth Kempe, eds., *The Battered Child* (Chicago: University of Chicago Press, 1987); Roth, "Child Murder in New England"; Sutton, *Stubborn Children*.

3. For the "little commonwealth" paradigm, see Demos, *A Little Commonwealth*. Holly Brewer argues that children became conceived as irrational with the absorption of Enlightenment philosophy. See Holly Brewer, "Age of Reason? Children, Testimony, and Consent in Early America," in Christopher Tomlins and Bruce Mann, eds., *The Many Legalities of Early America* (Chapel Hill: University of North Carolina Press, 2001). I am using "power" in the Foucauldian sense, in that power is not simply a confrontational or adversarial relationship but an externally imposed and internally realized invisible structure placed on free individuals to limit the possibilities of behavior. See Michel Foucault, *Discipline and Punish: The Birth of the Prison* (New York: Pantheon, 1977).

4. For an argument concerning the importance of child labor in the colonies at this time, see Vickers, *Farmers and Fishermen*.

5. Hugo Grotius, *The Jurisprudence of Holland*, 2 vols., Robert Warden Lee, trans. (Germany: Scientia Verlag Aalen, 1977), vol. I: I. 3. 8, vol. II: I. 7. 3.

6. Although in the commentary on the laws there appears to have been some controversy concerning whether both of these conditions needed to be met or only the separate-residence condition. Groenewegen Van Der Made, *ad* Cod. 8. 48 (49). 3. Grotius, *The Jurisprudence of Holland*, I. 8. 5.

7. Grotius, *The Jurisprudence of Holland*, vol. I: III. 34. 3.

8. Case of Andries Clazen vs. Jan Everzen Bout, from Berthold Fernow, ed., *Records of New Amsterdam*, vol. 3 (reprint Baltimore: Genealogical Publishing, 1976), 88, 93–94.

9. Daphne Blunt Bugental, Jay Blue, and Michael Cruzcosa, "Perceived Control over Caregiving Outcomes: Implications for Child Abuse," *Developmental Psychology* 25 (1989): 532–39; Cynthia A. Rhorbeck and Craig T. Twentyman, "Multimodal Assessment of Impulsiveness in Abusing, Neglecting, and Nonmaltreating Mothers and Their Preschool Children," *Journal of Consulting and Clinical Psychology* 54 (1986): 231–36; William D. Bauer and Craig T. Twentyman,

"Abusing, Neglectful, and Comparison Mother's Responses to Child-Related and Non-Child-Related Stressors," *Journal of Consulting and Clinical Psychology* 53 (1985): 335–43; David A. Wolfe, "Child-Abusive Parents: An Empirical Review and Analysis," *Psychological Bulletin* 97 (1985): 462–82; Sandra T. Azar and Cynthia A. Rohrbeck, "Child Abuse and Unrealistic Expectations: Further Validation of the Parent Opinion Questionnaire," *Journal of Consulting and Clinical Psychology* 54 (1986): 867–68.

10. Ordinance of the 15th of April, 1638, in *New York Historical Manuscripts: Dutch, Volume IV: Council Minutes, 1638–1649*, Arnold J. F. Van Laer, trans. (Baltimore: Genealogical Publishing, 1974), 4; Case of Schout Pieter Tonneman vs. Lambert Huybersen Mol and his son Huybert, Fernow, *The Records of New Amsterdam*, vol. 4, 205. The case against Gerrit Mannaet is found in ibid., vol. 4, 328.

11. Lourens Holst vs. Abel Hardenbroecx and wife, Fernow, *The Records of New Amsterdam*, vol. 3, 145–46; Abraham Pieterzen vs. Claas Tysen, the cooper, Fernow, *The Records of New Amsterdam*, vol. 3, 386, 392. I would like to thank Pieter Spierenburg for pointing out that the word "*wezen*" held both meanings in the statutes.

12. Case against Jan Creoly, *New York Historical Manuscripts*, 326–28.

13. Pieter Spierenburg, *Written in Blood: Fatal Attraction in Enlightenment Amsterdam* (Columbus: Ohio University Press, 2004), 3.

14. Cases against Willem Gilfoordt and Willem Gerritsz Wesselsz, *New York Historical Manuscripts*, vol. 4, 478, 482–86.

15. Brewer "Age of Reason?" Concerning modern debates over children and testimony, see Dana D. Anderson, "Assessing the Reliability of Child Testimony in Sexual Abuse Cases," *Southern California Law Review* 69 (September 1996): 2117–61; Rachel Sutherland, Julien Gross, and Harlene Hayne, "Adults' Understanding of Young Children's Testimony," *Journal of Applied Psychology* 81 (1996): 777–85; C. A. Elizabeth Luus, John W. Turtle, and Gary L. Wells, "Child Eyewitnesses: Seeing Is Believing," *Journal of Applied Psychology* 80 (1995): 317–26; Michael R. Leippe and Ann Romanczyk, "Reactions to Child (versus Adult) Eyewitnesses," *Law and Human Behavior* 13 (1989): 102–32.

16. The case against Nicolaes Velthuyzen is found in Berthold Fernow, ed., *Minutes of the Orphan Masters of New Amsterdam, 1655–1663* (New York: P. Harper, 1902–7), 87–89, 99–104, 106, 111–12, 118.

Chapter 6

"Improved" and "Very Promising Children"
Growing Up Rich in Eighteenth-Century South Carolina

Darcy R. Fryer

In 1764, Charleston merchant Henry Laurens penned a brief summary of his life in which he lamented the loss of "some very promising Children, particularly an improved Boy of Six and a clever Girl of Eight Years old."[1] Laurens was a fond father, who never let his multifaceted career deter him from pouring energy into childrearing. Yet when groping for language in which to describe his grief at his children's deaths, he turned to economic imagery. American colonists were deeply preoccupied with the project of "improving" their surroundings to make them both more civilized and, ultimately, more profitable. "Promising" also had economic connotations in Laurens's milieu; it implied investment in something that would yield future benefit. The economic imagery that Laurens applied to the children he loved and lost sums up the essence of affluent eighteenth-century Carolinians' beliefs about parenting: raising children (their own and, often, others') was an investment in the future of both individual planter and merchant dynasties and the emerging planter class as a whole. Childrearing was a central component of the vast colonial enterprises of estate building and community building.

This article explores two distinctive aspects of South Carolina merchant and planter families' childrearing strategies in the mid- to late eighteenth century. First, I examine the economic roles of children, teenagers, and young adults. Their responsibilities were often substantial; growing up rich in eighteenth-century South Carolina was as much about adding to the family fortune as it was about enjoying the privileges of wealth and rank. The shortage of educated white labor power, combined with low country settlers' economic ambitions, propelled upwardly mobile parents to entrust their older children with significant responsibilities as clerks, couriers, and assistants in family businesses. I then shift my focus to affluent Carolinians' preference for extensive parenting—their reliance on extensive networks of formal and informal guardians, whether kin, friends, business associates, or near strangers, to help bring up their children—rather than intensive parenting, in which parents invest more exclusively in their own biological offspring. Extensive parenting networks had dual significance for low country parents. They provided stability for children should their parents die before they were grown, but perhaps even more importantly, they allowed youths living on the margins of the British empire to maximize their educational, professional, and travel opportunities. In the conclusion, I argue that wealthy Carolinians' reliance on extensive parenting networks and emphasis on work as a source of social identity reflected their roots in Britain's commercial middle class as well as their colonial identity.

"[T]hough you are very young," Eliza Lucas Pinckney admonished her eldest son, Charles, in 1761, "you must know the welfair of a whole family depends in a great measure on the progress you make in moral Virtue, Religion, and learning."[2] These were the themes that resonated in the minds of most affluent low country parents and, indeed, most upwardly mobile middle-class parents throughout the British empire: virtue, education as the key to economic and social advancement, and family solidarity. But one of the crucial expectations of affluent South Carolina parents never made it into Pinckney's letter. Throughout the eighteenth century, low country planter and merchant parents set their children to work in the family business of managing plantations, trade, and slaves. The virtue of industry, and the urge for economic productivity, molded the low country gentry's approach to parenting.

In the decades preceding the American Revolution, most South Carolina planters and merchants envisioned themselves as members of an industrious network of upwardly mobile middling folk who were still very much in the process of building durable economic portfolios and accumulating wealth. They wanted to bring up diligent, capable daughters and sons who would tend and augment the family fortune, not wild blades and decorative belles who would squander it. Eighteenth-century planter children were trained to work—in fact, most of them were put to work in family businesses by their early teens. Certain chores that required some education but were too dull or time-consuming to be done by adult white men became young people's work, the province of teenagers and young adults of both sexes. The gentry's motives for setting its children to work were mixed, partly practical and partly pedagogical.

The labor of a merchant's or planter's children was potentially among his greatest economic assets. In fact, men pressed into service all the children in their households, including nieces, nephews, and wards as well as their own offspring. Children of the planter class began running errands for their parents by the age of seven or eight; Harry Laurens acted as his father's interpreter on a journey through France at that age. As elite children neared their teens, they assumed more substantial economic responsibilities. The onset of more rigorous economic training when children reached their early teens reflected a cultural judgment about the age at which children were mature enough to handle steady work; slave children were usually set to work full-time at the age of ten or twelve, and it is not surprising that their future masters' responsibilities were stepped up at about the same point.[3] The nature of the tasks that planter children were assigned also dictated the age at which they started to perform them. Wealthy children's economic responsibilities were largely secretarial, and by the age of eleven or twelve well-educated children could be counted on to write legibly, perform simple calculations, and keep records systematically and accurately.

The first administrative task in which boys and girls of the planter class were trained was writing and copying letters. The perilous nature of transatlantic voyages necessitated that careful correspondents send two or preferably three copies of each of their letters, by different ships, and keep yet another copy for themselves. Copying letters was a dull and time-consuming task, and adult men palmed it off on others whenever possible. When the men of the family were ill or unusually pressed for time, women and children took dictation or composed letters according to the head of the household's instructions. Teenagers with a taste for drawing, such as Jack Laurens, copied maps and diagrams on behalf of their parents.[4]

As they neared adulthood, children of the planter class entered the third phase of their economic training, in which they learned to manage and administer property. Although they continued to act as their parents' secretaries, they now began to serve as their deputies as well. Adults frequently placed teenagers in charge of particular household projects: a teenage girl might supervise a dairy, a kitchen garden, or the education of younger siblings; James Laurens asked his nephew Jack to plan a garden for him. In emergencies, planter families sometimes assigned enormous economic responsibilities to teenage children. When Colonel George Lucas was recalled to Antigua in 1740, his seventeen-year-old daughter Eliza took over the management of the family's three Carolina plantations, corresponding with her father and his Charleston business agent, directing the overseers, and experimenting with indigo and other new crops. Eliza was proud of her activities, both because they allowed her to help her financially embattled family and because they reflected her newly adult status. "I have the business of 3 plantations to transact," she bragged to her London foster mother, "which requires much writing and more business and fatigue of other sorts than you can imagine. But least you should imagine it too burthensom to a girl at my early time of life, give me leave to answer you: I assure you that I think myself happy that I can be useful to so good a father." In some families, teenagers and young adults of both sexes not only helped to administer property but also assisted their fathers in other aspects of their careers. Eliza Lucas zealously assisted her father in his pursuit of military promotion; fourteen-year-old Jack Laurens helped his father write a political pamphlet, *Extracts,* which was published in Charleston in 1769. A man's work was not considered to be a private, individual sphere of activity, but rather a family business. The entire family might assist the husband and father in his professional life, just as they assisted in managing the family's plantations and mercantile concerns.[5]

Young adults also acted as couriers, transmitting letters, messages, money, and goods on behalf of their households. Many gentry families delegated shopping responsibilities to young adults, especially young men, who traveled abroad; those who had no sons or brothers of their own abroad were not shy about employing neighbors and friends. As a young clerk in London in the 1740s, Henry Laurens selected painted floor cloths and scrubbers for Benjamin Smith, shipped silk gowns for Anne Loughton Smith and Miss Holmes, ordered a broadcloth suit for Robert Raper, and secured miscellaneous articles for Ann Ashby Manigault. As a law student a decade later, Peter Manigault positively begged his parents for errands to run. "You cant imagine how much pleasure it gives me, to be imployed by you," he assured his mother. Young women seldom ventured so far without their parents and consequently did not shop on the scale on which their brothers did, but they frequently ran errands for family and friends closer to home. Charleston teenager Margaret Izard did many odd jobs for her country cousin Mary Stead: purchasing a table, having Stead's handkerchiefs marked, and settling accounts with Stead's dressmaker.[6] Shopping, like copying letters, was a tedious, time-consuming task, so it naturally fell to the share of young, unmarried adults who had few other responsibilities.

Young women of the planter class received economic training that was nearly as extensive as their brothers' and similar in content, but the significance of children's tasks differed according to gender. For boys, copying letters, shopping, and supervising small business transactions were stepping-stones to greater responsibilities. Men carefully supervised their sons' progression from one task to the next. Jack Laurens, for example, began to help in his father's mercantile house, copying letters, when he was twelve or thirteen. This was a necessary secretarial task, but it also taught Jack the proper format of a business letter and allowed him to learn about his father's business. A few years later, Henry Laurens took Jack with him on his semiannual plantation tour so that he might view the family lands and meet the overseers and managers. In the fall of 1771, Laurens put Jack, now almost seventeen, in charge of purchasing stores for a transatlantic voyage. In England, Jack continued to act as his father's secretary and, increasingly, his deputy, conducting business by proxy. When Laurens returned to South Carolina in 1774, he authorized his son to select and ship plantation goods at his discretion.[7] By now Jack was not merely a secretary or apprentice but had acquired a status approaching that of a junior partner in his father's firm.

Teenage girls, including Jack Laurens's younger sisters, performed many of the same tasks their brothers did, but for them these jobs were laden with a different meaning. As daughters, sisters, wives, and to some extent even as widows, their role would always be managerial rather than executive. The economic responsibilities that they assumed as young teenagers were essentially the same ones they would bear for the rest of their lives. Wives formed the backbone of the family work force; they copied letters, transmitted messages and goods, shopped for provisions and household goods, and supervised routine plantation business much as teenage boys and girls did. Planters seldom designed graduated series of training tasks for their daughters, but they may have given their daughters *more* careful training than their sons in certain secretarial skills. Wealthy Carolinians paid close attention to the quality of their daughters' handwriting, not merely because good handwriting was a sign of gentility but also because it was a vital economic skill. In many families, women bore the primary responsibility for copying (and sometimes editing) letters; women also helped train younger family members in secretarial skills. A woman's good penmanship was thus an asset to the entire family. David Ramsay bragged that his wife "wrote very fast, and, at the same time, a round, distinct, legible hand. Her father pronounced her to be the best clerk he ever employed."[8]

Work was a vital source of social identity for the children of the eighteenth-century South Carolina gentry. Affluent parents' emphasis on productive work reflected both practical necessity and the value that Carolina colonists placed on early maturity and early assumption of authority. The shortage of educated white labor power in the eighteenth-century low country led ambitious fathers to press children (and women) into secretarial and managerial roles in the family business, whether it was planting, trade, or one of the professions. But many affluent Carolina parents evidently admired children who were socially poised, earnest, and intellectually precocious, eager to launch their careers and marry young, whether or not it was economically necessary for them to do so. Visitors like William Dillwyn of Philadelphia found this aspect of low country culture objectionable, but teenagers who grew up in South Carolina do not seem to have resented their families' expectations of them.[9] Many, like Eliza Lucas and Peter Manigault, gloried in the economic responsibilities that their parents ceded them and begged for more. They were keenly aware that their families, however wealthy, depended on their labor, and they viewed their contributions to the family economy as evidence of their impending accession to adulthood, authority, and power.

Affluent low country parents' preference for extensive parenting likewise reflected their colonial sensibilities, including anxiety about the high mortality rate, a desire to keep in touch with mainstream British culture, and eagerness to cultivate local social and economic networks. Henry Laurens provides an excellent case study. When Laurens's wife died in 17, Laurens broke up his nuclear household and cast his five children adrift to find their own mentors and parental figures among a varied cast of aunts, uncles, godparents, schoolmasters, and family friends that spanned both sides of the Atlantic. Laurens did not disappear from his children's lives, but henceforth he exercised his paternal authority largely in an epistolary manner, guiding his children towards other trustworthy advisors rather than supervising them on a day-to-day basis himself. Meanwhile, Laurens assumed similar authority for a diverse group of other South Carolina boys and girls: a niece, a nephew by marriage, sons of friends and business acquaintances.[10] The Laurens clan displayed, in slightly exaggerated form, the pattern of extensive rather than intensive parenting that characterized the eighteenth-century low country gentry. Parents did not concentrate all of their time and resources on their own children but reserved a portion for their nieces, nephews, wards, and young friends. At the same time, they gratefully accepted other adults' attentions to their own children. Growing up rich in eighteenth-century Carolina usually meant growing up within and under the supervision of a wide-ranging social network instead of, or in addition to, growing up in an intensive parent-child relationship.

Extensive parenting networks created a modicum of security for children growing up in a hostile demographic regime. Among the planter class, about 60 percent of children who lived to the age of sixteen lost at least one parent by that age. Orphans were surrounded by loose-knit circles of adult advisors, including kin, family friends, and parents' business associates; often they passed through a series of relatives' households. Guardianship arrangements were fluid and flexible, creating a seamless flow of adult supervision for children who might otherwise have been isolated by demographic catastrophe. Gabriel (Gay) Manigault Jr. had the misfortune to lose his primary English guardian soon after he arrived in Europe, but he knew the system and promptly selected a new guardian for himself: "[A]s I thought that my Grandfather would choose Mr. Manning to be my Guardian at present, I wrote him a Letter to that purpose, in which I hope I did right." When Gay's uncle William Wragg drowned off the Dutch coast a year later, leaving his seven-year-old son alone among strangers, Gay behaved with similar aplomb, calling on the sister of Wragg's deceased first wife and securing her assurances that she would "do all in her Power, for [Wragg's] Child's Advantage." Meanwhile, Gay's grandfather hurriedly wrote to London, authorizing Gay to draw on his own account for the care of his youthful cousin.[11] Gay, still young enough to be an object of guardianship arrangements, simultaneously moved into the role of guardian towards a child still younger than himself.

Guardianship networks were not merely a means of caring for orphans. Living parents relied on them to enhance the educational opportunities of their children (most commonly sons). Throughout the eighteenth century, low country boys as young as six or seven traveled to England for their education. Most went by themselves. Their parents entrusted them to acquaintances or friendly ship captains for the transatlantic passage; in England, they were delivered to "guardians" who had agreed to act as their foster parents abroad. Similar, though less formal, guardianship networks existed in the low country, where they served the same purpose of expanding elite children's educational opportunities. Families living in the countryside, Georgia, and Florida often sent their children to Charleston for schooling or vocational training, delegating administrative and disciplinary responsibility for the children to local families. Merchants often assumed personal as well as professional responsibility for young employees and apprentices. When traveling for pleasure came into vogue in the late eighteenth century, low country parents' willingness to entrust their children to the care of others for months or years at a time enlarged both boys and girls' travel opportunities. Fifteen-year-old Gay Manigault jaunted through New England, New York, and Philadelphia in 1774 with a motley party consisting of his spinster cousin Elizabeth Hasell, long-time family friend Dr. John Farquharson, and the governor's wife, Hannah Beale Bull—a remarkable travel opportunity that few American teenagers of the 1770s, however wealthy, enjoyed.[12] In the 1790s, Edward Rutledge's willingness to consign his fourteen-year-old daughter Sarah to the care of Thomas Pinckney, a relative by marriage, enabled Sarah to make a lengthy trip to England. Affluent parents today often rely on schools, camps, and summer programs to help their children gain unusual educational and travel experiences; eighteenth-century low country parents, lacking such formal opportunities, seized on extensive parenting networks to create comparable opportunities for their offspring.

In addition to expanding children's education and travel opportunities, extensive parenting networks provided a means (albeit a rather public one) of smoothing friction between parents and children. Guardians were inevitably drawn into the lives not just of individual children but of entire families. Sometimes they became the children's advocates, for children who were accustomed to extensive parenting networks quickly learned that when they disagreed with their parents, they might effectively appeal to their parents' friends. Brothers Billy and Charles Drayton, the eldest sons of a large and troubled family, often relied on their stepmother's brother, James Glen, and Eliza Lucas Pinckney, the mother of one of their schoolfellows, to ease their relationship with their father. They corresponded with Pinckney as teenagers, and when Billy grew dissatisfied with his allowance, Pinckney and another Carolina friend, Mr. Wright, "petition[ed] for 50 Sterling [in] addition to what your papa intended to allow you." Family friends sometimes tried to head off disputes before they occurred. In 1750, Andrew Rutledge warned nineteen-year-old Peter Manigault that Manigault's father had heard a rumor that Peter was devoting most of his time to the diversions of London rather than his legal studies. Rutledge assured Peter that he did not believe the rumors himself, but added that "as you know his temper as well as I do, your Study must be to please him."[13] Guardians and other adult mentors stood ready not only to replace natural parents if necessary but also to mold relationships between living parents and children.

The practical advantages that extensive parenting and guardianship networks offered children were clear: access to expanded educational and travel opportunities while their parents were alive; representation and mediation in family disputes; protection and stability in the case of parental death. But why did adults choose to act as guardians to other people's children? Their responsibilities varied but were often substantial. The Evance family looked after Charles Cotesworth and Thomas Pinckney for more than a decade, from 1758 until 1771. The Evances paid the boys' school fees, looked after their clothes, nursed them through childhood illnesses, hosted them for vacations, visited them at school, took Tommy on a tour of Bath, and arranged for Charles to study fencing. At judicious intervals they reminded the boys to write to their relatives, give Christmas presents to the servants, and pay their respects to family friends. "[H]ow many thousand Obligations are we all under to [Thomas Pinckney], who has treated you as his own Child, from the Moment I placed you under his Care," wrote Edward Rutledge to his daughter Sarah. "I hope you will never forget it, & that you will always love him with the tender affection of a Child, & his Children as a Sister." Some children became deeply attached to their English guardians, forming pseudofamilial relationships that endured for generations.[14]

Immediate pecuniary advantage was not the guardians' motive. Money changed hands, but it was only for the children's expenses; guardians were not supposed to glean any monetary profit from their charges. Some probably acted purely out of disinterested friendship. Some were childless themselves and may have found solace in vicarious parenting. Still others found guardianship an effective means to cultivate ties with current and future business associates and political allies. When Thomas Elliott Jr. traveled to London to complete his education in 1743, Charleston merchant Robert Pringle gave Thomas a letter of introduction to Pringle's brother Andrew, a ship captain based in London. Andrew Pringle mentored Thomas and corresponded with his father, first about his young charge but soon about other matters as well. In the winter of 1744 Thomas Elliott Sr. empowered Pringle to recover money owed him for fire damages; then he commissioned Pringle to purchase a chaise, a watch, and a "Chair for a Single horse" for him. Acting as a guardian for a wealthy South Carolina boy thus helped

Pringle expand his transatlantic mercantile business.[15] Indeed, the low country gentry's extensive reliance on English acquaintances to care for their children during lengthy stints abroad helped consolidate a close-knit Anglo-Carolinian community in London and the British hinterland. Guardianship arrangements cemented and extended ties based on kinship and joint economic ventures, welding the low country gentry and their British associates into a vast quasi-familial network.

Extensive reliance on guardianship networks, whether the natural parents were living or deceased, was perhaps the single most distinctive feature of eighteenth-century South Carolina merchants' and planters' childrearing strategy. Some combination of ambition and necessity nudged most upwardly mobile Carolina families into relying on guardianship networks to a greater or less extent. Parents usually explained their reliance on guardianship in terms of practical necessity. But it is clear that extensive parenting also fostered the growth of local and transatlantic economic networks. Moreover, it immersed children in these networks from an early age, thus providing them with social capital that could help them improve their estates and fortunes in later years.

Viewed together, low country planters' and merchants' reliance on extensive parenting networks and emphasis on their children's engagement in productive work from adolescence onward suggest that older children and teenagers were thoroughly integrated into the planter and merchant community. Though highly privileged, these children were not isolated in schools or other age-specific environments as affluent children have been from the Victorian era to the present. Boys who were sent abroad actively contributed to their families' social capital (by fostering social networks through guardianship) as well as to family businesses (by transporting goods and messages and shopping on behalf of those at home). Within individual households, older children and teenagers occupied a subordinate but essential niche, performing tasks that were imbued with both pedagogical and practical significance. Many affluent low country girls and boys took pride in their ability to contribute to the family economy and warmly embraced the guardians and mentors their parents chose for them.

Neither extensive parenting networks nor the centrality of work in affluent children's education was unique to the Carolina low country. Both were extensions, in slightly exaggerated form, of the childrearing practices of England's commercial middle class. In England, too, it was common for relatives and friends to participate in raising children, educating them, and launching them in careers; in England, too, it was common for teenagers of both sexes to undertake secretarial duties for their parents.[16] The low country gentry's childrearing practices thus highlight their middle-class British identity. Eighteenth-century South Carolina planters were entrepreneurs who established family businesses and maximized their access to human labor in the same way that British entrepreneurs did, by capitalizing on the labor of their dependents.

Yet these childrearing practices also reflect the extent to which British North America's wealthiest residents were shaped by the insecurities of colonial life. Extensive parenting networks had a rough-and-ready quality that underlines eighteenth-century South Carolina's high mortality rate. Low country children who were themselves only second- or third-generation Americans did not necessarily have large local extended families to turn to if they were orphaned; often, fictive family networks had to be created for them. Planters' and merchants' reliance on the labor of their adolescent children reflects the extent to which wealthy colonists remained absorbed in the creation of economic portfolios, even on the eve of the American Revolution. A leisured planter class, with leisurely and permissive childrearing norms, would not truly emerge in South Carolina until the nineteenth century. In eighteenth-century South Carolina, even the most affluent children participated actively and enthusiastically in the development of their families' economic and social capital.

NOTES

1. Henry Laurens to Mathew Robinson, May 30, 1764, *The Papers of Henry Laurens,* ed. Philip M. Hamer, et al., 16 vols. (Columbia: University of South Carolina Press, 1968–2003), 4: 295.

2. Eliza Lucas Pinckney to Charles Cotesworth Pinckney, April 15, 1761, *The Letterbook of Eliza Lucas Pinckney, 1739–1762,* ed. Elise Pinckney (Columbia: University of South Carolina Press, 1997), 167.

3. Henry Laurens to Richard Oswald, June 10, 1772, *Laurens Papers* 8: 368; Morgan, *Slave Counterpoint,* 197.

4. Henry Laurens to Lachlan McIntosh, January 15, 1770, *Laurens Papers* 7: 219.

5. Spruill, *Women's Life and Work in the Southern Colonies,* 76; Henry Laurens to James Laurens, April 15, 1772, *Laurens Papers* 8: 271; Eliza Lucas to Mrs. Boddicott, May 2, 1740, *Pinckney Letterbook,* 7, 8–9; Henry Laurens to William Fisher, March 1, 1769, *Laurens Papers* 6: 390.

6. *Laurens Papers* 1: 190–96, *passim*; Peter Manigault to Ann Ashby Manigault, April 9, 1752, "Peter Manigault's Letters," ed. Mabel L. Webber, *South Carolina Historical Magazine* 32 (1931): 50; Margaret Izard to Mary Stead, March 30, 1784, Manigault Family Papers, South Carolina Historical Society.

7. Henry Laurens to Andrew Turnbull, October 28, 1769, *Laurens Papers* 7: 178; Henry Laurens to Felix Warley, September 5, 1771, *Laurens Papers* 7: 564; Henry Laurens to Robert Deans, November 5, 1774, *Laurens Papers* 9: 630.

8. Griffin, "The Eighteenth-Century Draytons," 180–81; David Ramsay, *Memoirs of the Life of Martha Laurens Ramsay . . .* , 3rd ed. (Boston: Samuel T. Armstrong, 1812), 33.

9. William Dillwyn, "Diary of William Dillwyn during a Visit to Charles Town in 1772," *South Carolina Historical Magazine* 36 (1935): 73.

10. For a detailed account of extensive parenting within the Laurens family network in the 1770s, see Fryer, "In Pursuit of Their Interest," 59–68.

11. Fryer, "In Pursuit of Their Interest," 52 (demography); Gabriel Manigault Jr. to Ann Ashby Manigault, July 20, 1776, Manigault Family Papers, 1750–1900, South Caroliniana Library; Gabriel Manigault Jr. to Ann Ashby Manigault, October 8, 1777; Gabriel Manigault to Gabriel Manigault Jr., February 24, 1778, "The Great Fire of 1778 Seen through Contemporary Letters," ed. Samuel G. Stoney, *South Carolina Historical Magazine* 64 (1963): 22.

12. For example, see Henry Laurens's correspondence concerning his teenage apprentices Levi Durand and Alexander Wright: *Laurens Papers*, 3–6, *passim*. Gabriel Manigault Jr. to Ann Ashby Manigault, June 4, 1774, July 15, 1774, and October 17, 1774, Manigault Family Papers.

13. Eliza Lucas Pinckney to William Henry Drayton, April 16, 1761, *Pinckney Letterbook*, 169; Andrew Rutledge to Peter Manigault, December 16, 1750, Manigault Family Papers.

14. *Pinckney Letterbook*, 96, 105–6, 121, 146, 152–53; Edward Rutledge to Sarah Rutledge, April 2, 1796, Edward Rutledge's letters to his daughter Sarah, 1793–99, South Carolina Historical Society.

15. Robert Pringle to Andrew Pringle, March 1, 1743, February 7, 1744, November 19, 1744, December 6, 1744, *The Letterbook of Robert Pringle*, ed. Walter B. Edgar, 2 vols. (Columbia: University of South Carolina Press, 1972), 519, 642–43, 761, 772.

16. Grassby, *Kinship and Capitalism*, 279, 285–86; Hunt, *Middling Sort*, 22–23, 86.

"A Dutiful and Affectionate Daughter"
Eliza Lucas of South Carolina

Eliza Lucas was fifteen when her father, a British army officer, moved Eliza and her mother from Antigua, in the West Indies, to a plantation near Charleston, South Carolina, in 1738. As Eliza suggests in the following letters, with a mother in ill health and a father off campaigning with the army, Eliza was left to manage the family business. She is often cited as a pioneer in the effort to make indigo—a plant used to make a rich blue dye—a cash crop in South Carolina. Eliza wrote the following letters when she was only eighteen.

Eliza to Her Father, March 17, 1740

Hon[ored] Sir

Your letter by way of Philadelphia which I duly received was an additional proof of that paternal tenderness which I have always experienced from the most Indulgent of Parents from my Cradle to this time, and the subject of it is of the utmost importance to my peace and happiness.

As you propose Mr. L. to me I am sorry I can't have Sentiments favourable enough of him to take time to think on the Subject, as your Indulgence to me will ever add weight to the duty that obliges me to consult what best pleases you, for so much Generosity on your part claims all my Obedience, but as I know tis my happiness you consult [I] must beg the favour of you to pay my thanks to the old Gentleman for his Generosity and favourable sentiments of me and let him know my thoughts on the affair in such civil terms as you know much better than any I can dictate; and beg leave to say to you that the riches of Peru and [Chile] if he had them put together could not purchase a sufficient Esteem for him to make him my husband.

As to the other Gentleman you mention, Mr. Walsh, you know, Sir, I have so slight a knowledge of him I can form no judgment of him, and a Case of such consiquence requires the Nicest distinction of humours and Sentiments. But give me leave to assure you, my dear Sir, that a single life is my only Choice and if it were not as I am yet but Eighteen, hope you will [put] aside the thoughts of my marrying yet these 2 or 3 years at least.

You are so good to say you have too great an Opinion of my prudence to think I would entertain an indiscreet passion for any one, and I hope heaven will always direct me that I may never disappoint you; and what indeed could induce me to make a secret of my Inclination to my best friend, as I am well aware you would not disapprove it to make me a Sacrifice to Wealth, and I am as certain I would indulge no passion that had not your aprobation, as I truly am

Dr. Sir, Your most dutiful and affect[ionate] Daughter

E. Lucas

Eliza to Her "Good Friend, Mrs. Boddicott"

May 2, 1740

Dear Madam

I flatter myself it will be a satisfaction to you to hear I like this part of the world, as my lott has fallen here—which I really do. I prefer England to it, 'tis true, but think Carolina greatly preferable to the West Indies, and was my Papa here I should be very happy.

We have a very good acquaintance from whom we have received much friendship and Civility. Charles Town, the principal one in this province, is a polite, agreeable place. The people live very [Gentle] and very much in the English taste. The Country is in General fertile and abounds with Venison and wild fowl; the Venison is much higher flavoured than in England but 'tis seldom fatt.

My Papa and Mama's great indulgence to me leaves it to me to cho[o]se our place of residence either in town or Country, but I think it more prudent as well as most agreeable to my Mama and self to be in the Country during my Father's absence. We are 17 mile by land and 6 by water from Charles Town—where we have about 6 agreeable families around us with whom we live in great harmony.

I have a little library well furnished (for my papa has left me most of his books) in which I spend part of my time. My Musik and the Garden, which I am very fond of, take up the rest of my time that is not imployed in business, of which my father has left me a pretty good share—and indeed, 'twas inavoidable as my Mama's bad state of health prevents her going through any fatigue.

I have the business of 3 plantations to transact, which requires much writing and more business and fatigue of other sorts than you can imagine. But least you should imagine it too burthensom to a girl at my early time of life, give me leave to answer you: I assure you I think myself happy that I can be useful to so good a father, and by rising very early I find I can go through much business. But least you should think I shall be quite moaped with this way of life I am to inform you there is two worthy Ladies in Charles Town, Mrs. Pinckney and Mrs. Cleland, who are partial enough to me to be always pleased to have me with them, and insist upon my making their houses my home when in town and press me to relax a little much oftener than 'tis in my honor to accept of their obliging intreaties. But I some times am with one or the other for 3 weeks or a month at a time, and then enjoy all the pleasures Charles Town affords, but nothing gives me more than subscribing my self

Dear Madam,

Y[our] most affectionet and most obliged humble Serv[ant]

Eliza Lucas

During the next few years, Col. Lucas died in a French prison, the Lucas plantation was put up for sale, and Eliza married Charles Pinckney, the 45-year-old widower of the Mrs. Pinckney whom she mentions in her second letter! She gave birth to four children, one of whom, Charles Cotesworth Pinckney, rose to the rank of general during the American Revolution and signed the United States Constitution. When Eliza died in 1793, George Washington was one of her pallbearers. (Letterbook of Eliza Lucas Pinckney, 1739–1762, Pinckney Family Papers, 1708–1878, 37/038, South Carolina Historical Society, Charleston, S.C. Published with permission of the South Carolina Historical Society.)

"A Most Agreeable Family"
Philip Vickers Fithian Meets the Carters

We tend to think of people who lived in the distant past as being very different from ourselves. The technology that shaped their lives, the clothes they wore, the food they ate, the daily challenges they faced, the diseases that threatened their well-being, even the jokes they told were so different from the facts of our own lives that we often have a difficult time bridging the years to think of them as living, breathing people. The journal of Philip Vickers Fithian, a young tutor who worked for a time on a Virginia plantation, can help build that bridge to the past. Although the family with whom he lived in Virginia, the Carters, were fabulously wealthy by colonial—by any—standards, the behaviors and the relationships that he describes among the parents and many children are interestingly modern. (From Hunter Dickinson Farish, ed., *Journal & Letters of Philip Vickers Fithian, 1773–1774: A Plantation Tutor of the Old Dominion* [Charlottesville, VA: Dominion Books, 1957], 48–49, 63–66, 83, 116, 119, 193. Reprinted with permission of the University of Virginia Press.)

January 4, 1774

The Family is most agreeable! Mr Carter is sensible judicious, much given to retirement & Study; his Company, & conversation are always profitable —His main Studies are *Law* & *Music*, the latter of which seems to be his darling Amusement—It seems to nourish, as well as entertain his mind! And to be sure he has a nice well judging Ear, and has made great advances in the Theory and Practice of music—

Mrs *Carter* is prudent, always cheerful, never without Something pleasant, a remarkable Economist, perfectly acquainted (in my Opinion) with the good-management of Children, intirely free from all foolish and unnecessary fondness, and is also 'well acquainted' (for She has always been used) with the formality and Ceremony which we find commonly in high Life— Ben, the eldest [age eighteen], is a youth of genius: of a warm impetuous Disposition; desirous of acquiring Knowledge, docile, vastly inquisitive & curious in mercantile, and mechanical Matters, is very fond of Horsses, and takes great pleasure in exercising them—Bob, the other Brother [age sixteen], is By no means destitute of capacity, As Mr Marshal who was his last Tutor has asserted, & as many now supp. " He is extremely volatile & unsettled in his temper, which makes it almost wholly impossible to fix him for any time to the same thing—On which account he has made but very little advancement in any one Branch of Study, and this is attributed to Barrenness of Genius—He is slovenly, clumsy, very fond of Shooting, of Dogs; of Horses, But a very stiff untoward *Rider,* good natur'd, pleased with the Society of persons much below his Family, and Estate, and tho' quick and wrathful in his temper, yet he is soon moderated, & easily subdued—Harry the Nephew, is rather stoical, sullen, or saturnine in his make. He is obstinate, tho' Steady, and makes a slow uniform advance in his Learning, he is vastly kind to me, but in particular to my Horse, of his health or Indisposition—Miss *Priscilla,* the eldest Daughter about 16, is steady, studious, docile, quick of apprehension, and makes good progress in what She undertakes; If I could with propriety continue in the Family, I should require no stronger Inducement than the Satisfaction I should receive by seeing this young Lady become perfectly acquainted with any thing I propose so soon as I communicate it to her, but the situation of my affairs makes it out of my power to stay longer than a year; She is small of her age, has a mild winning Presence, a sweet obliging Temper, never swears, which is here a distinguished virtue, dances finely, plays well on key'd Instruments, and is upon the whole in the first Class of the female Sex.

Nancy the Second [age thirteen], is not without some few of those qualities which are by some (I think with great ill nature, and with little or no truth) said to belong intirely to the fair Sex. I mean great curiosity, Eagerness for superiority, Ardor in friend ship, But bitterness and rage where there is enmity—She is not constant in her disposition, nor diligent nor attentive to her business—But She has her excellencies, She is cheerful, tender in her Temper, easily managed by perswasion & is never without what seems to have been a common Gift of Heaven, to the *fair-Sex,* the "Copia Verborum," or readiness of Expression!—She is only beginning to play the *Guitar,* She understands the Notes well, & is a graceful Dancer.

Fanny next [age eleven], is in her Person, according to my Judgment, the Flower in the Family—She has a strong resemblance of her *Mama* who is an elegant, beautiful Woman—Miss Fanny seems to have a remarkable Sedateness, & simplicity in her countenance, which is always rather chearful than melancholy; She has nothing with which we can find Fault in her Person, but has something in the Features of her Face which insensibly pleases us, & always when She is in Sight draws our Attention, & much the more because there seems to be for every agreeable Feature a correspondent Action which improves & adorns it. Betsy next is young, quiet, and obedient—Harriot [age seven] is bold, fearless, noisy and lawless; always merry, almost never displeased; She seems to have a Heart easily moved by the force of Music; She has learned many Tunes & can strike any Note, or Succession of Notes perfectly with the Flute or Harpsichord, and is never wearied with the sound of Music either vocal or *Instrumental.*

These are the Persons who are at present under my direction, & whose general Character I have very imperfectly attempted to describe.

February 2, 1774

This day began Multiplication. We had also a large elegant Writing Table brought to us, so high that the Writers must stand.

February 4, 1774

I put Ben this day into virgil—We had our Room mended & came into it —at twelve I rode out to Mr Taylors about two Miles, in again by Dinner-Time—Dined with us one Mrs Hut—This Evening, in the School-Room, which is below my Chamber, several Negroes & *Ben,* & *Harry* are playing on a *Banjo* & dancing!—

February 8, 1774

Before Breakfast *Nancy* & *Fanny* had a Fight about a Shoe Brush which they both wanted—Fanny pull'd off her Shoe & threw at Nancy, which missed her and broke a pane of glass of our School Room. they then enter'd upon close scratching &c. which methods seem instinctive in Women. Harry happen'd to be present & affraid lest he should be brought in, ran and informed me—I made peace, but with many threats—

February 11, 1774

Last night I took Bob to my Room, after having in the course of the Day corrected him thrice, & reasoned with him concerning the impropriety of his Behaviour; at the same time I acquainted him with my final resolution to send him over for correction every Day to his Papa's Study, which had so strong an Effect on him (as all the Children are in remarkable Subjection to their Parents) that he firmly promised to attend to my advice, & thro' this Day has been punctual to his word.

I spent the evening with the Family to hear the music. For every evening Prissy & Nancy play the whole Evening for practice & besides every Week half of Tuesday, Thursday, & Saturday.

February 14, 1774

Mr *Randolph* this Morning happens to be Miss *Nancy's valentine* & Miss *Prissy* mine—

February 15, 1774

I have a call this morning from *Bob* & *Harry* for a Holiday, *for* Shrove Teusday; I shall dismiss them at twelve o-Clock. I gave Miss Carter my Verses for her Valentine.

February 15, 1774

I happened last monday to offend *Prissy,* She retains her anger & seems peculiarly resentful!—*Ben* agreed for half a Bit a Week to play the Flute every Night, or read, for me, twenty Minutes after I am in Bed.

March 21, 1774

At Breakfast Mrs Carter asked me who is foremost in Arithmetic; whether Bob, or Prissy? At which Mr Carter observed, that him of his Sons whom he finds most capable of doing Business when he leaves the World, & his Estate, Shall have the management of the whole, & support the Rest. It seemed to me to be not an ill-chosen Incentive to Diligence among the Boys—

June 6, 1774

At Dinner I had a long and useful conversation with Mrs Carter She told me openly & candidly the Several failings of her children, & indeed She knows them perfectly—in particular she knows not what to do with her perverse Son *Bob*—He abuses his Mama, Miss Sally, the children, Family, and is much given to slander. Poor unhappy youth, I fear he will come to an unhappy end! This afternoon I found it necessary to correct Bob severely for impertinence in School— . . .

June 7, 1774

The morning pleasant, cool & agreeable—I corrected Harry this morning for telling me a Lie—Stomachful & sullen as any youth—

June 11, 1774

. . . It is with considerable Difficulty that I keep the Children in School til twelve o Clock as they used to go out all the last winter at Breakfast—*Bob* especially is vastly vociferous on the Occasion—Our Bells for School & play-Hours are at present under good Regulations. The Children come in as soon as they rise and are Drest which is usually about seven—The Bell rings at eight for Breakfast—At nine it Rings for two purposes; for the Children to enter School, & for the Gardiners, Carpenters, & other workmen to, come into Breakfast—At ten it Rings them to work. At twelve it rings for the School play hours—At two it rings for us to Dine, & the workmen—And the las[t] bell is at three for School & for the workmen to go to Labour—I dismiss them by my watch at half after Five

September 20, 1774

Among the many womanish Fribbles which our little Misses daily practise, I discovered one to Day no less merry than natural; *Fanny* & *Harriot* by stuffing rags & other Lumber under their Gowns just below their Apron-Strings, were prodigiously charmed at their resemblanc to Pregnant Women! They blushed, however, pretty deeply on discovering that I saw them—

A few months later, Fithian returned home to New Jersey, where he was licensed as a Presbyterian minister and married. Early in 1776 he enlisted as a chaplain in the Continental Army; he died of dysentery later in the year.

Part III

Cares and Tribulations

The poet Anne Bradstreet ends "In Reference to Her Children" by imagining her own death, and by asking her eight children to teach their children —her grandchildren—that she had done all she could for them.

> In chirping languages oft them tell
> You had a Dame that lov'd you well,
> That did what could be done for young
> And nurst you up till you were strong
> And 'fore she once would let you fly
> She shew'd you joy and misery,
> Taught what was good, and what was ill,
> What would save life, and what would kill.
> Thus gone, amongst you I may live,
> And dead, yet speak and counsel give.
> Farewell, my birds, farewell, adieu,
> I happy am, if well with you.

Although Bradstreet's children all lived to adulthood and although her poem, while bittersweet, is generally quite upbeat, danger and disease and accident lurk in the background. Her metaphor of a mother bird minding her chicks conjures images of a hen frantically watching for predators, scrambling for food, worrying and clucking and darting here and there.

Colonial children faced all of the hardships and dangers faced by European children: the same diseases, the same open fires, the same sad states of medical knowledge and practice. Yet living in colonies far from the established institutions and extended families of long-settled European communities no doubt added to the strain of raising children—strains that are detailed in the three essays that follow. Two words that appear in their titles—"decrepit" and "fragility"—reveal the difficulties of growing up in the colonies, which, especially in the early years, could bring a whole new set of hardships to the already vulnerable world of children. The first details the terrible risks and consequence of the Pilgrims' decisions to carve new homes out of the wilderness, while the third shows that, even a century later and in relatively comfortable surroundings, no child or parent was every free of worry. In between, we learn about the legal and social challenges of raising mentally handicapped children on the frontier. Finally, one of Bradstreet's most famous poems strikes the hauntingly familiar tone of a parents' eternal concern for her children, no matter their age.

Chapter 7

"Decrepit in Their Early Youth"
English Children in Holland and Plymouth Plantation

John J. Navin

In his narrative history, *Of Plymouth Plantation,* William Bradford presents a compelling tale of persecution in England, refuge in Holland, and hardship in America. The main characters we know by name—Winslow, Standish, Brewster, etc.—but a lesser known cast of characters also populates Bradford's narrative: the children. They were the silent victims of religious enthusiasm and far-flung schemes that shifted them among households, towns, nations, and continents, dooming many in the process. Pawns in a world of adult conflict and enterprise, the sons and daughters of Plymouth's founders paid a high price for their parents' ambitions.[1]

Drawing from Bradford's account, we first encounter the sons and daughters of Plymouth's separatists when the "poor little ones" are cast into English prisons, "crying for fear and quaking with cold." A covert attempt to flee England in the spring of 1608 had come unraveled, leaving many fathers "in great distress" on a Holland-bound ship while their panic-stricken wives and children, left destitute on the Lincolnshire shore, were rounded up by the king's troops. The adults, not their offspring, had separated unlawfully from the Church of England, but the latter were treated as if they too were guilty of "rebellion and high treason." Hurried from jail to jail and court to court, the children endured "misery enough" despite their youth and innocence.[2]

The Lincolnshire fiasco was just the first of many instances in which physical and emotional hardships would be borne by these inoffensive youngsters. In their quest for spiritual salvation, itinerant separatists who fled to the Netherlands unwittingly steered their sons and daughters into hazardous employments and an invidious and highly infectious culture.

Ironically, these conditions would eventually prompt some noncon-
formists to migrate once again, this time for America . . . yet another decision with dire consequences for many of them and their offspring.

Many of the separatists who fled to Holland in 1608, and others who
came after, took up residence in the bustling city of Leiden. There they
gathered a church under the pastorship of John Robinson, a defrocked
Anglican clergyman who, like his followers, had fled the "antichristian
estate" of England to seek refuge in the Low Countries. What set out as a
tight-knit group from England's northeast midlands gradually became a
"great congregation" of some three hundred communicants. Concomitant
with that expansion was a dramatic increase in the number of English
children in Leiden, many of whom were born in that city.[3]

In exile, certain traditions could not be maintained. Many of Robinson's followers were accustomed to "plain country life, and the innocent
trade of husbandry."[4] Removal to a walled Dutch city meant that boys
with rural origins would not inherit the land or lifestyle of their fathers
and grandfathers. The sons of artisans also faced altered circumstances. In
England they might serve an apprenticeship, rise to journeyman, and
eventually become a master craftsman. But immigrant status forced many
men into new occupations, denying boys the opportunity to learn their
fathers' trades or to work as apprentices for a relative or neighbor. Separatists' daughters faced their own uncertainties. In Holland their chances
of finding an English husband with the means to support a family were
greatly diminished. Marriage would probably come at a later age and, for
many, their link to agrarian tradition was similarly shattered.

Seventeenth-century Holland was a whirlwind of commercial activity.
Its vibrant trade fostered opportunities aplenty, but more so for Dutch
nationals than recent immigrants. In Leiden, most English separatists were
constrained to the lower rungs of the socioeconomic ladder. Many were
compelled to seek employment in the textile industry; the work was unin-
spiring, low paid, and difficult. Bradford wrote that many "could not
endure that great labor, and hard fare . . . some preferred and chose the
prisons in England, rather than this liberty in Holland, with these afflic-
tions."[5] Children performed some of the more mundane tasks in textile
production, and their meager earnings soon became an essential part of
many families' incomes. Thus the sons and daughters of English separatists exchanged playtime and schooling in traditional occupations for
mindless and debilitating drudgery, much as the children of Irish immigrants would labor in New England mills two centuries later.

This work took a heavy toll: many children were "so oppressed with their heavy labors . . . their bodies bowed under the weight of the same, and became decrepit in their early youth; the vigor of nature being consumed in the very bud as it were."[6] Burial records reveal just how utterly consumed some were. Between 1609 and 1623, Pastor John Robinson and his four deacons interred nine of their own children (and three spouses). At least one-third of the male separatists who would embark for New England in 1620 lost one or more children during their stay in Leiden. The frequency of death within the separatist community must have been staggering. Not only were children at great personal risk, but they also had to deal with the loss of parents, siblings, and friends.

As if the prospect of untimely death was not sufficiently unnerving, the separatists also worried that they might lose their sons and daughters in an entirely different sense. To their utter dismay, Robinson's followers discovered that their new surroundings inhibited the transmission of cultural norms and values from one generation to the next. When they first arrived in the Low Countries, many separatists thought they had "come into a new world." But the unfamiliar landscape and strange customs that discomposed adult refugees proved more inviting to their children, many of whom were born in Holland or conveyed there in their infancy. Eventually the separatists' offspring became so totally immersed in their Dutch environment that their heritage became unclear and their obedience fleeting. To their mothers' and fathers' increasing alarm, children were "drawn away by evil examples into extravagant and dangerous courses, getting the reins off their necks, and departing from their parents."[7]

The "goodly and pleasant city" of Leiden turned out to be a place of "great licentiousness" and "manifold temptations." Some English boys became soldiers, others went to sea, and still others, perhaps girls as well, pursued "worse courses, tending to dissoluteness, and the danger of their souls; to the great grief of their parents, and dishonor of God." Robinson's followers realized that "their posterity would be in danger to degenerate and be corrupted" if they did not take dramatic action. Had they resigned themselves to the hardships and drawbacks imposed by the rigors of that urban setting, had they consented to gradual but inevitable assimilation into Dutch culture, and had they rationalized the growing independence exhibited by their children as the price of their own religious freedom, the members of Robinson's congregation could have stayed in Leiden indefinitely, as indeed some did. But those who refused such concessions struck a bargain with a group of London investors who were willing to finance a settlement in the "northern parts of Virginia." There the separatists hoped to establish a devoutly Christian community of incontrovertibly English character . . . and regain control of their offspring in the process.[8]

According to separatist Edward Winslow, it was agreed that "it was best for one part of the church to go at first . . . the youngest and strongest part." Most adults who volunteered for the advance party were married, though only a few families traveled intact. Recognizing the expedition's inherent dangers, prospective colonists employed a variety of strategies. Some men decided to leave their wives and children in Leiden on the understanding that they would migrate later. Others traveled alone or brought their eldest son. A few couples brought only their youngest offspring. One separatist brought two sons, ages three and five, but left his wife and daughter in Leiden, perhaps because some claimed that females "could never be able to endure" the ocean crossing.[9]

Some separatists brought wards; others were accompanied by servants or apprentices they hired in Holland or had agents recruit in England. Twelve-year-old John Hooke had been apprenticed to separatist Isaac Allerton, a tailor, for twelve years. Allerton agreed to provide for Hooke as he would for his own child and to instruct him in reading, writing, and religion. The contract with Allerton was arranged by the youngster's mother and stepfather.[10] "Putting out" children as servants or apprentices in neighboring households was not unusual in that era, but the establishment of colonies in the Americas added an entirely new dimension— transatlantic passage and permanent separation. The practice became a means by which desperately poor parents could unload their children, shipping them off as servants (more often to Virginia than New England), perhaps making a small profit in the process. Some reasoned that their family's dire circumstances justified their actions, which gave their sons or daughters a chance to "make it" in the New World; others were simply pleased to have one less mouth to feed.

In a development that accentuated the powerlessness of both children and women in this era, Samuel More placed four youngsters between the ages of four and eight in the care of the departing separatists. His wife had given birth to them, but he was not their father. It was best, he reasoned, to send these bastard offspring far away, sparing them future disgrace and sparing himself their humiliating presence. His distraught wife, whose marriage had been arranged when she was in her teens in order to maximize family landholdings, opposed the removal of her children, but in vain.[11]

By the time the first Leiden separatists boarded ship in 1620, their colonization scheme was already in danger of ruin. In order to obtain financing, Robinson's followers had to promise investors that they would work six days per week for seven years—not just the adults, but their children as well. Some separatists considered the agreement "fitter for thieves and bond-slaves, than honest men" and abandoned the enterprise.[12] To replace them, investors in London hurriedly recruited colonists, including five couples with children. To their dismay the members of the separatist vanguard soon found themselves outnumbered by voyagers with no connection to their church. A company of hired hands and servants, some in their teens, also joined the expedition. When the *Mayflower* finally embarked from England in early September it carried 102 passengers. Fourteen were between the ages of thirteen and eighteen, and nineteen were twelve or younger. Two additional children were born aboard ship; another was stillborn.

By the time they chose the location for their settlement and constructed the first building, some passengers had lived below decks for nearly four months. Lacking adequate food and shelter, the colonists began to succumb to exposure, malnutrition, and disease. In the spring of 1621, only fifty of the 102 colonists remained. Six of Plymouth's twenty-two families had been completely wiped out, six suffered the loss of one parent (thirteen of the eighteen married women perished), and in six others only one child survived. Disease also struck down ten of the twelve youths who arrived without adult kin, including three of the four illegitimate More children entrusted to the care of the separatists. Six orphans, four wards, and the only remaining servant boy were hastily shifted to new guardians.

Directly or indirectly, sickness, deprivation, and staggering mortality affected every child who sailed on the *Mayflower*. This differentiated these firstcomers from the majority of boys and girls who would migrate to Plymouth afterwards. In the end, New England proved a much healthier place to live than England or other parts of Western Europe, where smallpox and other diseases sporadically ravaged the population. But that was not the case for "pilgrim" families, many of whom unwittingly fled the hardships and worldly distractions of Leiden (or, in the case of Plymouth's nonseparatists, the economic distress in England) for an early grave in America. Pastor John Robinson's followers may have had their children's best interests in mind when they decided to abandon Holland, but it was the religious convictions of those adults, not their offspring, that steered them away from England and into a land some claimed would be likely "to consume, and utterly to ruinate them," as indeed it did.[13]

The first winter's ordeal mercifully ended but fear still gripped the plantation. Disease and starvation were not the only perceived dangers. In May 1621, sixteen-year-old John Billington Jr. became lost and "wandered up and down some five days, living on berries and what he could find." The boy ended up among Indians who had attacked the *Mayflower*'s landing party the previous December. When heavily armed colonists set out to recover young Billington, a renewal of hostilities seemed imminent. Instead, a breakthrough in relations occurred as Aspinet, the Nauset sachem, "delivered us the boy, behung with beads, and made peace with us."[14] This was the first of many encounters that children in Plymouth would have with Native Americans. Most had encountered foreigners but few if any had come in contact with members of another race. The biases that would influence their future relations with Indians and Africans were as yet nonexistent or derived mainly from parents whose ethnocentricity stemmed largely from ignorance and misinformation.

Although hostilities marked the colonists' first encounter with Native Americans, the two groups prevented major outbreaks of violence in Plymouth Colony—at least until the 1670s—by mutual accommodation, occasional intimidation, and a series of treaties. Thus Plymouth's children did not experience interracial warfare until they reached adulthood, and some not at all. Yet these young colonists lived in the shadow of war: a stockade surrounded their homes, men conducted regular militia drills and carried muskets to religious services, and twice weekly the children joined in prayer in the colony's blockhouse—pulpit on the first level, mounted cannon on the second, and perched on a pole high above the rest, the head and blood-drenched shirt of a slain Indian "conspirator."[15] In disease-ridden England and Holland these children had witnessed premature death, but none so calculated or potentially horrific as in New England. During every waking hour and even as they slept, imminent destruction was a genuine possibility. As the New England Primer later reminded young readers,

> I in the Burying Place may see
> Graves shorter there than I;
> From Death's Arrest no Age is free
> Young Children too may die.[16]

It may have been the case that the separatists' religious intensity caused them to overestimate or exaggerate the likelihood of child mortality. After the first winter, life expectancy for the survivors and subsequent immigrants was actually longer than it would have been across the Atlantic. But as historian David Stannard has argued, New England Puritans appear to have deliberately inculcated their sons and daughters with a sense of impending doom. Just how this affected the young psyches of young colonists is impossible to tell, but death and damnation represented dual terrors.[17]

In subsequent decades many children who crossed the Atlantic would mature, marry, and migrate to new towns in the interior, thereby exposing their own offspring to physical and emotional hardships on a westward-moving frontier. The sense of ever present danger that accompanied resettlement in a potentially hostile environment would characterize a peculiarly American brand of childhood for two and a half centuries. What the children on the *Mayflower* shared with later generations of youthful pioneers was their lack of choice in such ventures.

In late 1621 and the summer of 1622 more settlers arrived at Plymouth; the majority were "lusty young men, and many of them wild enough," according to Bradford. Ironically, the only married newcomer to bring his family died within a year, leaving two children fatherless (one of whom was born the day the family arrived at Plymouth). With the addition of so many bachelors, the colony shifted even further away from a family-based society, and maintenance of law and order became more difficult. For a few tumultuous months, women in the plantation found themselves outnumbered by men by a ten-to-one ratio. The colony's five teenage girls, four of whom were orphans, must have been guarded closely. Although circumstances would ameliorate, Plymouth would suffer a gender imbalance for years. This meant that girls' adolescence would be brief: proposals of marriage could be expected when they reached their midteens. Had they remained in Holland or England, betrothal was more likely to occur at age twenty-three. Early marriage also meant that female colonists were likely to experience more conceptions. Indeed, four of the aforementioned five teenagers would give birth to ten or more children; the exceptional fifth returned to England by 1623 and apparently never married. Conversely, the prospect of marriage for young men in Plymouth would remain unfavorable for years. Seven years after the *Mayflower* arrived, there was only one unmarried female over the age of sixteen in Plymouth

—slim pickings for the colony's twenty-two bachelors. For at least a decade one's prospects for marriage clearly depended on one's gender.[18]

In Plymouth, a child's gender also determined what role he or she could aspire to in household, town, and colony. It was a man's world, a patriarchal society in which women bore a full measure of the work and hardships but an unequal portion in terms of authority, rights, and entitlement. Through the course of their lives Plymouth's females would remain subordinate to their father, minister, magistrates, and, eventually, a husband as well. In some ways their childhood—a brief span in which they escaped the scrutiny of all but their parents (or guardians)—represented their period of greatest independence.

During Plymouth's first several years, food shortages plagued the colony. "Some say you are starved in body and soul; others, that you eat pigs and dogs that die alone," wrote Robert Cushman in London. Quite simply, the colonists were not growing sufficient crops to feed themselves. The colony's young men objected to working "for other men's wives and children." The women, few as they were, deemed it "a kind of slavery" to be commanded to work for unrelated men. Searching for a solution, Plymouth's leaders decided to assign every family a parcel of land for planting. This "had very good success, for it made all hands very industrious." The long-suffering women of Plymouth "now went willingly into the field, and took their little ones with them to set corn." Bradford's description of events reveals that children shared in the fieldwork, even at an age when they still clung to their mothers or female guardians. Dressed in plain linen shifts (boys and girls alike), the children enjoyed a world of simple distractions until they reached an age—six or seven years—when serious instruction and individual responsibilities complicated their young lives. Girls would be trained in housewifery and gardening, boys in husbandry, trades, fishing, hunting, and other mature engagements. In manner and habit, even in attire, these children would resemble "miniature adults," obscuring to some degree their passage from youth to adulthood.[19]

Scholars have made much of the Puritan practice of "putting out," whereby children were assigned to other households at an early age. Except for the placement of orphans and wards in the wake of the first winter's devastating mortality, there is only limited evidence of this phenomenon in early Plymouth. Other than children who sailed to America as wards or apprentices, few lived apart from their parents prior to 1630. The putting out of children would become more common in the colony in later decades, especially as families grew beyond men's ability to provide for them. Francis Billington, who arrived on the *Mayflower* at age thirteen, proved unable to support his growing family; in 1642 the magistrates removed five children (including three stepchildren) from his home and placed them with other families. This left Billington and his wife with just an infant, but the couple produced at least five more offspring.

It also became increasingly common for the sons and daughters of widows to be shifted to new homes. Even though widows remarried quickly in Plymouth, their new husbands often elected to place stepchildren in other households, not due to financial considerations but as a way to avoid marital disputes and problematic parent-stepchild relationships. The practice of placing boys in apprenticeships also increased as time passed and more men were able to make their living as artisans rather than as farmers.

The arrival of ninety-two settlers on the ships *Anne* and *Little James* in 1623 instantly doubled the size of the colony. Among the newcomers were at least thirteen couples, several single women, and the wives (and, in four cases, children) of seven men who had arrived beforehand. Approximately three dozen dependents arrived from Holland or England on the two vessels, increasing the number of children aged sixteen and under in the colony to approximately sixty-four, or slightly more than one-third of the total population. Although there might have been little discernable difference between the children who traveled on the *Mayflower* and those who arrived afterward, the experiences they had internalized were very dissimilar. The trauma of the first deadly winter, the deconstruction and subsequent reconstitution of families, the lack of adequate food and shelter, and the other hardships and dangers linked to the frontier undoubtedly left emotional scars on children in the Plymouth vanguard. Those who arrived afterward, or who were born in the plantation, entered an austere but comparatively settled environment. Though some of the adult newcomers "fell a-weeping" and "wished themselves in England again" when they saw the "low, and poor condition" of Plymouth's inhabitants, their sons and daughters would generally grow up in stable households and enjoy the fruits of the land without having to undergo a traumatizing initiation.[20] Of course, those young newcomers who lost a parent in 1620–21 while they remained safe in Holland or England also felt the effects of the first winter's devastation, but at a distance.

Within a year of the arrival of the *Anne* and *Little James,* the number of married couples in the plantation soared from seven to thirty-two. But just as the colony seemed to be gaining material and demographic stability, new religious and political intrigues involving an Anglican minister sent by Plymouth's financial backers impelled several dozen inhabitants, including nine children, out of the settlement and into the New England wilderness or back to England. Once more, the quarrels of their parents would dictate the erratic course of those youngsters' lives.

In 1626 the investors in London sold their interests in the colony to its inhabitants. Plymouth's leaders decided to award every person twenty acres of land and a portion of the plantation's livestock. They also granted proprietor status to all heads of families and to single young men who were neither servants nor sons of householders. Twenty-eight of the fifty-two men who received ownership shares were unmarried, including every male orphan or ward from Leiden, regardless of age. The distribution of land may have had unforeseen consequences for Plymouth's adolescents. Because sons were better suited to heavy field work, couples had more reason to prefer male offspring. Whether this would have implications in terms of the way children were treated is uncertain, but expanded land-holdings undoubtedly meant more work for all family members beyond the toddler stage. Young men without land of their own may have been expected to labor not just for their fathers but for other landowners as well.

The land division also had potential implications in regard to patriarchy and inheritance. In Plymouth the English practice of primogeniture was not maintained; at death a man's estate would be equally divided among his children, except that the oldest son was entitled to a double portion. But fathers often gave their sons land long before they expired. In the last half of the seventeenth century, when land became dearer in southern New England, men sometimes forestalled their sons' marriage by denying them an early inheritance.[21] When lands were held in common in Plymouth, men lacked this stratagem (since they had no land to withhold from their offspring). But following Plymouth's first major land distribution, colonists such as Francis Cooke, whose allotment included shares for his twenty- and eighteen-year-old sons, assumed greater control of their destinies since they were less likely to establish their own households unless he gave them land to do so. These young men were also excluded from the list of proprietors entitled to future land distributions. Although Plymouth's land distribution strengthened patriarchal control for a time, the creation of new towns throughout the region soon presented impatient male heirs with opportunities to secure land grants elsewhere. This encouraged secondary migration and a cyclical process of town planting, growth, and out-migration, increasingly to the west.

In 1627 a roster of inhabitants was drawn up for the pending division of cattle. The list included 156 colonists, the oldest of whom was 61–year-old William Brewster and the youngest of whom was his five-week-old grand-child. At that time the colony housed thirty-eight boys and thirty-five girls below the age of seventeen. Of the thirty married couples then living in Plymouth, only four had no offspring living with them, though they had young men or bachelors sharing their homes. The twenty-six other cou-ples had one or more sons or daughters living under their roof. Altogether, the thirty families in Plymouth accounted for 131 of Plymouth's 156 inhab-itants.[22] The fact that so many inhabitants lived with kinfolk attests to the great strides the colonists had made in fashioning a family-centered settle-ment. But we must be mindful of the nature of those households if we want to appreciate the inner workings of Plymouth's "Little Common-wealths" and some of the factors shaping the outlook and personalities of its children. Even in 1627 the colony's devastating first-year mortality was reflected in the structure of many families. In the Winslow, Cuthbertson, Kempton, and Bradford households, all four women had been widowed (two twice). Similarly, the husbands in three of these households had also lost their first spouses. Consequently, two of Susannah Winslow's sons were actually stepchildren (she had lost two of her own in Holland), none of Cuthbert Cuthbertson's three dependents was his progeny, and Manas-sas Kempton was father to five stepchildren and perhaps his wife's nephew, but had no offspring of his own. William Bradford had remarried and fathered two children at Plymouth, but his first son was still languish-ing in Holland and his two stepsons were still in England, not having seen their mother since 1623. The specter of patchwork households becomes even more vivid when we consider that these descriptions account for family members only—in 1627 Bradford's household may also have included four wards or servants.

At most, only thirteen of Plymouth's thirty households included a cou-ple whose first marriage was still intact and whose children were the prod-uct of that union. Many families may have been characterized by insecurity and emotional distance; their social fabric can hardly be described as a seamless quilt. We have no way to measure the affection and cohesiveness or, conversely, the hostility and mistrust that existed, but we should not ignore the complex dynamics within Plymouth's households and we certainly should not assume that "in terms of the overall stability of family life it [death] was not a factor of the first importance," as one historian has written of Plymouth Colony.[23]

We think of Plymouth as an English settlement, but only fifteen of the seventy-three colonists aged sixteen and under in 1627 had emigrated directly from England. Nearly one-third of the colony's youth had dwelled in Holland, and fourteen others who were slightly older had also been born in Holland or had emigrated there at a very young age with their parents. Thus many of Plymouth's children probably spoke some Dutch and shared memories not of London or rural Lincolnshire but of the waterways, alleys, and bustling marketplaces of Leiden. It was, after all, partly their inclination toward Dutch ways that prompted their concerned parents to concoct the Plymouth venture. Because they had lived in Holland, it is not unlikely that these children's mannerisms, speech, and outlook reflected a duality of cultural influences. The colony's remaining thirty-six youth, or nearly a quarter of the total population in 1627, had been born in Plymouth or during the Atlantic crossing. America was the only land they had known; they had never seen an alley, marketplace, or cathedral. The disdain that some colonists felt for others—the "stranger" versus separatist dichotomy first evident on the *Mayflower*—may have been due, at least in part, to the different cultures from which they emerged.

Beginning in 1630 the arrival of thousands of Puritans at nearby Massachusetts Bay Colony meant that Plymouth's inhabitants suddenly had a burgeoning market for their crops and livestock. To capitalize on the opportunity, they "scattered all over the Bay," and the plantation that had been a decade in the making was "left very thin, and in a short time almost desolate."[24] Once again, sons and daughters were uprooted in response to their parents' ambitions. But this time many of the adults who decided that they and their families should pack up and move elsewhere on the New England frontier were individuals who had themselves been torn from their familiar surroundings in Holland or England. In their youth they had experienced the hardships of resettlement in the American wilderness; now they were the instigators.

One tragic consequence of this "scattering" was increasing encroachment upon Native American lands. As colonists planted new homes and towns in the interior, their contact and conflicts with neighboring Indians often increased. Eventually this exposed some settlers and their children, and later their grandchildren, to the horrors of frontier warfare. In 1675, King Philip's War—America's deadliest conflict in proportion to population—would erupt in Plymouth Colony. Once again there would be ample and tragic proof that in the colonial world, a child's birthright included a full share in the consequences of decisions in which he or she had no voice. Like their parents, the sons and daughters of some of Plymouth's firstcomers, and their progeny in turn, would be weaned in hardscrabble circumstances, tutored in pragmatism and prejudice, and traumatized by the sudden loss of parents, siblings, and friends—additional sacrifices on America's altar of westward migration.

NOTES

1. William Bradford, *Of Plimoth Plantation,* reprinted in a spelling-modernized edition and also in original manuscript format (scanned), in "The Complete Works of the Pilgrims," *MayflowerHistory.com's CD-ROM Reference Collection,* version 1.01, copyright Caleb Johnson, 2003.

2. Ibid., 4–8.

3. In 1596 separatist Francis Johnson stated unequivocally that "all that will be saved must with speed come forth from this Antichristian estate." Francis Johnson, *A true confession of the faith* (Amsterdam, 1596), art. 32, cited in Stephen Brachlow, *The Communion of Saints: Radical Puritan and Separatist Ecclesiology, 1570–1625* (New York: Oxford University Press, 1988), 54; Bradford, *Of Plimoth Plantation,* 11.

4. Bradford, *Of Plimoth Plantation,* 7.

5. Ibid., 13.

6. Ibid., 13–14.

7. Ibid., 10–14.

8. Ibid., 14; the reference to the "northern parts of Virginia" occurs in the Mayflower Compact.

9. Edward Winslow, *Brief Narration* [appendix to *Hypocrisy Unmasked*] (London, 1646), 55, reprinted in *MayflowerHistory.com's CD-ROM Reference Collection,* version 1.01; Bradford, *Of Plimoth Plantation,* 14.

10. Jeremy D. Bangs, "The Pilgrims and Other English in Leiden Records: Some New Pilgrim Documents," *England Historical and Genealogical Register* 143 (1989): 195–99.

11. Sir Anthony Wagner, "The Origin of the *Mayflower* Children: Jasper, Richard, and Ellen More," *New England Historical and Genealogical Register* 114 (1960): 163.

12. Bradford, *Of Plimoth Plantation,* 29.

13. Ibid., 14.

14. [William Bradford, Edward Winslow, and Anon.], *Mourt's Relation: A Relation or Journal of the Beginning and Proceedings of the English Plantation Settled at Plymouth in New England* (London, 1622), 29, reprinted in *MayflowerHistory.com's CD-ROM Reference Collection,* version 1.01.

15. Thomas Morton, *New English Canaan* (Amsterdam, 1637), 47, reprinted in *MayflowerHistory.com's CD-ROM Reference Collection*, version 1.01.

16. "The Dutiful Child's Promises," in *The New England Primer* (1727 version), reprinted in *The Heath Anthology of American Literature*, 3rd ed., ed. George McMichael (New York: McMillan, 1993), 54.

17. David E. Stannard, *The Puritan Way of Death: A Study in Religion, Culture, and Social Change* (New York: Oxford University Press, 1977).

18. Bradford, *Of Plimoth Plantation*, 55; Stone, *The Family, Sex, and Marriage in England*, 40.

19. Robert Cushman to William Bradford, et al., January 24, 1623/4 in Bradford, *Of Plimoth Plantation*, 81; ibid., 70–71; Demos, *A Little Commonwealth*, 139–41.

20. Bradford, *Of Plimoth Plantation*, 74.

21. Greven, *Four Generations*, passim.

22. Nathaniel B. Shurtleff and David Pulsifer, eds., *Records of the Colony of New Plymouth, in New England* (Boston, 1855–61), 12: 9–13.

23. Demos, *A Little Commonwealth*, 66.

24. Bradford, *Of Plimoth Plantation*, 147.

Chapter 8

Idiocy and the Construction of Competence in Colonial Massachusetts

Parnel Wickham

Idiocy captured the imaginations of Puritan colonists with vivid portrayals of impairment. Cotton Mather depicted the horror and fear of idiocy in a story of two sisters who lived in the town of Dunstable:

> A gentleman there, whose name is Mr. S———, under paralytic affects, is yet the father of two daughters, whereof the one is now nine, the other three, years of age. They continued for several months after their nativity in the same circumstances of sensibility that other infants of their age use [*sic*] to have. But anon they were taken with odd convulsive motions, which carried a little of an epileptical aspect upon them. The fits would be short, and many of them in an hour; but after some while the fits grew seldomer, and lasted longer, and the screeches of the little wretches in them would be very doleful. These fits anon left them wholly deprived of almost everything in the world, but only a little sight, and scent, and hunger. Nothing in the whole brutal world so insensible! They move not their limbs: you may twist them, and bend them to a degree that none else could bear, and they feel it not. They take notice of nothing in the world, only they seem to see and smell victuals, at the approach of which they will gape, and be very restless, and make something of a bray. They are in good health, and eat rather more than other children of their age. But they let their excrements pass from them without the least regard. The elder is ever drivelling, the younger never has any salival discharge. They shed no tears. They never sneeze. They have no speech. They have no way to discover any sentiments of their minds. They never use their hands to take hold of anything. Was *idiocy* ever seen so miserable![1]

Mather's account rings with fear and revulsion. What was it about the girls that repelled and frightened him? Why did he associate the sisters with idiocy and what did this mean? Did Mather's reaction represent other colonists' responses to idiocy? The answers to these questions offer some insights into the ways New England colonists understood idiocy and the standards that determined whether or not one was competent. These standards linked idiocy with parenting and child-rearing in a negative association, for idiocy represented the antithesis of Puritan parents' aspirations for their children.

Where parents invested hope and effort in raising children to become competent adults, idiocy represented disappointment and loss; and where parents were judged by their children's maturity, idiocy introduced failure and inferiority. With idiocy, parents lost their purpose in raising respectable youngsters. Religious conversion, the most important child-rearing issue in Puritan New England, was irrelevant when idiocy was involved. In addition, the prospects for a chosen calling and meaningful work were beside the point, and relationships in the social institutions of families and communities were problematic. All three, conversion, calling, and social duties, constituted the chief aims of Puritan parents, and all required competencies that idiots presumably lacked. The loss of parental purpose and the anticipation of failure for afflicted children and their parents all contributed to colonists' aversion to idiocy.[2]

It is well established that parents in the colonies feared for the safety and healthy development of all their children. They worried when children became ill or were injured, agonized over their absences, and despaired when they died, yet few of the problems encountered by parents in the New World were entirely unknown. Settlers brought with them most of the difficulties experienced in England: trauma and death at childbirth, disease and disability in later childhood. Furthermore, the fears of parenting were exacerbated by the uncertainties of settling in a foreign land, the great expanse of ocean that distanced family and friends from one another, and the more ambiguous anxieties of predestination associated with Calvinist belief.[3]

Children in seventeenth-century colonial New England fared better than those in other parts of the country, and for the most part, better than their compatriots in England. In the more rural regions close to one in ten infants died, while in the larger towns of Salem and Boston, the number was about three in ten. The relatively high birth rate indicates that nearly every family in the seventeenth century experienced the death of a child.

Complications resulting from childbirth were frequent causes of infant mortality, and the first weeks introduced risks, especially with feeding. Birth defects took their toll. Illness associated with poor diets included scurvy and rickets. Epidemics of smallpox, first reported in 1631, measles, influenza, diphtheria, and yellow fever were most debilitating with the weak and the young. Other communicable diseases, including chicken pox, diphtheria, dysentery, measles, mumps, scarlet fever and whooping cough, were common among children. Colds and convulsions were noted frequently in colonists' diaries. Accidents caused painful injuries and sometimes death: untended children fell into wells and rivers, drowning or nearly so; beans and nutshells found their way into noses; worms plagued skin and intestines; teeth deteriorated with painful frequency; fires claimed young lives or left the living seriously disabled; and horses trampled young and old, while carriages overturned upon their riders. Colonial children who survived these and other hazards were possibly disabled, disfigured, or both.[4]

An essentially hopeless condition, idiocy was understood by colonists to afflict children at birth or shortly thereafter. It held no promise for treatment, nor was there hope for a cure. Some colonists thought that idiocy implied a physical malformation of the brain, but unlike their English counterparts, they took little interest in the problem unless there were difficulties of a practical nature, such as personal neglect and the need for guardianship. Traces of idiocy appeared in public laws and records of the New England colonial courts, colonists' personal writings, and Puritan sermons that adopted images of idiocy as religious symbols. Although there is little evidence of the condition in colonial Massachusetts, there is even less in the other colonies; this fact helps to explain why the Massachusetts Bay Colony is the focus of this study.[5]

Idiocy and its many constructed meanings can be traced from ancient Greece and Rome through the European Middle Ages and into seventeenth-century England. Idiocy appeared in English law regarding criminal proceedings as early as the twelfth century; it was first recognized as a medical problem in the technical writings of Thomas Willis; and the language of idiocy found a place in the plain-style sermons of English Puritan preachers. Throughout history, the concept of idiocy has been marked with consistent interpretations of human inferiority, incompetence, and degeneracy. Paradoxically, although idiocy was thought to be a permanent, inborn condition for which there was no hope of recovery, its utter failure suggested a state of innocence akin to infancy, and indeed throughout history, idiocy has been associated with the helpless, pathetic circumstances of early childhood. Pitiable in its childishness, idiocy inspired tolerance in courts of law, while at the same time it signaled God's creative and retributive powers. These complex and sometimes contradictory meanings were carried by settlers to America and can be found today in the condition's contemporary analog, mental retardation. Although there are significant differences between the concepts of idiocy and mental retardation, they both tend to portray the paradoxical interpretations of base inferiority paired with childlike innocence.[6]

The comparison with childhood tends to soften the more comprehensive interpretation of idiocy as a deplorable representation of the human condition. Yet interpretations of childhood changed over the ages, while the construct of idiocy remained stable until the middle of the nineteenth century. In colonial America idiocy was more closely associated with the early period of childhood than it would ever be again once the new republic was established. Newborns and idiots were closely linked by the perilous, fragile nature of their existence and the consequent parental anxiety regarding both physical and spiritual futures. In fact, however, the term "idiot" appeared only in the literary language of Puritan ministers and in the abstractions of public laws. It was, indeed, largely a construct, for a careful review of Massachusetts court records revealed no cases of idiots, although there were several unfortunate individuals described with words related to idiocy but less demeaning, such as "simple," "incapashous," and "foolish," and there is Cotton Mather's case history of the two sisters whom he called idiots.

Linguistic variations indicate that colonists understood that some people were more impaired than others, even as more formal texts from the period imply a unitary concept, and colonists differentiated between idiocy and other mental impairments. Although the language was often ambiguous, people with problems similar to mental illness were referred to, for example, as "crazy," "mad," "lunatic," and the most common term, "distracted." These mental disabilities were thought to be temporary conditions acquired later in life. Distractedness suggested an intermittent situation that was often frightening with its unpredictable and sometimes violent behaviors while idiocy, though a stark portrayal of inferiority, suggested a relatively harmless, innocent condition.[7]

Negative interpretations of idiocy contrasted with Puritans' cautious optimism, which stemmed from the knowledge, if not certainty, that God favored his covenanted people with grace and forgiveness. Despite the difficulties they might encounter in the wilderness of the New World, Puritan believers rarely doubted that God intervened in their lives for a purpose, and that His purpose was essentially good. Just as they depended on one another for comfort and assistance, they turned to God for assurance that they did not suffer in vain. If they were besieged with problems in this world, they hoped the next one would be better, and at least they might learn from the difficulties they faced. Nevertheless, Puritans' guarded optimism was tempered with fear for the possibility that they might not be counted among the elect and would suffer accordingly, since none knew God's purpose, and all were tainted with sin. This conflicted psychological environment, rooted in Puritan conviction, helps explain the generally negative approach that colonists took toward idiocy.[8]

Despite the glimmer of hope implicit in faith, Puritans doubted that children who were permanently impaired would develop sufficiently to emerge from under the cloud of sin. To Puritan parents who worried about their children's souls, and they all did, idiocy was devoid of possibilities for regeneration, since incompetent children would never acquire the skills for regeneration, such as reading scripture, comprehending sermons, and affirming their faith. Unable to profess their faith, both infants and idiots might die as sinners unless God provided a third, mysterious way, and some agreed that he did. Presumably one might always worry about the souls of idiots, but infants would eventually grow into comprehending adults who would need to experience conversion first-hand. More liberal ministers, such as the English Puritan Richard Baxter, got around the problem of original sin with the claim that "Personal Believing was never commanded to Infants or Ideots, nor required as necessary to their Salvation." If parents were faithful members of church fellowship, Baxter professed, there was a good possibility that their children, no matter how young or incompetent, would experience salvation, although even Baxter would not go so far as to admit them to church membership. Other Puritan ministers, such as Samuel Parris, took a hard line when it came to the sacraments. In 1693 Parris wrote, "Infants cannot examine themselves, & therefore are not meet Subjects for this Ordinance. . . . Fools & Idiots are not meet subjects for this ordinance. For those being void of Reason cannot examine themselves. There is a degree of knowledge . . . required in all communicants."[9]

Indeed, idiocy reminded Puritans of the brutish qualities that might intrude upon a child's life and destroy the promise of humanity if his or her natural tendencies were left alone. Like infants, idiots were considered neither fully human nor entirely animal, but there was a critical difference between the two: young children might eventually grow into competent, repentant humans, while idiots were permanently suspended in childhood between humanity and the lesser animals. Fearful for their children's souls, parents pushed and prodded little children to grow straight and upright physically, to develop sound minds, and to practice Christian virtues. Until they acquired Christian attributes, reversion to the animal state remained a serious threat. Methods of childrearing stressed the human capacities in order to eliminate the animalistic. One might be very young, but one should not be childish: "Childlike was childish, foolish, degrading, and animalistic," wrote Calvert. Likewise, Puritan parents initiated reading instruction at an early age in order to develop their children's intellect. With the ability to read came evidence of children's moral superiority and parents' diligence as well as practical necessity: children who could read were better prepared to manage personal and business affairs. Illiterate adults suffered the indignities of life-long incompetence in religious, personal, and business matters.[10]

Ever vigilant to find signs of God or the devil, Puritans brooded over rumored and real malformations among fetuses and newborns. Such anomalies represented violations of the human form and signified deviations from the natural order of God's creations. They were explained by various interpretations such as the displacement of the father at the time of conception and the substitution of the devil in his place, perversions in copulation, or the mother's distraction with unwholesome preoccupations such as disturbing or fanciful images. Monstrous births signified the "spiritual waywardness" of the birth mother and represented the "inverse of conversion," a violation of God's ordered creation. In seventeenth-century New England, reports of monstrous births involving Mary Dyer and Anne Hutchinson linked human deviance with religious heresy. Cotton Mather, like others of his time, was fascinated with these kinds of alleged natural distortions. His interpretations linked monstrosities, including the cases of idiocy, with immorality, degeneracy, and human deviance.[11]

While Mather wrote about monstrosities and ministers haggled over sacramental eligibility, parents were concerned with practical matters. The expectation for a life-long childhood extinguished parents' hopes for their children's productive work and the responsibilities of family and community life. Puritan parents prepared children from an early age for a calling that would sustain them both economically and spiritually. Every job was valuable, no matter how mundane: "Wee should so take up duties, so order them that one should bee helpful to another, and not a hindrance. . . . As it is with a Wagon, the little Wheeles goe before to make way for the greater that come after them, and the greater follow after, and serve to drive on the former." No occupation was too menial, if it contributed to the welfare of a family or the surrounding community, and indeed, simplicity was a virtue, as long as the little wheels actually turned. If, however, wagons were idle because certain people failed to do their jobs, the laws of both God and man were broken, and there was a price to pay. Capable but useless people were severely chastised if they were unemployed. Incapable people who were counted among the worthy poor were better tolerated, but useless nonetheless.[12]

Vocational preparation involved direct teaching in the home, modeling by relatives and neighbors, and apprenticing outside the home. Boys needed skills for the trades and professions, and for the privileged, the management of property, while girls were trained for household tasks. Both boys and girls were prepared for their own roles as parents to the next generation of Puritan children. Competence required a partnership between men and women who needed one another to create and sustain the ideal Puritan family. More specifically, however, the concept of competence centered on the masculine responsibilities associated with accumulating resources, including a family, and making a living independent of outside support. Mature men were noted for their economic self-sufficiency, rational wisdom, and self-control. Parents of boys succeeded with child-rearing when their offspring were pious and law-abiding, and no longer needed their assistance. Parents of incapable children were burdened not only with the care of their offspring but also with the shame of having failed at their task. Presumably they suffered more when life-long dependency involved boys.[13]

Despite the potential for parental disappointment and shame, colonists took into account the real possibility that incompetent individuals might require special provisions not just for their personal care, but in legal matters as well. The early settlers singled out for special dispensations certain kinds of people whom they thought were weak and vulnerable, thoroughly incompetent, or both, including children, idiots, and people who were distracted. The publication of Massachusetts' first legal code in 1641, the *Body of Liberties,* introduced protections for such individuals and their property and provided means to expedite business transactions when a person was considered incapable of managing his or her affairs. The ability to handle one's material possessions and specifically one's real property provided a critical test of competence in the colonies. The *Body of Liberties* determined that people were capable of making responsible decisions regarding the disposition of their property at age twenty-one, as long as they were "of right understanding and meamories." Children under the age of twenty-one and those with mental impairments, such as idiots, distracted persons, and aged individuals with dementia were traditionally denied such rights due to their presumed incompetence with decision making.[14]

An adaptation of English law, Liberty 52 granted special dispensations to "Children, Idiots, Distracted persons, and all that are strangers, or new commers to our plantation" who faced criminal charges. The diversity of the group suggested a tolerance toward people who may have been unfamiliar with the laws, designed to attract foreigners who might settle in the area. Liberty 52 introduced in America provisions to deal leniently with children and people considered mentally incompetent who were brought before criminal courts. It laid the groundwork for future debate over mental competence, moral responsibility, and culpability in criminal convictions and sentencing. In the seventeenth century, both children and the mentally disabled presumably lacked the ability to plan and actually commit a serious crime, although special dispensations went just so far when Puritan principles were violated.[15]

Beyond the legal constraints, social custom ensured that the values associated with child-rearing were respected in Massachusetts. Tight-knit families and community ways imposed conformity in terms of behavior as well as mores. Parental responsibilities were grounded both in law and in the expectations of family members, neighbors, and ministers. When children failed to learn the requisite skills at home, parents were taken to task. Demands on parents could be intense if children were rebellious; likewise, parents were suspect when children failed to learn expected skills such as reading. In some cases families failed to provide the necessary setting and instruction for children's learning, while in other cases children lacked abilities to learn necessary skills and behaviors. Pressures at home suggest a potential for significant abuse when children proved unable to learn simple skills and behaviors, regardless of the cause. Fear of censure coupled with the shame of failure may have driven parents of incompetent children to desperate ends.[16]

Nevertheless, reports of incompetence that appear in court records suggest that colonists were more tolerant of their disabled neighbors than might be expected, for there was a considerable gap between colonists' hopes and expectations for their children and perceptions of actual incompetent adults whose stories appear in court records. Although colonial parents set the standard for adult maturity with their vision of children's learning practical skills, correct behavior, and piety, when competence was questioned for legal purposes, most likely jurists conducted the same simple tests that were in use in England and were described by John Brydall, English author of legal treatises, in 1700:

> ... Among the English Jurists, *Idiot* is a Term of Law, and taken for one that is wholly deprived of his Reason and Understanding from his Birth; and with us in our common Speech is called a *Fool Natural*; of whom there has been given a Description by several of our Law-Authors. Master Fitzherbert describes an Idiot thus: He *who shall be said to be an Idiot from his Birth, is such a Person, who cannot account or number twenty pence, or cannot tell who is his Father or Mother, or how old he is, &c. So that it may appear that he hath no understanding of Reason, what shall be for his Profit, or what shall be for his Loss.*[17]

The outcome of a court case might depend on the credibility of a witness or a defendant, although there is no evidence that formal tests of competence were conducted in Massachusetts. In 1690 Mary Phips was considered by her neighbors to be incapable of illegal sexual behavior. Her innocence was established on the basis of the following testimony:

> [She is] void of common reason and understanding that is in other children of her age, not capable of discerning between good and evil or any morality
> . . . but she knows persons and remembers persons. She is next to a mere naturall in her intellectuals.
> . . . She is incapable of resisting a rape have[ing] one side quite palsied.
> . . . [We] have to help her as a meer child.[18]

Mary Phips's age is unknown, but she was considered a child and "a mere naturall," rather than an idiot. Incompetence in Mary Phips's case apparently extended to sexual behavior in addition to mental deficiencies and included physical disability as well.

Samuel Hadley was another individual who, in 1670, was considered incompetent due to his failure to learn to read and his inability to hold a job:

[Deponent] and his sisters took a great deal of care and diligently instructed [Hadley] in reading and he was also put to school, but he did not gain much of what might have been expected. "In his ordenary imployment he was incapashous that I neuer saw one of that age soe unfit for larning & any work in which was needfull to haue discresion used."[19]

One more example serves to illustrate the ways colonists thought about the inadequacies of their neighbors. In 1647 Michael Smith was brought into court for casting three votes in an election:

It is ordered, yt ye fine of Mighill Smith for his puting in of three beanes at once for one mans election, it being done in simplicity, & he being pore & of an harmles disposition, it is ordered his fine is suspended till further order from ye Generall Corte.[20]

In Smith's case, incompetence combined with poverty and an inoffensive nature secured his acquittal. All three individuals, Phips, Hadley, and Smith, shared characteristics ascribed to idiocy: simple, childlike behavior, a lack of reading or counting ability, a failure to tell right from wrong, and an inability to work at a meaningful job. Their neighbors' attention to reading, working, and reasoning reinforces the definition of competency among colonial adults and the values they placed on those skills. The emphasis on simplicity and innocence expands the meaning of incompetence with a suggestion of tolerance and pity that was more typically reserved for children.

There is considerable disparity between Cotton Mather's observation of the two sisters in Dunstable and the court reports of Phips, Hadley, and Smith. The differences speak to the diversity in colonists' perceptions of disability and incompetence. Whereas Phips, Hadley, and Smith seemed to meet none of the standards for capable adults, none of the individuals was actually called an idiot in court documents. "A mere natural," in the case of Mary Phips, is as close as it gets. Nevertheless the three shared the main characteristics of intellectual incompetence—an inability to read, to work, and to reason—and additional factors played a role in one or another case: poverty, simplicity, physical disability, and childishness. There was nothing threatening about any of these three individuals, and nothing that might frighten someone else. To the contrary, Smith's harmlessness helped win his acquittal and Phips's childlike demeanor suggested a kind of innocence associated with immature sexuality. As adults, Hadley and Smith presented a timeless quality that blurred the boundaries between childhood and adulthood. Even Phips, considered still a child, was physically mature yet essentially undeveloped in other aspects of life. Both agelessness and gender neutrality accompanied immaturity and the perceived permanence of incompetence of these individuals.

Even though Mather wrote his letter about the girls from Dunstable in 1713 and the court testimony about Smith appeared as early as 1647, the difference in time is not as meaningful as the difference in perspective. Because Mather intended his writing for publication, he wrote in a style that conformed to the work of intellectuals with whom he wanted to be associated. The topics that he wrote about, the point of view, and the language were intended to impress his readers. Like many other colonials with a scientific bent, Mather adopted an ostensibly objective perspective to study aberrations in the natural world. Distanced from the objects he observed, Mather tried to maintain a cool detachment to prove his intellectual veracity. More telling, however, were his emotional outpourings, which reflected his personal sense of shame and foreboding at witnessing such a disaster. Missing altogether was an expression of empathy that might have betrayed Mather's identification with his subjects. Perhaps his greatest fear was that he too might suffer the humiliation and burden of caring for such children if he should provoke God either knowingly or unknowingly.[21]

Although Cotton Mather has been criticized for self-promotion and embellished writing, he was also driven by ministerial duties of religious instruction and acts of benevolence. His reaction to the girls reflected both personal piety and public preaching. To Mather the minister, the girls' deformities represented animalistic qualities found just below the surface in all people, a suggestion of evil to be subdued. Here, then, was a portrayal of raw, unredeemed human nature that violated every aspect of God's ordered universe. Physical deformities, combined with a failure to control the most basic human functions, frightened and disgusted Mather. Even God, he concluded, had abandoned these children. With their grotesque deformities the girls represented the possibility of extreme deviations from God's planned and ordered universe that only God could explain. As such they represented moral failures that dashed every hope that Puritans might have for their children's independence and respectable maturity.

In contrast to Mather's description of these extreme cases of idiocy, the informal, personalized accounts of Phips, Hadley, and Smith portrayed the three as merely incompetent, pitiful characters. Whereas Mather depicted the sisters in ways that violated the ideal image of Puritan childhood, the individuals described in court represented unfortunate but more ordinary people who aroused sympathy and understanding. Court testimony, in contrast to Mather's attempts at scholarship, consisted of informal, spontaneous verbal accounts of familiar family members and neighbors. Lacking artifice, these accounts convey an authenticity which is missing in Mather's letter. Nevertheless, it is likely that the two sisters from Dunstable were considerably more disabled than Phips, Hadley, or Smith. The differences suggest that mental disability in Puritan Massachusetts took many forms that ranged from the severity of the disabilities of Mather's report of two sisters from Dunstable to the more typical people who appeared in court.

Despite the diversity of perceptions, tolerance went only so far: the social fabric of Puritan communities required moral and behavioral conformity grounded in religious principles. Defined as incompetent, Phips, Hadley, and Smith were excluded from the company of respectable adults, although their exclusion earned them status as worthy recipients of colonial benevolence. Christian charity, after all, required objects in order for Puritans to practice good intentions, and the practice of charity was a Puritan duty.[22]

In summary, idiocy, along with all its variations of intellectual disability in colonial Massachusetts, provides an example of childhood gone awry. Put another way, it offers a negative example of everything that was most important to Puritans about parenting and child-rearing. In the abstract, idiocy violated the religious and moral precepts that grounded Puritan society. In reality, idiocy and lesser forms of intellectual disability disappointed parents' expectations for their children and extinguished their hopes. Worthy but permanently dependent, idiots and others with intellectual disabilities failed to attain the minimal standards determined by literacy, useful work, and religious commitment. These standards established, in part, the competencies required for the respectable maturation of children into adulthood. Puritans may have found purpose in intellectual disability, but it was consistently negative: the deviancy of idiocy served as a measure of incompetence; the condition satisfied Puritans' charitable obligations; and it reminded Puritans of the unfathomable mystery of God's creativity. More significantly, idiocy contradicted the colonists' optimistic expectations for their children with visions of lifelong dependency, inferiority, and failure.

NOTES

1. Cotton Mather, *Selected Letters of Cotton Mather,* compiled with commentary by Kenneth Silverman (Baton Rouge: Louisiana State University Press, 1971), 139.

2. Morgan, *Puritan Family.*

3. Fischer, *Albion's Seed.*

4. Vinovskis and Moran, *Religion, Family, and the Life Course,* 34–35; Linda Pollock, comp., *A Lasting Relationship: Parents and Children over Three Centuries* (Hanover, NH: University Press of New England, 1982), 93–94; William M. Schmidt, "Health and Welfare of Colonial American Children," *American Journal of Diseases of Children* 130 (1976): 694–701.

5. Parnel Wickham, "Conceptions of Idiocy in Colonial Massachusetts," *Journal of Social History* 3 (2002): 938–48.

6. C. F. Goodey, "Mental Retardation: Social Section—Part I," in *A History of Clinical Psychiatry: The Origin and History of Psychiatric Disorders,* ed. German E. Berrios and Roy Porter (New York: New York University Press, 1995), 239–48.

7. Mary Ann Jimenez, *Changing Faces of Madness: Early American Attitudes and Treatment of the Insane* (Hanover, NH: University Press of New England, 1987), 22.

8. Miller, *The New England Mind,* 365–97.

9. Richard Baxter, *Universal Redemption of Mankind, by the Lord Jesus Christ: Stated and Cleared by the late Learned Mr. Richard Baxter. Whereunto is added a short Account of Special Redemption, by the same Author* (London: Printed for John Salusbury . . . , 1694), 477; Stephen Mayor, *The Lord's Supper in Early English Dissent* (London: Epworth Press, 1972), 130; James F. Cooper Jr. and Kenneth P. Minkema, eds., *The Sermon Notebook of Samuel Parris, 1689–1694* (Boston: Colonial Society of Massachusetts, 1993), 299.

10. Calvert, *Children in the House,* 52; Morgan, *Puritan Family.*

11. Michael W. Kaufman, *Institutional Individualism: Conversion, Exile, and Nostalgia in Puritan New England* (Hanover, NH: Wesleyan University Press, 1998), 91; Anne Jacobson Schutte, "'Such Monstrous Births': A Neglected Aspect of the Antinomian Controversy," *Renaissance Quarterly* 38 (1985): 85–106.

12. Thomas Hooker, *A Godly and Fruitfull Sermon: The Plantation of the Righteous* (London: Printed by M. P. for John Stafford, 1639), 124–25.

13. Lombard, *Making Manhood*; Lila Wilson, *Ye Heart of a Man: The Domestic Life of Men in Colonial New England* (New Haven, CT: Yale University Press, 1999).

14. *The Laws and Liberties of Massachusetts, 1641–1691: A Facsimile Edition, Containing also Council Orders and Executive Proclamations,* compiled with an introduction by John D. Cushing (Wilmington, DE: Scholarly Resources, 1976), 696.

15. Ibid.

16. Greven, *Protestant Temperament*; Wall, *Fierce Communion*.

17. John Brydall, *Non Compos Mentis; or, The Law Relating to Natural Fools, Mad-Folks, and Lunatick Persons, Inquisited, and Explained, for Common Benefit* (London: Printed by the Assigns of R. & E. Atkins, for I. Cleave, 1700), 6.

18. Roger Thompson, *Sex in Middlesex: Popular Mores in a Massachusetts County, 1649–1699* (Amherst: University of Massachusetts Press, 1986), 138.

19. Massachusetts, *Records and Files of the Quarterly Courts of Essex County, Massachusetts*, Vol. 4, *1667–1671*, ed. George F. Dow (Salem, MA: Essex Institute, 1914), 219.

20. *Records of the Governor and Company of the Massachusetts Bay in New England: Printed by Order of the Legislature*, ed. Nathaniel B. Shurtleff (Boston: W. White, 1853), 189.

21. Silverman, *Life and Times of Cotton Mather*, 197–202.

22. Stephen Foster, *Their Solitary Way: The Puritan Social Ethic in the First Century of Settlement in New England* (New Haven, CT: Yale University Press, 1971).

Chapter 9

"My Constant Attension on My Sick Child"
The Fragility of Family Life in the World of Elizabeth Drinker

Helena M. Wall

In 1707, the *Boston News-Letter* advertised "A Token for Mourners," a ser-mon addressed to a woman who "bewailed the loss of her dear and only son." The sermon promised to explain God's design and console the griev-ing family; it was, moreover, a work "Wherein the Boundaries of Sorrow are duly Fixed." This advertisement draws our attention to a deeply embedded, defining element of life in early America: the precariousness of life in that world and the ways in which people tried to make sense of that precariousness. More particularly, it impresses upon us the impact of diff-erent kinds of insecurity on family life, and on the experiences of parents and children, and the strategies families pursued in search of security and solace.

This essay examines one piece of the larger problem, the ways in which a sense of fragility shaped the experience of families, and especially chil-dren and childrearing, in early America, through a close reading of the diary of Elizabeth Sandwith Drinker. Drinker (1735–1807), a Philadelphia Quaker of the gentry class, kept a very detailed diary from 1758, shortly before her marriage, through the birth of nine children and the death of four of them, to just before her final illness in 1807. It would be an under-statement to say that Drinker showed a keen interest in all forms of pre-cariousness, particularly as they affected the well-being of her children. Indeed, the reader can open at random to any page in the diary and find a catalogue of fevers, headaches, toothaches, riding accidents, kitchen fires, smallpox, and whooping cough. Her diary encompasses the daily tribulations of her family as well as the impact of the Revolutionary War on Philadelphia, miscarriages as well as the great yellow fever epidemic of 1793, fears of childbirth as well as, with increasing frequency, reports of urban disorders such as crime and arson and threats of uprising by Philadelphia's black community.

Consider only part of a single entry, from 12 September 1777:

> This has been a day of Great Confusion to many in this City; which I have in great measure been kept out of by my constant attension on my sick Child. part of Washingtons Army has been routed [in the Battle of Brandywine, in which Washington failed to halt the British advance on Philadelphia], and have been seen coming into Town in Great Numbers; the perticulars of the Battle, I have not attended to, the slain is said to be very numerous.—hundreds of their muskets laying in the road. . . . I was a little fluttered this Afternoon by hearing a Drum stop at our Door and a hard knocking succeed; it proved to be, men with orders for HD [Henry Drinker, her husband] to appear or find a Substitute.

And well might she have been "a little fluttered" by the appearance of soldiers at her door: many of her pacifist Quaker neighbors had been exiled to Virginia that very week for failing to swear allegiance to the revolutionary cause. The private and public worlds of Elizabeth Drinker, the many positions she inhabits, converge here, and the common theme is a sense of anxiety and vulnerability. Drinker is at risk as a mother whose child may succumb to consumption; as a wife whose husband may be impressed into the army; as a Philadelphian well aware of the advance of the British, despite her preoccupation with her sick child; and as a Quaker subject to banishment for insufficient patriotic fervor. Our task is to understand not only Elizabeth Drinker's experience of these risks but also how her experiences, her perceptions, and her responses shaped the lives of her children as well.[1]

This task is complicated by a fact so obvious that it is easy to overlook. Historically speaking, children have been seen and not much heard from. Children appear in the historical documents as the subjects of advice books, as the objects of affection or punishment, and as the victims of accident and illness. We see children almost exclusively through the recorded perceptions of others. The few exceptions to this in early America are *so* exceptional that they only underscore the general point. The conversion narratives of adolescents in the Northampton religious revivals or the testimony of the "afflicted" girls in Salem in 1692 offer rare glimpses into the minds and feelings of nonadults—but these can hardly be relied upon as guides to common experience.

This is an unlucky fact for the historian of childhood, but it is a fact that we can work around. The historians of other groups once deemed voiceless or lost to history have overcome similar obstacles to produce rich portraits of the poor, the enslaved, the female. And there is one paradoxical advantage for historians of childhood in relying on the observations of adults, especially parents, to make sense of children's experience: children themselves rely on and respond to and incorporate their parents' perceptions and actions as they come to understand themselves and the world around them. Parental conduct, expectations, attitudes, even moods shape children's immediate world and their entry into the larger world. Here is a fact that we can work with and not simply around: to understand Elizabeth Drinker's experience of the fragility of family life is at least one way to begin to understand the experience of her children as well.

Drinker's diary does not give us a typical or ideal representation of the effects of precariousness on parents and children in early America. As a Quaker, she adopted a "moderate" approach to childrearing, to use Philip Greven's term; financially comfortable, she did not experience—although she did observe and report—the effects of poverty and economic desperation on families; and as a Philadelphian, she was spared the dangers of life on the frontier. But much of her story and her sensibility was widely shared or can be discussed in comparative terms; in its detailed mapping of one family's life over half a century, her diary gives us considerable insight into how the Drinker family, in common with all other early Americans, faced, and sought to "fix," the boundaries of sorrow in their daily lives.

"Birth, and copulation, and death. / That's all the facts when you come to brass tacks," T. S. Eliot's Sweeney reminds us. "Birth, and copulation, and death." These facts, along with sickness, do form the brass tacks of Drinker's diary and most of the defining experiences and rhythms of the Drinker household. Sickness—or its apprehension or aftermath, and not only their own sickness but that of their siblings and their mother—was a constant presence in the lives of the Drinker children. How they responded to this atmosphere is something we can only guess at, but the diary gives us a clear look at what they had to absorb. The Drinkers had the usual run of childhood illnesses and minor accidents, as well as the conditions idiosyncratically described in eighteenth-century terms: bloody fluxes, disordered bowels, swellings, fevers. Drinker herself noted that "'tis hard to ascertain the real disorders of young Children." Along with eighteenth-century disorders, they submitted to the hazards of eighteenth-century medical practice: they were bled and purged and dosed with laudanum and "physick" at rates that shock the modern reader.[2]

There were larger threats as well. Ironically, the most devastating medical crisis of Elizabeth Drinker's lifetime, the Philadelphia yellow fever of 1793, was one from which her family was largely buffered. The Drinkers, like most wealthy Philadelphians, retreated to their country estate when signs of the summer complaints and fall fevers began to appear. This retreat protected them not only against infection but also against equally dangerous medical treatments. Dr. Benjamin Rush, the most famous and assiduous of Philadelphia's practitioners, mustered more courage than efficacy in his ministrations. An advocate of "heroic" medicine who advised bleeding patients of up to 80 percent of their blood, Rush expressed puzzlement at the high death rates of those under his care. William Cobbett saw the situation more clearly, calling Rush's cure "one of those great discoveries which are made from time to time for the depopulation of the earth." Far from Philadelphia, and Rush, the Drinkers weathered the 1793 yellow fever.[3]

Physical protection, however, is not the same as emotional protection. Throughout Drinker's lifetime, other outbreaks of yellow fever and smallpox visited Philadelphia in the sickly summer and fall seasons. Removing the family to the countryside became a seasonal ritual and a reminder of what they were escaping. Drinker paid very close attention to the signs of impending sickness in town, and from her country house she followed the reports of sickness, the mortality rates, the wrenching stories of orphaned children and victims abandoned by their neighbors. She even recorded the deaths of children in separate tallies from the whole. These disease outbreaks were very much on Drinker's mind no matter where she was, and her preoccupation and expressions of anxiety would have permeated the household.

And if their exposure to serious epidemic disease was at a remove, the Drinker children experienced first-hand major illness and tragedy. William, born in 1767, suffered a bout with tuberculosis from which he seems never fully to have recovered. Alone among the Drinker children who reached adulthood, he never married; he continued to live with his parents well into his maturity, and Elizabeth monitored his every ache, every mood, every spell of weakness. He emerges from the diary as a young version of Emma Woodhouse's father: mild, given more to frets than temper, a valetudinarian whose leading characteristic was how rarely he complained of feeling unwell. William, at least, survived. Four other Drinker children did not. Mary died at fourteen months; Harry, just short of three months; Elizabeth, in less than a year and possibly during or just after birth; and the youngest, Charles, sickly from birth, died at age two-and-a-half. All of the Drinker children experienced the death of at least one sibling when they were old enough to know what was happening. In addition, at least three of these sibling deaths came after sustained periods of illness, periods marked by bedside vigils, doctors' visits, periods of worry and distraction for the whole family.

This points to another powerful determinant of the Drinker children's environment, the physical and emotional well-being of Elizabeth Drinker herself. This issue is surprisingly difficult to approach, given the diary's focus on just this area. But the diary is *so* preoccupied with Elizabeth's health, she is so attentive to every twinge and misery, that it is hard to form a sense of proportion. As the scholar who knows her diary best put it, "She considered herself a sickly person, and indeed, she seemed assailed with more than her share of eighteenth-century maladies. Yet against what standard does one measure her constant malaise?"[4] Still, we may venture a few points. It seems clear that for Elizabeth Drinker, as for so many eighteenth-century Americans, toothache, joint ache, headache, indigestion or worse brought on by spoiled food, and all kinds of bowel disorders, were frequent companions. To read the diary is to appreciate the miracles of aspirin and antibiotics—although Drinker had her own mother's little helpers in laudanum and opium. From early middle age on, her health and physical strength declined noticeably—reflected in curtailed outings, prolonged confinements, multiplied complaints—reducing her eventually to near invalidism.

Furthermore, there is the central fact of her childbearing. Drinker carried nine pregnancies to term and suffered two miscarriages. Like most women of her time and class, she is frustratingly delicate in her references to pregnancy and labor. In most instances, though, the diary entries in the weeks before she went into labor refer obliquely to the discomforts of her "situation," to more frequent retreats to her chamber, to more admissions of feeling "unwell." She clearly seems to have found pregnancy difficult. On the pain of childbirth, she gives us a little more to work with. On her birthday in 1800, she thinks "of my dear mothers situation on the eve of my birth. . . .—I have never brought a child into the world," she writes almost twenty years since her last pregnancy, "without thinking how much my dear mother might have suffered with me." Her unusually pointed comment about menopause offers the most explicit retrospection on her childbearing years. One day before her sixty-second birthday, she wrote, "I have often thought that women who live to get over the time of Child-bareing, if other things are favourable to them, experience more comfort and satisfaction than at any other period of their lives."[5]

But far more terrible than the pain of childbirth was the grief of losing children. Most of Drinker's diary is notable for its lack of emotional expressiveness. The death of Charles Drinker, her youngest child, occasions one of the most striking exceptions. "Our dear little one after diligent nursing had out grown most of his weekness and promised fair to be a fine Boy, became much oppress'd with phlegm," prompting the doctor to administer a purgative. This

> did not work, and in little more then 20 minits from the time he took it, he expired aged 2 years 7 months and one day—about a week before he was fat, fresh and hearty—he cut a tooth a day before he died—thus was I suddenly depri[v]ed of my dear little Companion over whome, I had almost constantly watchd, from the time of his birth, and his late thriving state seem'd to promise a [reward] to all my pains—he dyed the 17 march, fourth day [of the religious week].[6]

And what of the surviving Drinker children? What did it mean to them to grow up watching their mother cope with bouts of illness and grief, with multiple and apparently difficult pregnancies, all the while tending to the care of small children? What did it mean to them to watch their siblings suffer sickness, submit to often gruesome medical treatments, and in four cases die? Modern psychological studies of children who experience the death or chronic illness of siblings, and of those who grow up with a parent who experiences frequent or chronic illness, confirm what common sense would tell us. Depending on the precise circumstances, the dynamics of the family, and the age of the child when bereaved, such children may be more vulnerable to depression, fears of attachment, and feelings of guilt and unworthiness; and as adults they may replicate the symptoms they observed in their chronically ill parent. In the case of the Drinker children, such findings may be suggestive but nothing more: we have no way of testing them, and Elizabeth herself never commented on the responses of her surviving children to the loss of their siblings. It may be worth keeping these psychological studies in mind for other research into the history of childhood, however, especially as we note a striking gap in the historical literature: although it is a chestnut of family history to analyze the responses of parents to the death of a child, virtually no historical work examines the impact on children of losing a parent or sibling.[7]

All the more reason to look closely at the fragments of evidence available to us. Although the diary gives us no direct comment on the Drinker children's reactions to their siblings' deaths and mother's condition, it does point to some clear disruptions in the household. We know, for example, that Elizabeth put at least three of her children out to nurse, though she did so reluctantly and disliked the periods of separation. She explicitly attributes this decision in the case of Henry to her own ill health. Writing in July 1771, she complained, "I have been unwell all Day. . . . Dr. D says I must wean my little Henry or get a nurse for him, either seems hard —but I must submit." Another period of disorder seems to have followed the death of the first Henry in August 1769. Elizabeth did not confide to her diary anything like the access of grief she would later lay open after Charles's death. Quite the opposite. Henry last appears in the diary on July 25, "not very well." His death nearly a month later is never mentioned. Yet in its silence Elizabeth's diary is as eloquent here as in the death of Charles. In sharp contrast to her usual daily entries, for the rest of that year Elizabeth writes only a handful of perfunctory notes, some apparently added after the dates. One senses a household in a kind of hibernation, with the usual routines suspended. Finally, the Drinker family tree gives a small hint of the impact of these sibling deaths, an echo of loss in the next generation. Henry Sandwith Drinker, born in 1770 and christened with the same name as the brother who had died one year earlier, was fourteen when Charles died. In 1808, he named one of his own sons Charles and then, when that boy died in 1809, another son became Charles the following year. Henry, it seems, twenty-five years on, had not forgotten his younger brother Charles.[8]

If we must rely on imagination to form a picture of the emotional atmosphere of the Drinker household, we are on much firmer evidentiary ground in charting the practical buffers against precariousness and their strategies for responding to distress. The most obvious of these was wealth, derived from Henry Drinker's successful mercantile house. We have already noted the Drinkers' country house, which afforded them protection against Philadelphia's sickly seasons. Wealth also brought them the services of the best doctors in town, however dubious some of their methods, along with a nutritious and varied diet, and a substantial, secure home. It ensured a steady supply of servants, too, young girls and slaves and newly arrived immigrants, who provided child care as well as household labor. Troublesome they might be—and Elizabeth Drinker frequently comments on nurses who didn't suit and girls who were too saucy —but Drinker, unlike, say, Martha Ballard, never had to complain that she had no one to cut firewood for her. The diary gives us another clue to the financial safety net available to the Drinkers: insurance. When Elizabeth paid "four Dollars to renew the Insureance on our House" in 1777, she reentered the ranks of property holders who could take advantage of this fairly recent innovation—insurance for personal property as opposed to business assets—to protect their homes and families.[9]

Alongside wealth as a protection against precariousness, and in some ways closely related to it, was family, both nuclear family and extended kin, and an even broader network of friends and, in the Drinker case, fellow Quakers. The importance of these forms of "social insurance," to use Nancy Tomes's term, winds unmistakably throughout the diary. Elizabeth was not quite twenty-one when her mother died, and her father died two months later. She and her sister, Mary, were taken in by a prominent Quaker, Thomas Say, living in his household for fourteen months. They then lived for four years with another Quaker, Ann Warner, and it was from her house that Elizabeth married the widowed Henry Drinker. Mary Sandwith never married and lived throughout her life with Elizabeth and Henry—as a spinster, the beneficiary of their familial support, as well as a useful contributor to a household soon filled with young children. The diary contains hundreds of entries attesting to the importance of female friends and coreligionists as sources of solace, invaluable news, and practical help. Elizabeth repaid these attentions to her friends and to her adult children, nursing them through illness, shepherding them through pregnancy and childbirth, minding grandchildren, and, throughout, nurturing a dense web of personal contacts. Elizabeth acknowledged her good fortune in these personal ties when she reflected on the counterexample of James Logan, after a visit from him in 1798: "A poor Solatary Man, No one to attend on him in his advanced life, 'tho abundantly sufficient of wealth, No Child, or near female relative, the case seems hard—how greatly, is a near, and dear and feeling friend to be prised, a disinterested friend who will attend out of pure Affection and regard."[10]

Wealth, family, and a broader social network, each important in its own right, also worked together, often in deliberately cultivated ways, to protect families; and in the case of the Drinkers, they also converged to create the "Quaker tribalism" that some historians have seen as characteristic of this elite group. Nancy Tomes has studied closely the visiting patterns of Quaker women in the late eighteenth century, and Drinker's diary exhibits every one of them. Quaker women visited each other's families for ceremonial calls, to help in times of sickness and childbirth, and to enforce religious discipline. From the recreational to the quasi-coercive, Quaker visiting served an important set of purposes, as Tomes notes. "Visiting helped to maintain an informal social 'insurance'"; through visiting, "the community built a network of mutual obligation and social knowledge in a society where few institutional forms of assistance existed."[11]

If Quaker visiting was primarily female and familial, Quaker connections among men and households provided another layer of economic security. The Philadelphia Yearly Meeting's Book of Discipline enjoined upon members honesty and prudence in business dealings. The enforcement of this ethic—through word of mouth, through formal disciplinary measures, and through the conferral of "certificates in good standing"— gave Quakers "an edge in international business," Mary Schweitzer has concluded. "A professed Quaker could be trusted in business"—especially by other Quakers. Henry Drinker's own dealings attest to the intermeshing of business, religion, and social ties, which stretched from the West Indies to Philadelphia. On several occasions, he arranged for the sons of trading partners or their friends to be given places as apprentices or junior clerks, primed to learn the business, in one of Philadelphia's trading houses, including his own.[12]

Bound by trust, business, friendship, and favors, mercantile families were also frequently bound by marriage as well. Quaker discipline forbade "marrying out of unity," although this ban on intermarriage had lost much of its force by the late eighteenth century. For socially prominent Quakers, however, such a taint still carried a strong sting. And marriage within the group held many advantages for them beyond social approval. Intermarriage helped the Philadelphia Quaker gentry consolidate its class position and authority. Furthermore, doing business with family members who could be trusted, or at least monitored, provided a hedge against the uncertainties of the market and the potential treachery of strangers, as well as an efficient way to pool capital. As Naomi Lamoreaux has shown, "insider trading"—nepotism, mixing family and business—was the most reliable form of trading there was, a familial buffer against economic risk. Family and wealth, social networks and business alliances, all converged to protect people like the Drinkers from several kinds of loss, or at least cushion their impact.[13]

And if Drinker's diary attests to the effectiveness of these familial and financial strategies for promoting security, it also gives us glimpses into how the other half lived, including the children of the other half. One sure way to locate families in trouble in early America is to look for children who are placed or bound out as servants or apprentices. Such arrangements, usually although not always formalized through indenture, sometimes served to educate children or train them in a craft or business. The boys whom Henry Drinker placed in the great counting houses of Philadelphia were not, it seems, at all disadvantaged. On the contrary, they were upwardly mobile, and they were the exceptions. Most children bound out came from families in crisis: poverty, illegitimacy, parental illness, parental abandonment, parental death—these were the usual suspects in the decision, or need, to bind out children. In January 1807, Elizabeth Drinker reports that a "new born babe, to all appearance, was found in an Alley downtown . . . it was taken to a poor woman in the Neighborhood who has a sucking child, who engages to take care of it, if the overseers [of the poor] will pay her for her trouble." Here was a child bound for indenture, if it survived wetnursing. Such children found their way to the Drinkers' house as well. An unsatisfactory applicant appeared in April 1798: "A well duped Woman of the Name of Mary Scott, with a little tidy girl between 2 and 3 years old, and a little boy of 7 months in her arms, came to desire I would take her child 'till she was 18 years of age, that she might go out to service with her other child." This child was too young to be of any use to Drinker but over the years, she took in several more suitable children and adolescents as servants.[14]

Thus did the alchemy of the labor market transform one family's desperation into another's privilege, one child's hardship into another's indulgence. Drinker recognized the advantages of her position—both the wealth that enabled her to hire such servants and the legal indentures that protected her investment and her rights—but she saw them as her due. One adolescent servant, the frequently impertinent Sally Johnson, had given birth to an illegitimate child, who shortly thereafter died, while in the Drinker household. Her mother then "very willingly agree'd to Sallys staying with us two months longer as we shall be cleaning house &c." Then off came the velvet glove: "—she is, I expect, sensible, that we might, if inclined so to do, oblidge her to serve us near a year longer for the expences we have been at on her and Childs account, instead of giving her freedom Cloaths &c—." This is what it meant to be on the *other* side of Quaker tribalism.[15]

The Drinkers' family life, then, was framed by the abiding facts of birth, copulation, and death, and by the embedded support system of wealth and social networks. These basic facts of life were not immutable, however, and the Drinkers did not live in a static world. Some of the changes they experienced reflect deeper changes in late colonial society, and some of them bear directly on the experience of family and childhood. The protective cocoon around the Quaker gentry began to unravel in the late eighteenth century. Quakers declined as a proportion of Philadelphia's population as the city grew larger and more diversified, and as more Quakers married "out of unity." The decline of Quaker authority came home to the Drinkers when daughter Molly eloped with a man of whom her parents disapproved and in defiance of the Quaker meeting. Molly and her husband reconciled with both her parents and the meeting but the elopement was a signal that even respectable Quaker girls might not become quite the respectable Quaker matrons their mothers had been. Quaker political authority had eroded considerably even before the revolution but the most vivid challenge came during the war when a number of prominent Quakers, Henry Drinker included, were sent into internal exile for several months. Henry's absence opened a period of great anxiety in the household and a palpable sense of the loss of male protection. It even occasioned a rare comment from Elizabeth about her children being frightened.[16]

Henry's detention was highly disruptive to the household, but it was involuntary and exceptional. Longer-term changes, rooted in business and public life, pulled him away from his family more frequently over the years, just as they did many other ambitious, successful men of the new republic. And the reaction of upper-class wives such as Elizabeth was also becoming more familiar. In December 1795, she expects—hopes, really—that bad weather will prevent Henry from traveling: "a little relaxation from business may be useful to HD—I am not acquainted with the extent of my husbands great variety of engagements, but this I know, that he is perpetually and almost ever employed; the Affairs of Society and the public, and private, out of his own family, or his own concerns, I believe takes up ten twelfths of his time."[17] Occasionally, Elizabeth expresses admiration for Henry's industry but more often she voices frustration, loneliness, and melancholy; and his absences become sufficiently regular that she enlists male neighbors and servants to stay with her and the children, for protection. That this added tension to the Drinker marriage is unmistakable. It is less clear what Henry's absences meant to the children, but they may have contributed to Elizabeth's notably close relationship with her children, especially her daughters, well into their adulthood.[18]

The employments of men like Henry Drinker and Elizabeth's attendant focus on her home and children reflect broader changes in the household economy of the late eighteenth century, and the movement of families like the Drinkers toward a class-specific domesticity. Elizabeth's diary over the years also hints at a growing self-consciousness of class boundaries, a perceived increase in urban dangers and public disorders. She hints as well at greater uncertainties in the marketplace, arising from strangers' untrustworthiness and greed and more frequently resulting in reverses or even bankruptcy. Her sense of the multiplying hazards of city streets, combined with her declining health and physical mobility, drew Elizabeth—and her children—deeper into the sanctuary of her home, her family, her own kind.

Her diary thus gives us some sense of the ways in which the middle- and upper-middle-class family incubated class consciousness and class values, and promoted the separation—cultural, physical, residential, psychological—of one class from another by the turn of the nineteenth century. It was, after all, a sense of rising disorder in urban culture and among lower-class youths that led gentry groups to appropriate the working-class, carnivalesque rites of Christmas and transform them into the safe, wholesome—and wholly domesticated—middle-class family celebration of the Victorian era. Here is one final way in which Elizabeth Drinker's diary alerts us to the changing face of precariousness in late-eighteenth-century America. Birth, copulation, and death are universal facts of life. But as upper-class families such as the Drinkers found more ways to guard against or cope with childhood mortality or epidemic disease, they grew more concerned with challenges to their peace of mind, their class authority, the security of their family and their possessions, and the molding of their children into respectable adults. The Drinkers and others like them faced a new set of dangers to their family and their world as the nineteenth century began, and the family itself, as their class defined it, formed a major bulwark against those dangers.

NOTES

1. Elaine Forman Crane, ed., *The Diary of Elizabeth Drinker,* 3 vols. (Boston: Northeastern University Press, 1991) [hereafter ED], I, 229.

2. T. S. Eliot, "Sweeney Agonistes," in *The Complete Poems and Plays, 1909– 1950* (New York: Harcourt, Brace and World, 1971), 80–81; ED, I, 509.

3. J. Worth Estes and Billy G. Smith, eds., *A Melancholy Scene of Devastation: The Public Response to the 1793 Philadelphia Yellow Fever Epidemic* (Philadelphia: Science History Publications, 1997), quotation on 157.

4. Elaine Forman Crane, "Introduction," ED, I, xix.

5. ED, II, 1279, 893.

6. ED, I, 420.

7. Betty Davies, *Shadows in the Sun: The Experience of Sibling Bereavement in Childhood* (Philadelphia, 1999); Jonathan Bloom-Feshbach and Sally Bloom-Feshbach, eds., *The Psychology of Separation and Loss* (San Francisco: Jossey-Bass, 1987); Elaine Forman Crane, "'I Have Suffer'd Much Today': The Defining Force of Pain in Early America," in Ronald Hoffman, Mechal Sobel, and Frederika Teute, eds., *Through a Glass Darkly* (Chapel Hill: University of North Carolina Press, 1997), 383–84.

8. ED, I, 162, 149–50, lxxiv.

9. ED, I, 253.

10. ED, II, 1060.

11. Nancy Tomes, "The Quaker Connection: Visiting Patterns among Women in the Philadelphia Society of Friends, 1750–1800," in Michael Zuckerman, ed., *Friends and Neighbors* (Philadelphia: Temple University Press, 1982), 181.

12. Mary Schweitzer, *Custom and Contract: Household, Government, and the Economy in Colonial Pennsylvania* (New York: Columbia University Press, 1987), 60; ED, II, 768 n.5.

13. Naomi Lamoreaux, *Insider Lending: Banks, Personal Connections, and Economic Development in Industrial New England* (New York: Cambridge University Press, 1994).

14. Wall, *Fierce Communion,* ch. 4; ED, III, 2008; II, 1018–19.

15. ED, I, 791.

16. ED, I, 258; II, 829 ff.

17. ED, I, 759–60.

18. Terri Premo, *Winter Friends: Women Growing Old in the New Republic, 1785–1835* (Urbana: University of Illinois Press, 1990), 21, 23, 57–58, 61–62.

"I Had Eight Birds Hatcht in One Nest"
Anne Bradstreet Writes about Parenthood

Anne Bradstreet is known to most high school and college literature students as one of the first American poets, as one of the first American women to publish a book (a collection of poems published in England in 1650 without her permission), and as a chronicler of the kinder, gentler side of Puritanism. As an eighteen-year-old, she and her family had been among the first settlers to travel to the new Massachusetts Bay Colony in 1630. She married a childhood sweetheart, gave birth to eight children (Samuel, Dorothy, Sarah, Simon Jr., Dudley, Hannah, Mercy, and John)—all of whom lived to adulthood—over the course of about ten years, and died in 1672 at the age of sixty. Although her poetry covered many aspects of the Puritan experience in early New England, her touching reflections on raising her many children and on her inevitable separation from them seem surprisingly modern.

In Reference to Her Children (1659)

I had eight birds hatcht in one nest,
Four Cocks were there, and Hens the rest.
I nurst them up with pain and care,
No cost nor labour did I spare
Till at the last they felt their wing,
Mounted the Trees and learned to sing.
Chief of the Brood then took his flight
To Regions far and left me quite.
My mournful chirps I after send
Till he return, or I do end.
Leave not thy nest, thy Dame and Sire,
Fly back and sing amidst this Quire.

My second bird did take her flight
And with her mate flew out of sight.
Southward they both their course did bend,
And Seasons twain they there did spend,
Till after blown by Southern gales
They Norward steer'd with filled sails.
A prettier bird was no where seen,
Along the Beach, among the treen.
I have a third of colour white
On whom I plac'd no small delight,
Coupled with mate loving and true,
Hath also bid her Dame adieu.
And where Aurora first appears,
She now hath percht to spend her years.
One to the Academy flew
To chat among that learned crew.
Ambition moves still in his breast
That he might chant above the rest,
Striving for more than to do well,
That nightingales he might excell.
My fifth, whose down is yet scarce gone,
Is 'mongst the shrubs and bushes flown
And as his wings increase in strength
On higher boughs he'll perch at length.
My other three still with me nest
Until they're grown, then as the rest,
Or here or there, they'll take their flight,
As is ordain'd, so shall they light.
If birds could weep, then would my tears
Let others know what are my fears
Lest this my brood some harm should catch
And be surpris'd for want of watch
Whilst pecking corn and void of care
They fall un'wares in Fowler's snare;
Or whilst on trees they sit and sing
Some untoward boy at them do fling,
Or whilst allur'd with bell and glass
The net be spread and caught, alas;
Or lest by Lime-twigs they be foil'd;

Or by some greedy hawks be spoil'd.
O would, my young, ye saw my breast
And knew what thoughts there sadly rest.
Great was my pain when I you bred,
Great was my care when I you fed.
Long did I keep you soft and warm
And with my wings kept off all harm.
My cares are more, and fears, than ever,
My throbs such now as 'fore were never.
Alas, my birds, you wisdom want
Of perils you are ignorant.
Oft times in grass, on trees, in flight,
Sore accidents on you may light.
O to your safety have an eye,
So happy may you live and die.
Mean while, my days in tunes I'll spend
Till my weak lays with me shall end.
In shady woods I'll sit and sing
And things that past, to mind I'll bring.
Once young and pleasant, as are you,
But former toys (no joys) adieu!
My age I will not once lament
But sing, my time so near is spent,
And from the top bough take my flight
Into a country beyond sight
Where old ones instantly grow young
And there with seraphims set song.
No seasons cold, nor storms they see
But spring lasts to eternity.
When each of you shall in your nest
Among your young ones take your rest,
In chirping languages oft them tell
You had a Dame that lov'd you well,
That did what could be done for young
And nurst you up till you were strong
And 'fore she once would let you fly
She shew'd you joy and misery,
Taught what was good, and what was ill,
What would save life, and what would kill.

Thus gone, amongst you I may live,
And dead, yet speak and counsel give.
Farewell, my birds, farewell, adieu,
I happy am, if well with you.

Part IV

Becoming Americans

The broadside condemns to "HELL's dark shore" Ebenezer Richardson, a Boston customs officer who, in February 1770—less than a fortnight before the more famous Boston Massacre—had shot and killed an eleven-year-old boy named Christopher Seider. Although he was convicted by an American jury, two years later he received a royal pardon, prompting protests in America and inspiring the following breathless, outraged declaration of American anger and principles:

> Bear in Remembrance that on the 22d Day of February, 1770, the infamous EBENEZER RICHARDSON, Informer, and tool to Ministerial hirelings, most *barbarously* MURDERED CHRISTOPHER SEIDER, an innocent youth! Of which crime he was found guilty by his Country on Friday April 20th, 1770; but remained Unsentenced

Two years later, officials were informed that the king was considering a pardon.

> Let THESE things be told to Posterity! And handed down from Generation to Generation, 'till Time shall be no more! Forever may AMERICA be preserved, from weak and wicked monarchs, Tyrannical Ministers, Abandoned Governors, their Underlings and Hirelings! And may the Machinations of artful, designing wretches, who would ENSLAVE THIS People, Come to an end, let their NAMES and MEMORIES be buried in eternal oblivion.

Seider's funeral attracted hundreds of mourners; he became one of the first martyrs of the movement that would lead to the American Revolution. The drive toward independence reflected a growing sense of "Americanness" among the British subjects crowded along the eastern seaboard of North America. That Seider, the young son of German immigrants, came to be a symbol of that American spirit is an exaggerated version of a common development in the eighteenth century, as colonists nurtured their own institutions and attitudes and realized that they had become a separate people.

The essays and documents in this section address the Americanization of colonial children in very different contexts: the experiences of German Catholic girls in British and French colonies, the public debates over the education of youth in Pennsylvania, and the participation of boys and young men in Boston's revolutionary movement. The autobiographies of John Barnard, a relatively unknown minister, and the famous Benjamin Franklin, provide reflections on what it meant to be a boy and to become a man in eighteenth-century America. Most of the children and youth who appear in these essays probably did not realize it, but they were in the process of becoming, in their respective communities, the first true Americans.

Chapter 10

From German Catholic Girls to Colonial American Women

Girlhood in the French Gulf South and the British Mid-Atlantic Colonies

Lauren Ann Kattner

German Catholic girls arrived in two waves of immigration to North America between 1720 and 1741. Originating in the same general locales south of the Main and on either bank of the Rhine River, some of the girls traveled with their parents to French Gulf South colonies while others wended their way to British Mid-Atlantic colonies. Since all of these girls had the same origins but different destinations, their lives offer an interesting opportunity for comparing and contrasting growing-up experiences in colonial North America. We may further gain insight by contrasting the lives of their American-born sisters and daughters.

Jean Pierre Purry was the first to see the potential for recruiting German Catholic colonists. In early 1717, he noted in a conversation with his friend the Duke d'Orléans, regent for the seven-year-old King Louis XV, that German Protestants had displayed a strong work ethic in the British colonies. He envisioned German Catholics with this same work ethic in French colonies. People west of the Rhine and south of the Main rivers especially impressed him. However, Purry's suggestion was temporarily set aside. The leader of the French Gulf South colony, Crozat, stepped down before Purry's ideas could be implemented.[1]

In 1719, Scotsman John Law entered the scene not only as a friend but also as financial adviser to the Duke d'Orléans. Law's Company of the West united with others to form the Company of the Indies and took over the leadership of the infant colony, which enabled the vision of German emigration to the French Gulf South to become a reality. As Law appealed to prospective emigrants, he painted the French colonial South as "the land of their dreams." With the prospect of a better life, couples (farmers and craft workers) with either very young children or marriageable sons and daughters eagerly left Europe as indentured servants.[2]

Thirteen years later, the British finally allowed German Catholics to enter their American colonies. The sudden appearance of German Catholics on British colonial shores seems unusual given the unwavering anti-Catholicism of the English. Although about one hundred thousand Germans lived in the British colonies at the time, none was openly Catholic. Yet the English apparently changed their policy in the early 1730s. Perhaps England's new king, George I (in reality, a northern German from Hanover), accepted the greater religious tolerance of the dominant political party, the Whigs. Whig merchants seeking cheap labor may have put pressure on Parliament and local colonial officials to loosen restrictions on the immigration of Catholic workers. Or northern Alsatian parents may have begun to christen their children in both Catholic and Lutheran churches. Whatever the case, at least twenty-two Catholic or part-Catholic families left for Philadelphia in the autumn of 1732, with at least five more boatloads arriving in the subsequent nine years. Unlike the earlier immigration to the French Gulf South, few German Catholics arrived on the British Mid-Atlantic shore as indentured servants.[3]

Growing-up situations differed from one colonial context to the other. For example, children in British colonies had more educational opportunities than those in the French Gulf South. In terms of religious life, German Catholic girls in the French Gulf South were more likely to participate in class- and race-based activities than elsewhere. The extent and nature of work inside and outside the home also differed from one colony to the next. Finally, though both colonial contexts brought with them the likelihood of interaction with people of different ethnicities, the specific details of that interaction differed.

European Roots

The backgrounds of two representative German Catholic girls suggest some of the assumptions they had about growing up. Marie Solome Zehringer was born in 1707 at Village Neuf in Alsace. Her father was a carpenter and her grandfather was the village schoolteacher. Solome probably attended her grandfather's school. Each town and village in Alsace, except for Strasbourg and Haguenau, had its own distinct religious orientation, and girls wore distinctive clothing and head coverings indicative of their Catholic, Mennonite, or Lutheran orientation.

When Solome was thirteen, just before her confirmation, a recruiter came to her village looking for workers to go to the French Gulf South. Her father signed an indentured-servant contract in return for his family's passage to the French Gulf South, where they went with sixty other families to Biloxi, Mississippi.

A few years after Solome left for the French Gulf South, Eva Marie Kuhn was born in a small Bavarian town. Her father was also a carpenter, and Eva had the same educational opportunities and religious life as Solome during her childhood years. And, like Solome, she joined the migration of German Catholics to America. From about 1732 to roughly 1740, hundreds of German Catholic girls left Alsace, Bavaria, and the Kraichgau region. The teenaged Eva and her family traveled to the Netherlands, where they boarded a ship bound for the British Mid-Atlantic colonies. Unlike Solome, Eva and her family did not sign an indentured servant's contract, but paid their own way to America.[4]

When they left for French and British American colonies, respectively, Solome and Eva took with them growing-up expectations acquired in Europe. Those assumptions included attitudes about literacy and education, religious life, work inside and outside the home, and courtship. In addition, differences between town and rural life, free and unfree labor, and economic classes had a profound effect on growing-up patterns.

Townspeople had privileges limited somewhat by class. In accordance with the Treaty of Westphalia, two types of citizenship existed in Alsace: free town and French citizenship. Male residents of free towns throughout German-speaking Central Europe, such as Strasbourg, had the right to vote in the Electorate and to keep their unique customs. Moreover, they had legal jurisdiction within their walls. Residents of ten other Alsatian towns enjoyed full French citizenship. They could practice local customs, but they also had to agree to the quartering of troops in their towns. Emigrants from Switzerland to the Rhine Valley region retained their Swiss citizenship. This included the right to vote in their home towns and to have their children's births registered. Citizenship also entailed the privilege of receiving a better formal education than one might find in a rural area. Despite the semblance of equality along the lines of citizenry, carefully orchestrated seasonal processions accented the higher social standing of the upper and upper-middle classes. Only members of these classes walked in the parades. Those of the lower classes were expected to show their deference as observant bystanders.[5]

In the countryside, families were set apart by their status as free-born families or as serfs. In early eighteenth-century Zurich Canton, Switzerland, and in other parts of German-speaking South Central Europe, German Catholic families toiled side by side as serfs on large farms owned by wealthy families or by the church. Serfs generally worked for no pay and could not move off the land without the owner's permission. When a certain piece of land passed from one hand to another, all of the serfs who lived on that acreage also went to the new landowner. In freer rural areas, especially along both banks of the Rhine River, German Catholics were more likely to be freeborn laborers. They grew grapes, tobacco, and flax and, by the late 1730s had begun selling their excess linen and canvas material on the open market. Other families raised sheep, traveling with the seasons up and down the Rhine River's west bank. Whether under free or unfree conditions, rural people did not place much emphasis on formal schooling.[6]

For German Catholic girls in South Central Europe, childhood varied according to the economic system in which they were born and their residence in towns or in the country. For instance, rural and seasonally migrating girls seldom went to school. If we measure the ability to write signatures at the time of marriage in the late teens or early twenties, we find emigrating teenaged girls and young women had a lower literacy rate than others of the Rhine region. In general, 40 percent of the Rhine-area brides could write their names. My sample of 278 German Catholic teenaged girls aged fifteen to nineteen and young women in their early twenties reveals a stark contrast. Marrying at Haguenau or Phalsbourg, France, these teenagers and young adults mainly originated on the right bank of the Rhine River. Between 1720 and 1740, only eighteen (12.2 percent) could write their names. In part, this may be due to the likelihood that most grew up in rural or seasonally migrating families.[7]

Unlike their rural counterparts, girls in towns began attending school or taking embroidery classes before the age of confirmation (generally, by the age of fourteen or fifteen). We may see this reflected in the way they wrote their names or created symbolic "signatures" as teenagers and young adults. In all, girls learned to express themselves in myriad ways: from Gothic to Latin script, from printed initials to self-designed symbols. Among those who could write their names, literate girls with citizen fathers more likely wrote in Latin than in German script. That is because the daughters of settled citizens had a greater likelihood than those of more transient noncitizens to acquire a bilingual education. This included Latin or French alongside German. The teenaged girls and young women of my sample, especially the daughters of citizens, tended to express themselves symbolically more often than through signatures. One explanation of the use of symbols may be traced to childhood attendance at schools or in-home training in needlework. Indeed, these symbols often resemble cross-stitch or embroidery patterns and could represent an artistic "signature." Although every Catholic parish in the Alsace-Lorraine region had a schoolmaster by this time, girls did not necessarily attend schools. Town girls also had more occasions to learn embroidery, reading, and writing by the age of fourteen. Moreover, they may have had more free time than their rural or migratory counterparts.[8]

In addition to formal schooling, town girls learned their place in society through their observation of seasonal processions. Though girls of the upper and upper-middle classes could walk in such parades, girls of the lower classes could not. Rather, these girls were consigned to the position of bystander and expected to show deference to their superiors.[9]

German Catholic girls in rural areas—especially those belonging to serf families—were more likely than town girls to work at home. Country girls worked alongside men, women, and boys during the planting and harvesting seasons. In addition, they helped their mothers clean, cook, spin flax, weave and bleach linen cloth, and sew modest clothing.[10]

Whether in a rural setting or in a town, free-born teenaged girls generally completed the growing-up process under unfree conditions. Girls began working outside of their homes soon after confirmation (at about fourteen or fifteen). Most rural-born teenagers worked on neighboring farms without pay. Some went to live in nearby towns. Girls living in towns found themselves at the greatest risk for living under unfree conditions as domestic servants and prostitutes. At Strasbourg, for example, they did domestic chores, cooked, and performed related services within the elegant homes of wealthy French government workers, the lesser nobility, and Catholic clergy. In Swiss cities, Catholic girls did the same sort of work for German patricians or for noblemen or clergy from various ethnic backgrounds. Wherever eligible teenaged country girls lived, local ordinances made them hold paid jobs during their stay in the town. But such legal measures did not control the nature of these girls' work. Their final job placement relied on local demands coupled with the skills of teenaged girls.[11]

Although girlhood in South Central Europe generally ended in marriage to men of their own faith, some girls experienced a very different coming of age. Catholic domestics sometimes had affairs with soldiers of both Lutheran and Catholic faiths. Quite often, a maid's work turned into a "job" as a mistress to a wealthy Frenchman. A number of Catholic domestics were forced to grow up quickly when they became unwed mothers. And with the large soldier population in the area, it was not unusual for Catholic domestics to become prostitutes if they could not obtain any other position.[12]

In all, we have seen that emigrants had particular ideas about what unfree versus free teenaged girls should expect to do for work. A large part of these expectations pivoted around the quasi-unfree nature of servitude during the time between confirmation and marriage or unwed motherhood. Additional expectations revolved around the nature of teenaged girls' work under serfdom. These assumptions would be challenged by the move to the French and British colonies in North America, where local conditions would add additional contexts to the lives of emigrant girls like Solome and Eva.

Girlhood in the French Gulf South

From 1720 to 1740, German Catholic girls like Solome and their families settled in four distinct areas of the French Gulf South. At first, they lived in the vicinity of Old Biloxi (today's Ocean Springs, Mississippi). That is where Anna Margaretha Zweig's father died. Some of her sister travelers went eastward to the Mobile area as temporary indentured servants. Anna Margaretha and her mother traveled to New Orleans, where some of their company decided to settle. Such was the case of Solome, her sister Felicite, and their brothers and parents. Anna Margaretha bid New Orleans farewell when she and her mother trekked to the German Coast (today, St. Charles and St. John the Baptist Parishes). Like other German Coast families, mother and daughter raised cattle and grew indigo, rice, and truck crops. Many of their neighbors worked in crafts. Until her teenaged years, this is where Anna Margaretha stayed. Moving northward, a handful of German families—mainly associated with the military—lived in and near present-day Natchez, Mississippi. A few German families lived as subsistence farmers in southeastern Arkansas during the early years of settlement before moving to Pointe Coupée, Louisiana. They were replaced by

German cattlemen and their families. Included among the latter was Louisiana-born Marie Anne Lepine.[13]

Within this setting, German Catholic girls grew from childhood to adolescence to womanhood. Specifically, their lives were touched by a lack of educational opportunities. In addition, high male-to-female ratios and migration patterns shaped their growing-up experiences. These factors would influence changes and continuities between European and French Gulf South situations.

As in Europe, town girls in the French Gulf South had a greater opportunity to attend school than their rural or migrating counterparts. In New Orleans, girls like Felicite had the advantage of going to the all-girl Ursuline school. The Ursulines had arrived in the summer of 1727, mainly from a Parisian convent. Their vocation included hospital work alongside teaching. By 1737, one of the sisters was teaching about thirty white and black female orphans in addition to regular day students. Black and Indian women attended school for two hours a day. French-speaking boarding students also came to the academy from wealthy plantation homes. Even so, girls in New Orleans could attend despite social station or ethnic background.[14] Soon, Felicite qualified to attend.

Adapting to the French colonial context, the academy's curriculum differed somewhat from that of schools in European towns. First and foremost, those who could not speak French soon learned to do so. Then, as mandated by the governor of Louisiana, black and Indian girls learned to care for silkworms and made silk fabrics. Fine silk needlework would fit into the curriculum for other students. But the girls of color were not the only ones who learned practical arts. All students learned to make jellies and preserves. Not surprisingly, religion and music were also included in the curriculum. Music lessons not only involved the singing of hymns and motets but also singing while marching to the beat of a military band.[15]

Like European towns, New Orleans had formal processions, but French colonial attitudes about whites and blacks influenced their desired outcomes. The procession honoring the dedication of the Ursuline Convent provides an example. Unlike processions in Europe, which were limited to the upper classes, those conducted in colonial New Orleans involved the entire community. Even so, the organization of the pageantry followed class, age, and racial lines. Those processing in honor of the Ursuline Convent came in the following order: male citizens; orphans and day-school pupils; forty "principle ladies" of New Orleans; twenty wealthy young boarders dressed in white; one young lady dressed in a fine robe, representing St. Ursula, surrounded by a dozen of the lightest-skinned African American girls dressed as angels; the Ursuline nuns; the clergy, Governor Bienville and his staff; Intendent Salmon; and finally, the rest of the general population. Soldiers lined both sides of the procession.[16] Felicite, the daughter of a master carpenter and citizen, would have walked with the day-school pupils, apart from wealthier, French girls.

As in Europe, rural and migrating girls lacked literacy. Though Capuchin Fr. Philip offered schooling to boys at the German Coast northwest of New Orleans, he did not extend that offer to girls. Young men could at a minimum write their initials at the time of marriage, and in many cases, their entire names with Latin letters. However, all brides but one could do neither by 1768. Margret Reinchart was the only girl able to write her name. An immigrant from Ingwiller in Alsace, Margret spent her early childhood in a home that emphasized biblical literacy. Her mother was Lutheran and her father was a Calvinist.[17]

The uneven gender ratio within this rugged colonial context changed the social circumstance of teenaged girls who lived on the German Coast. At Marienthal, Augsburg, and Hoffen, Louisiana, for example, teenaged girls saw local circumstances halt the usual "growing-up" customs known in their homeland. One casualty was the traditional girls' experience of domestic servitude. Because men heavily outnumbered women, teenaged German girls did not stay single for a very long time. Thus, they worked only briefly as domestic or farm servants. By 1724, all but thirteen of the eligible teenaged girls had married at the German Coast of Louisiana.[18]

Anna Margaretha took a more traditional path. Sometime between the ages of thirteen and seventeen, she moved to New Orleans. Given her social station, she most likely went there as a domestic servant. While there, she met and married a French soldier in 1729.[19]

As Anna Margaretha's experience shows, migration and greater contact with people of other ethnicities affected courtship along the Mississippi River. Marie Anne, the colonial-born daughter of a German mother and Dutch father, provides another example. Marie Anne arrived in southeastern Arkansas with her parents in 1731 as a four-year-old. Her family owned an old crippled Indian woman, Theresa, an African woman in her twenties, and two African men. These slaves helped clean the home and take care of the cattle. Following the pattern of most rural German Catholic girls in the French Gulf South, Marie Anne most likely helped with the field work. Without a school nearby and only an itinerant priest to meet religious needs, Marie Anne did not learn to write even the initials of her name. Between 1740 and 1743, Wilhelm Bienvenu, a stout Franco-German trader from Bern, Switzerland, became a close acquaintance. Making frequent trips between New Orleans and the Arkansas Post, he could not help but notice the blossoming Marie Anne. Finally, he married her in 1743.[20]

The colonial experience mixed different ethnic groups much more readily than in Europe. Thus, teenaged German Catholic girls like Marie Anne and Anna Margarethe came into greater contact with Frenchmen. We do not yet know specific courtship practices, but we do know that teenagers who lived along the Mississippi River had frequent contact with French traders. We also know that residence in New Orleans or Natchez placed these teenaged girls in contact with many French soldiers as their potential suitors. This was a colonial circumstance that differed from the Central European situation where most resident soldiers were German. An analysis of 193 marriages between 1719 and 1768 reveals the extent of contact and marriage with Frenchmen. During that time, sixty-two (about one-third) of the girls married a Frenchman.[21]

From school age to marriage German Catholic girls of the French Gulf South lived in a very different environment than they had experienced in Europe. Limited educational opportunities and the presence of more men than women heavily influenced growing-up patterns among German Catholic girls in the French Gulf South. Religious processions taught additional, more complicated lessons. Fewer girls worked as domestic servants, more married non-Germans, and virtually none resorted to prostitution.

Growing Up in the British Mid-Atlantic

German Catholic girls like Eva and their families found themselves in a wider range of locales along the British Mid-Atlantic than did their counterparts in the French Gulf South. In addition to several Pennsylvania counties, where by 1757 Germans made up about three-fourths of the 1,365 Pennsylvania Catholics aged thirteen and older, at least 4,000 lived in Maryland, and a few others lived in Virginia near the Maryland border and in New Jersey and Delaware near the Pennsylvania border. Apparently better off than most German Catholic families of the French Gulf South, these Catholics were less likely to work as indentured servants and more likely to be independent farmers, miners, teachers, and traders. Mary Magdalena Eck of Ridge Valley, Montgomery County, Pennsylvania, offers a glimpse at German Catholic colonial life on a farm. Magdalena's father and brothers grew hemp and flax that she, her mother, and her sisters made into clothes. All family members helped with outdoor chores, including the growing and harvesting of corn, buckwheat, rye, and beans.[22]

A number of differences between the lives of girls in the Catholic Gulf South and in Protestant Pennsylvania emerge. Unlike German Catholic girls in the French Gulf South, in British Pennsylvania girls had just as many opportunities to learn their ABCs in rural areas as in towns. Another difference appeared in the procession culture in which they lived. In New Orleans processions emphasized race and class, but in Pennsylvania such rituals actually broke down class barriers. In terms of work, we see family members working side by side with no mention of domestic servitude in extant Pennsylvania sources. We also see German Catholics in Pennsylvania coming into contact with Mennonites and Moravians who encouraged literacy and jointly sponsored a school for local farmers that girls could attend. In addition, Moravian women in the small town of Bethlehem offered embroidery lessons to girls regardless of religious preference. Finally, although they did not marry outside of their faith, teenaged girls and young women in their early twenties did frequently marry non-Germans or non-Catholics, as did girls in the French Gulf South.

Catholic and Protestant educators taught children from both religious traditions. Arriving in 1741 a Jesuit priest from Heidelberg, Fr. Theodore Schneider, decided to teach German Catholic and Protestant children on his mission circuit. He established several Catholic schools in Pennsylvania and possibly one or two in New Jersey. We know of four: near present-day Allentown, at present-day Bally, at Bethlehem, and at Haycock.[23]

Johann Helfer went to Bethlehem as a teacher at this time. He and his wife, Maria Appolonia, together with an infant son, had arrived in Philadelphia in 1732 from Lembach, Alsace. His new position at Bethlehem placed him in the heart of a Moravian community. Within a year, Maria Appolonia gave birth to her namesake. By the time the younger Appolonia reached the age of seven in 1749, Moravian women had formed a boarding school for girls. At that school, girls learned flower embroidery on satin or Eastern silk. Flower embroidery may have fostered a love of nature, but it did not entail the creation of alphabets. In this, the Moravian school at Bethlehem differed in focus from English sampler schools attended by young girls elsewhere.[24]

Students at the St. Paul School in present-day Bally and, most likely, at Cedar Creek near present-day Allentown, attended one-room, log-cabin schools four months of the year, a routine revealing that schooling followed seasonal work patterns. Though taught by Catholics, the St. Paul school by 1754 stood across the road from the Mennonite church and was attended by Mennonite as well as Catholic children. By February 1764, Father Schneider had appointed Mr. Fredder as schoolmaster. He may have done so in response to religious discrimination during the French and Indian War that prevented him from staying in one place long. It was believed locally that Catholics favored the French during that war since the French were also largely Catholic. Two years later, at the close of the war, Father de Ritter appointed Mr. Breitenbach as schoolteacher.[25] Although these schools existed, we do not know for sure whether or not girls attended.

As in Europe and the French Gulf South, a look at signatures in British Pennsylvania would help us to determine the extent of formal education by the time of marriage, at least to the extent that women could sign their names on legal documents. In Berks County, Pennsylvania, some teenaged girls and young women in their early twenties had learned to write Latin capital letters by the date of their land purchase with their new husbands. Thus, they wrote the initial of their last name. In addition, the use of Latin capital letters for German words appears on the one surviving tombstone from colonial days: that of Anne Bewer.[26]

We do not see symbols used in signatures at this time. In part, this fact may reflect the absence of a needlework school outside of Bethlehem. After the American Revolution, women of English descent would form another school of embroidery in Reading. Because of the background of their teachers, German Catholic girls who would attend the latter school in Reading would learn to read and embroider in English.[27]

Families of German Catholic girls attempted to recapture traditionally German Catholic activities under the leadership of the clergy. As soon as St. Paul Chapel was built in present-day Bally at the beginning of the French and Indian War (in the summer of 1754), informal religious education began to involve holy day rituals similar to those in New Orleans. In 1755, German Catholic girls of this rural community began to celebrate the Feast of Corpus Christi along with other parishioners. This celebration involved a procession under the gold-starred ceiling of St. Paul Chapel that ended in the grassy green church cemetery. Beginning in 1765 (during the time of Father de Ritter), girls joined others in celebrating All Soul's

Day. On that day, they helped to decorate the hand-carved tombstones and light candles. Unlike the case of New Orleans girls, these girls and their families did not walk in any particular order that would reflect class or race.[28]

German Catholic fathers sometimes tried to control marriage patterns as they may have done in Europe. Such was the case of Eva Marie's Uncle Heinrich. Her cousin Anna Margaret wanted to marry at the young age of sixteen. Heinrich would not hear of it, but Anna Margaret did so anyway in 1760. In a rage, Heinrich officially disowned her and asked Father Schneider to document his action.[29] This situation differed from the French Gulf South context, where teenaged girls more commonly married soldiers or traders at younger ages than in Europe.

As in the French Gulf South, German Catholic girls came into contact with non-Germans during their teenaged years. Catholic leaders in Philadelphia made a concerted effort to separate German- from English-speaking Catholics. However, the French and Indian War caused an influx of French speakers during the Acadian Diaspora, which led to an increase in the number of teenaged German girls marrying non-Germans. Before 1754, Jesuit fathers performed seven such marriages, but afterward, they performed twenty-six. All told, from 1739 to 1763, thirty-three (27 percent) of the 123 German Catholic girls in extant records married non-Germans, mainly in Philadelphia. Since this percentage is slightly lower than that of the French Gulf South, we may conclude that either priests or community leaders successfully shielded German Catholic girls from interaction with non-Germans, particularly outside of Philadelphia.

We have examined a cross-section of the lives of German Catholic girls, mainly in their teenaged years. In so doing, we have ascertained changes and continuities between Old and New Worlds. The changes marked a transition from being a German Catholic girl to a colonial American woman. In both colonies, we see an end to teenaged German Catholic prostitution, with marriage marking the end of girlhood. That end came earlier to girls in the French Gulf South than in British Pennsylvania. Both colonial contexts brought with them a greater likelihood of interaction with non-Germans and non-Catholics. Other changes involved choices made by community leaders with the concurrence of the populace. When learning their place in society, German Catholic girls actually participated in processions in America instead of simply observing them as in Central Europe. Yet, as we have seen, the French colonial view went beyond class standing to include lessons on the place of race in what would become a hallmark of the colonial South. The growing-up experiences of German-Catholic girls in colonial North America varied regionally. Although immigrant girls brought with them growing-up expectations with regard to education, religious life, work, and courtship, they saw those expectations altered in different ways within diverse colonial contexts.

NOTES

1. Rudolf Cronau, *Drei Jahrhunderts Deutschen Lebens in Amerika: Eine Geschichte der Deutschen in den Vereinigten Staaten* (Berlin: Dietrich Reimer, 1909), 11–12; Reinhard Kondert, "German Immigration to French Colonial Louisiana: A Reevaluation," in *Proceedings of the Fourth Meeting of the French Colonial Historical Society, April 6–8, 1978, University of Mississippi, Oxford, Miss.,* ed. Alf Andrew Heggoy and James J. Cooke (Washington, DC: University Press of America, 1979), 71–72; Winthrop Pickard Bell, *"Foreign Protestants" and the Settlement of Nova Scotia* (Toronto, Canada: University of Toronto Press, 1961), 97; J. Hanno Deiler, *The Settlement of the German Coast of Louisiana and the Creoles of German Descent* (Philadelphia: Americana Germanica Press, 1909), 19, 51, 59, 94.

2. Tyge W. Fourtner, "French Slavery in the Mississippi Valley" (M.A. thesis, Southern Illinois University at Carbondale, 1996), 3–5, 12; analysis of ship records, 1719–1721, G1 464, Archives Nationales, Section Outre-Mer, Paris, France (ANO), and Louisiana Governor-General, Census of 1719, 1724, 1727, and 1731, État Civil Recensements, 1706–1741, G1 464, ANO; Bell, *"Foreign Protestants,"* 93–94.

3. Linkage of data contained in Annette Kunselman Burgert, *Eighteenth-Century Emigrants from the Northern Alsace to America* (Camden, ME: Picton, 1992), reconstructed passenger lists, Palatine Project, ed. Gary T. Horlacher (1998–Aug. 2003), http://www.palproject.org/, and "saddlebag" marriage and christening records kept by Fathers Schneider and de Ritter, 1741–1768, copies located in the Church of the Most Blessed Sacrament Museum and Archive, Bally, Pennsylvania. The Palatine Project is now under the direction of the ProGenealogists Group.

4. Lauren Ann Kattner, "Confronting Slavery: German-American Catholics, 1719–1836," ms. (being revised for possible publication by University of Missouri Press); Aaron Spencer Fogleman, *Hopeful Journeys: German Immigration, Settlement, and Political Culture in Colonial America, 1717–1775* (Philadelphia: University of Pennsylvania Press, 1996), 39–41, 44, 56, 62–65.

5. Robert Darnton, "A Bourgeois Puts His World in Order," in *The Great Cat Massacre and Other Episodes in French Cultural History* (New York: Basic Books, 1984), 106, 110–11, 133.

6. Friedrich Lütge, *Geschichte der deutschen Agrarverfassung vom frühen Mittelalter bis zum 19.Jahrhundert,* Deutsche Agrargeschichte, no. 3 (Stuttgart, Ger-

many: Euygen Ulmer Vlg., 1970), 162–63; James Q. Whitman, *The Legacy of Roman Law in the German Romantic Era: Historical Vision and Legal Change* (Princeton, NJ: Princeton University Press, 1990), 151, 154; Bell, "Foreign Protestants," 88–102; Fogleman, *Hopeful Journeys*, 37–39, 56.

7. Harvey J. Graff, *The Legacies of Literacy: Continuities and Contradictions in Western Culture and Society* (Bloomington: Indiana University Press, 1987), 187; Louis Henry and Jacques Houdaille, "Célibat et âge au marriage aux 18ᵉ et 19ᵉ siècles en France. II: Age au premier marriage," *Population* 34 (March 1977): 403–41; analysis of literacy evidence in the following sources: St. Nicholas Catholic Church (Haguenau), Parish Registers, 1720 and 1740, Archives départementales de Bas-Rhin, Strasbourg, France, St. George (Haguenau) Catholic Church parish registers, 1720, Archives départementales de Bas-Rhin, Strasbourg, France, and Phalsbourg Catholic Church parish register, 1720, Archives départementales de la Moselle, St-Julien-les-Metz, France. Heidelberg also stood as an entrepôt between 1719 and 1745, but the marriage records available to this author for the Holy Ghost Jesuit Catholic Church in Heidelberg do not provide signatures.

8. Analysis of bride signatures in the following records: St. Nicholas Catholic Church (Haguenau), Parish Registers, 1720–1740, Archives départementales de Bas-Rhin, Strasbourg, France, St. George (Haguenau) Catholic Church parish registers, 1720–1740, Archives départementales de Bas-Rhin, Strasbourg, France, and Phalsbourg Catholic Church parish register, 1720–1740, Archives départementales de la Moselle, St-Julien-les-Metz, France; Graff, *The Legacies of Literacy,* 145–47, 194–96; Henry and Houdaille, "Célibat et âge au marriage," *Population* 34 (March 1977): 403–41; François Furet and Jacques Ozouf, *Lire et écrire: L'alphabetisation des Français de Calvin à Jules Ferry* (Èditions de Minuit, 1977), vol. 1; Georges Klein, *Das Elsassische Museum in Strassburg* (Strasbourg: Musées de Strasburg), 118–22; Moriz Dreger, *Künsterische entwicklung der weberei und stickerei innerhalb des europäischen kulturkreises von der spätantiken zeit bis zum beginner des XIX jahrhundertes* (Vienna, 1904), vol. 1.

9. Darton, "Bourgeois," in Darton, *Great Cat Massacre,* 106, 110–11, 133.

10. Hidemi Uchida, "Le Tabac en Alsace aux XVIIème et XVIIIème Siecles," diss., University of Strasbourg, France II, 1990, 383; Jacob M. Price, *France and the Chesapeake: A History of the French Tobacco Monopoly, 1674–1791, and of Its Relationship to the British and American Tobacco Trades* (Ann Arbor: University of Michigan Press, 1973); Bell, "Foreign Protestants," 95 ; Suzanne Dreyer-Roos, *La Population Strasbourgeois sous L'ancien regine,* Publications de la Sociètè savant d'Alsace et de Regions de l'Est Recherces et Documents 6 (Strasbourg, France: Librairie Istrea, 1969), 53. Haguenau Catholic marriage records document the importance of shepherding on the Rhine's West Bank. See: St. Nicholas Catholic Church (Haguenau), Parish Registers, 1720–1740, Archives départementales de Bas-Rhin, Strasbourg, France, and St. George (Haguenau) Catholic Church parish registers, 1720–1740, Archives départementales de Bas-Rhin, Strasbourg, France.

11. Dreyer-Roos, *La Population Strasbourgeois,* 51–53, 133–35, 167, 188, 195; Jacques Hatt, *Liste des Members du Grand Sénat de Strasbourg: Des Stettmeistres, des Anmeistres, des Conseils des XXI, XIII et des XV du XIIIe Siécle B 1789* (Strasbourg, France, 1963), 632.

12. Dreyer-Roos, *La Population Strasbourgeois,* 134–35, 188, 195.

13. Kattner, "Confronting Slavery."

14. P. J. K., "Louisiana," *Woodstock Letters* 15 (1886): 37; "Expulsion of the Jesuits from Louisiana," *Woodstock Letters* 5 (1870): 161; John G. Shea, *Life and Times of the Most Rev. John Caroll, . . . , Embracing the History of the Catholic Church in the United States, 1763–1815* (New York, 1888), 569; "Old Ursuline Convent," accessed 6 Aug. 2005, http://www.accesscom.net/ursuline/.

15. M. A. C., "Education in Louisiana in French Colonial Days," *American Catholic Quarterly Review* 11 (Jan.–Oct. 1886): 404, 406, 410.

16. Ibid., 407.

17. St. John the Baptist Parish, Loose Papers, 1743–1768 (microfilm, The Church of Jesus Christ of Latter-day Saints, #382837)

18. Analysis of Louisiana Governor-General, Census of 1724, G1 464, ANO.

19. 1724 Louisiana Census; New Orleans marriage records.

20. Using ages in the Chenal/Lincto marriage contract, New Orleans, La., 18 Apr. 1744, we may approximate the year of birth for Marie Anne. Her marriage record gives her place of birth. At the time of her death, Marie Anne's mother still owned Theresa, by then aged fifty-five. See Orleans Par., La. Estate #03-S-069-001-1785, in Afro-Louisiana History and Genealogy, 1719–1820, database, ed. Gwendolyn Midlo Hall, http://www.ibiblio.org/laslave/.

21. Analysis of the following records: St. Louis Cathedral Records, Dept. of Historical Records, Archdiocese of New Orleans (Louisiana), 1719–1768; St. John the Baptist Parish (Edgard, Louisiana) Records, Dept. of Historical Records, Archdiocese of New Orleans (Louisiana), 1744–1768; St. Francis of Pointe Coupée Parish Records, Dept. of Archives, Diocese of Baton Rouge (Louisiana), 1728–1768; Louisiana District Court, Loose Papers, 1753–1768, St. John the Baptist Parish Courthouse, Edgard Louisiana; Louisiana District Court, Original Acts and Misc. Court Records, 1741–1768, St. Charles Parish Courthouse, Hahnville, Louisiana.

22. Shea, *Life and Times of John Caroll,* 52, 54; Mary Magdalena Eck, "Reminiscences of Mary Magdalena Eck," as recorded by her granddaughter, 1856, in *Eck Families,* comp. Helen E. Arkey (1992), 26.

23. Correlation of names, residence, and years of schoolmasters as found in Berks Co., Pa., Deed Book A, vols. 1–8 (1734–1768), and in "saddlebag" marriage and christening records kept by Fathers Schneider and de Ritter, 1741–1768, copies located in the Church of the Most Blessed Sacrament Museum and Archive, Bally, Pennsylvania; Shea, *Life and Times of John Carroll,* 64–65; Letter, Father Farmer, 1764, in Lambert Schrott, *Pioneer German Catholics in the American Colonies*

(New York: American Catholic Historical Soc., 1933), 92; William J. Buck, ed., *Account of Bucks County, Pennsylvania* (Philadelphia, 1893).

24. "John and William" ship record, in Reconstructed passenger lists, Palatine Project, ed. Gary T. Horlacher (1998–Aug. 2003), http://www.palproject.org/; Catholic records kept by Father Schneider, copies located in the Church of the Most Blessed Sacrament Museum and Archive, Bally, Pennsylvania; Candace Wheeler, *The Development of Embroidery in America* (New York: Harper & Bros., 1921), 62–66.

25. "Search for Evidence of the Catholic Schoolhouse across the Road from the Mennonite Meetinghouse before 1797" (typescript, 2005), Church of the Most Blessed Sacrament, Museum and Archive, Bally, Pennsylvania; "saddlebag" marriage and christening records kept by Fathers Schneider and de Ritter, 1741–1768, copies located in the Church of the Most Blessed Sacrament Museum and Archive, Bally, Pennsylvania. Since Fathers Schneider and de Ritter traveled as itinerant priests, their sacramental records encompass congregations throughout southeastern Pennsylvania and western New Jersey.

26. Manuscript church records kept by Fathers Schneider and de Ritter; Berks Co., Pa., Deed Book A, vols. 1–8 (1734–1768); tombstone of Anne Bewer, located in Church of the Most Blessed Sacrament, Old Goshenhoppen Churchyard, Bally, Pennsylvania.

27. The first known needlework school in this vicinity was opened at Reading, Pennsylvania, in about 1790. It was attended by German Catholic and Protestant girls in the area.

28. 3 July 1755, Berks County, Pennsylvania Justices of the Peace Report to Gov. James Hamilton; Schrott, *Pioneer German Catholics,* 86; Shea, *Life and Times of John Caroll,* 29–31.

29. Eilean Scheckelhoff Stemley, comp., *The Catholic Kuhns, Kuhn, Coons Families of Goshenhoppen, Berks County, Pennsylvania, 1730–1830,* 40, undated typescript, Berks County Historical Society, Reading, Pennsylvania.

Chapter 11

"Let Both Sexes Be Carefully Instructed"
Educating Youth in Colonial Philadelphia

Keith Pacholl

Poor Hilario. How could his life have crumbled apart so quickly? He was the kind of person whom others envied, the one who had it all: money, looks, charm. But alas, it was all for naught. According to *The Pennsylvania Packet and General Advertiser,* Hilario had been born into "an easy fortune" and started life with all the advantages a person could ever desire. In fact, he was considered by all who met him as "a most agreeable fellow." Unfortunately for Hilario, such a luxurious lifestyle didn't bring him the ultimate happiness he had anticipated; instead, a life of cards, women, and wanton spending slowly whittled away his wealth. By the time he was thirty-five, the process was complete. His wealth was gone, no woman would marry him, and even his good looks had failed him. In fact, his "dissipation" and "debaucheries" landed him in jail with little hope for a future. The article concluded with a warning to the "young men of the age" to lead a virtuous life rather than to spiral into oblivion like poor Hilario.[1]

Stories like Hilario's abounded in newspapers and magazines throughout the eighteenth century and provided readers with useful information on how best to raise their children. The proper training of Pennsylvanian youth had always been a priority since the very beginnings of the colony. For example, William Penn declared in 1682 that "all wicked and scandalous living may be prevented" if children were trained "in virtue and useful knowledge and arts." In 1696, the governor and Provincial Council of Pennsylvania were called upon to provide for "the good education of youth."[2] This desire to create a virtuous citizenry proved to be a boon for the ephemeral print industry as magazines and newspapers became an important repository for this crucial knowledge by the time of the American Revolution. Most importantly, periodicals offered an additional means of educating Philadelphia youth beyond formal schooling by presenting didactic pieces intended to improve personal behavior. The articles and poems found in periodical print thus provided society with specific examples of virtuous behavior (or the lack thereof) and the kinds of education that would best train children to achieve these lofty standards. The rest of this chapter will explore what eighteenth-century Pennsylvanians meant by "virtue" and "a good education" for their young by examining the periodical literature of newspapers and magazines published in Philadelphia.

Many recognized the important contributions of the periodicals to the public discourse regarding education. Noah Webster, for example, claimed that the information found in newspapers provided a tangible public service to America. "Newspapers are not only the vehicles of what is called news," he wrote; more importantly, "they are common instruments of what is called social intercourse, by which the citizens of this vast Republic constantly debate with each other on subjects of public concern." According to one essayist in *The American Weekly Mercury,* periodicals provided an avenue where the revelation of "truth" dramatically improved society. The printers of *The Independent Chronicle* succinctly articulated the relationship between knowledge and newspapers: "The diffusion of knowledge, essentially necessary in promoting the most important interests of society, is undoubtedly effected, in some measure, by the circulation of newspapers."[3] Periodicals thus fundamentally contributed to the intellectual advancement of society, and nowhere is this clearer than in the emerging discussion over the proper education of a child. In Philadelphia, the periodical industry provided a new public forum where ideas over education could be explored and debated. In addition, they offered stories and essays that explored various dimensions of virtuous living, and throughout the course of the eighteenth century were viewed by many Americans as a vital contributor to American discourse on citizenship.

A number of printers articulated this goal. In their very first issue, the printers of *The American Magazine or Monthly View of the Political State of the British Colonies* promised to "improve the Understanding" of their readers in "every Branch of Work." The knowledge imparted would hopefully influence people in their "Idea of Learning, Wisdom, and Abilities" by focusing upon matters of "Taste, Politeness, Customs, Manners, Morals, Religion and Politics." *The American Magazine and General Repository* offered similarly lofty goals; its pages would contain material "for promoting useful knowledge" that they believed would "be of public utility." Enoch Story and Daniel Humphreys declared in their proposal for *The Pennsylvania Mercury and Universal Advertiser* that their main objectives for the paper included "improving" and "instructing" the public as well as including material of a "moral" nature. From the perspective of the Hermit, a regular contributor to *The American Magazine and Monthly Chronicle for the British Colonies,* periodicals should be praised for their advancement of "virtue and knowledge." In the case of *The American Magazine,* he praised the magazine "for promoting a design that appears so well calculated for the public good."[4] The goals set forth by colonial printers reflected the prevailing sentiments shared by others: in effect, the essays and articles published would provide the community with important information on how to become a better person.

A number of articles and essays addressed the philosophical direction that youthful education should take. For example, one author declared that the triumvirate of learning, religion, and liberty were the ultimate goals of a childhood education. An education based upon "good morals" would result in the creation of "virtuous and good men" in that properly trained children would evolve like the "tender plant" into "a great tree" whose roots would provide the foundation of a stable and successful society. In 1775, *The Pennsylvania Magazine or American Monthly Museum* published "A New Plan of Education," which argued that the successful future of America rested upon training its children properly. "Many schemes have been formed by ingenious men for this purpose," the author declared, but his personal solution lay in a curriculum "by which science and morality are planted in the youthful mind." The same magazine also published "A Series of Letters on Education" over the course of a year that explored the concept of youthful education in greater depth, this time focusing upon the religious dimensions of a proper education. The anonymous contributor of these letters encouraged parents, both husbands and wives, "to conspire and co-operate in every thing relating to the education of their children." When training their children, parents should "be purified by the principles, and controuled or directed by the precepts, of religion." A religious education could be valued as "profitable" for a child, concluded the author, since religion was "a venerable thing in itself, and it spreads an air of dignity over [a] persons whole deportment." Most importantly, "the real dignity of religion" lies in its ability to create an "excellence" of character where individuals choose a life of virtue rather than one of "dissolution."[5]

The overall instruction offered by these and other authors of eighteenth-century American periodicals was informed by the principles of rational Christianity, or by what Henry May terms the "Moderate Enlightenment." Influenced by the writings of Locke, Newton, and the Scottish "Common Sense" philosophers, learned elites reconciled new scientific thought with existing religious principles. The use of one's rational faculties, conjoined with observations of the natural world, buttressed one's faith in a benevolent God. The end result would be balance, harmony, and order.[6] A growing number of newspaper and magazine articles in Philadelphia emphasized the tenets of "rational Christianity." One writer in *The American Magazine or General Repository* clearly articulated this idea of a rational God working within the laws of nature when he declared, "What comfort then does the human soul want, who firmly relies upon this rational and Scriptural assurance, that tho' Providence acts by general laws, which may not (for wise and good reasons partly unknown to us) and will not, break in upon, to prevent their operation, 'till the universal scheme is perfected?" Humanity must understand, he concluded, that "moral and natural events have a manifest implication, connection, and dependence."[7] Central to this discussion of an "enlightened" education was the emphasis upon morality and science as the cornerstone of youthful education rather than the traditional Christian focus upon matters of theology and salvation. Focusing upon these twin pillars of learning caused education to become quite utilitarian in transforming children into virtuous citizens.

A key aspect of this enlightened education was the need to instill good moral values in American youth. Periodicals heavily emphasized the need for a moral education as the foundation of a good citizenry. A review of the numerous articles in newspapers and magazines on this topic reveals that contributors defined morality in a number of different ways. In 1731, an author in the *Pennsylvania Gazette* asserted that charity was the crucial component of morality. He declared that the "Great Author of our Faith, Whose Life should be the constant Object of our Imitation," had always shown the greatest compassion to those who were less fortunate. For this writer, charity was exemplified by those who helped the sick, since "this branch of charity seems essential to the true Spirit of Christianity," and he offered the parable of the good Samaritan as the best example of charitable behavior. In another case, one magazine writer believed that goodwill and benevolence were the basis of happiness and contentment among humans. Since God was the supreme example of goodwill and benevolence, "he is beheld with pleasure" by all those who try to achieve these lofty goals. According to an essayist in *The Royal American Magazine,* the human attribute of generosity "may be justly considered as the noblest work of the Creator," and a generous demeanor included a good nature and forgiving personality.[8]

The future was bleak for those who failed to live up to these moral standards. Testimony to this emerged in the execution speeches given by condemned criminals moments before they tied the knot. In one case, Terence Rogers, executed in 1734 for murder, hoped that his last speech would serve as a warning for others, particularly those who were young and still impressionable. After leading an immoral life of "drinking, whoring, and swearing," Rogers sank to such depths that he eventually took the life of another man. Realizing the errors of his way, he asked that all people pray for him, "a poor miserable Sinner, and take warning by my unhappy end, which is come to me by not regarding the Advice of Parents and Friends." Immoral citizens did not have to be convicted felons, however. Playing cards on the Sabbath, for example, was a sign of a "less serious and virtuous person." Gaming on Sunday indicated a number of character flaws, including "covetousness," "drinking," "idleness," and "knavery." In fact, such people would "degenerate" over time and eventually "become a burthen and nuisance" to society. Thus, parents had to train their children against this vice out of fear of them becoming "dissolute and worthless" adults. According to a moralist in *The Pennsylvania Packet,* ill nature, defined as "malevolence of temper," proved to be one of the most common faults of humanity, and unfortunately, "no vice is attended with more disagreeable consequences, either to the person himself or his neighbors." Another essayist in the same newspaper declared that drinking was far and away the "most dangerous" vice a person could engage in, and the ultimate results of such activity would eventually leave a person "very rude, very stupid, or very mad." In 1775, *The Pennsylvania Magazine* listed a series of scriptural passages from Proverbs, Psalms, and Ecclesiastes that admonished its readers against committing such vices as theft, covetousness, suicide, revenge, and fornication.[9]

The second area of emphasis in education was the value of science. Scientific knowledge trained youthful minds to think in rational ways that would serve them well as adults. In addition, science not only illustrated the logical workings of the universe, but it also provided the foundation for understanding the nature of the divine mind. If science was such an important component in the development of virtue and citizenship, then it was necessary to inform readers on the basics of scientific thought. A vast array of articles informed readers about fields of study like astronomy, mathematics, geology, zoology, and even the fledgling study of electricity. Periodicals proved critical in communicating this new scientific thought, because as one author in *The Pennsylvania Magazine* pointed out, "the bulk of mankind have neither leisure nor opportunity to apply to books of science for information." Instead, magazines provided "a means of conveying some degree of philosophical truth to those who would never look for it in any other place." Most people, he concluded, were "unacquainted with the first principles of philosophy and the laws by which nature is governed [and] are apt to assign super-natural causes to effects they cannot otherwise account for." Thus, instruction in scientific knowledge was critical in preventing such "vulgar errors" from occurring. *The American Magazine and General Repository* reminded readers that "the mind of man is an active principle, incapable of continuing any time in a state of idleness" and thus should turn to magazines as a source of scientific knowledge since "many persons that would not buy or read a large work on this subject probably might purchase a Magazine, and be induced to read short detached treasures, which might not only furnish them with knowledge, but inspire them with an inclination to pursue and study nature."[10]

By the time of the American Revolution, the ideas of an "Enlightened" education had become firmly entrenched, and according to contemporary periodicals, the two emphases of eighteenth-century education were now morality and science. This did not mean that religion itself had become displaced; rather, the idea of what religious education meant had now been redefined according to a new understanding of the world. Christian learning, as exemplified by Christ and other pious individuals, now emphasized moral behavior; logic and science now made understandable the natural world that had been created by God. One supporter for the College and Academy of Philadelphia extolled this enlightened education in *The American Magazine and Monthly Chronicle*. What better instruction could be provided, the author asked, than an education "where due regard to religion is kept up" while at the same time students learn about "the superstructure of the sciences?" An enlightened education would also provide children with the "acquisition of solid Wisdom," bestow upon them the "sublime" learning that had been intended by "Our Maker," and even encourage them to greater learning as adults.[11]

Periodicals also delved deeply into the issue of a female education. Given the changing nature of American society over the last half of the eighteenth century, a female's place in the educational system became a subject of enormous debate. Historians Mary Beth Norton and Linda Kerber have shown how educational reforms for women had become an integral part of American society by the end of the eighteenth century. The necessity of having intellectually competent mothers raising virtuous republican children necessitated an overhaul of the traditional constraints that had been placed upon female education. Because education began at home with the mother, it was essential that women be prepared for this enormous responsibility.[12] Periodicals thus provided parents with knowledge on how to properly train not just their sons but also their daughters.

A number of periodical writers commented on the overall neglect of female learning in Philadelphia and insisted that women receive a much more inclusive education. From the perspective of these authors, such neglect had a negative impact not only on females themselves but also on society as a whole. For example, the essayist Clio lamented "how many female minds, rich with native genius and noble sentiment, have been lost to the world, and all their mental treasures buried into oblivion." Prior limitations on female education could not be justified since "the human mind was made for improvement, and 'knowledge is sweet to the soul.'" In fact, Clio waxed eloquent about the unlimited possibilities should women become better educated: "When Man shall consider the Female Mind as the first object under the sun upon which he should bestow his wisdom to improve, then will the halcyon days dawn, and human nature appear in its highest beauty and perfection." The author Sylvia was more scathing when assessing the limited educational opportunities available to women. For Sylvia, it made no sense that women were "utterly debarred from some particular studies merely because some gentlemen think their sex have an exclusive right to them." The author lambasted negative assessments regarding the intellectual capacities of women and urged her readers to reevaluate their preconceived notions about females: "Let those who conceit themselves lords of the creation, and misunderstand, and, in the vanity of their minds, often misapply the language of St. Peter in calling a woman the weaker vessel, begin a reformation at home, and among the rest of their own sex."[13]

As the bearers of virtue in society, women were expected to conform to certain standards of behavior. In fact, greater demands were placed upon females than on their male counterparts. Nowhere was this more clearly articulated than with the sexual chastity of a woman. Periodicals warned women about the wiles of men and the need to guard their chastity at all costs. The innate character of men drove them to almost any lengths in their attempt to have their way with women. Despite the aggressiveness of males, women were still perceived as equally responsible for sexual activity and loss of virtue, no matter how trusting and innocent a woman might have been in the process. One concerned author offered this counseling to female readers in the *Pennsylvania Packet*:

> Trust not to man, we are by nature false;
> Dissembling, subtle, cruel, and inconsistent.
> When a man talks of love, with caution trust him;
> But if he swears, he'll certainly deceive thee.
> Such is the fate unhappy women find,
> And such is the curse entail'd upon our kind,
> that man, the lawless libertine! may rove,
> Free and unquestion'd thro' the wilds of love;
> While women, sense and nature's easy fool,
> If poor weak woman swerves from virtues rule;
> If, strongly charm'd she leave the thorny way,
> And in the softer paths of pleasure stray,
> Ruin ensues, reproach, and endless shame,
> and one false step intirely damns her fame;
> In vain with tears the loss she may deplore,
> In vain look back to what she was before,
> She set, like stars that fall, to rise no more.[14]

Women, not men, would ultimately suffer if they gave in to temptation. For parents, training their daughters to be guardians of their sexual virtue was thus paramount.

Periodicals focused on other factors of female morality beyond chastity. As with men, religious education remained at the core of female learning. In 1769, one magazine offered this poetic advice that emphasized the importance of Christianity for female instruction:

> Let pure Religion's dictates fire your soul,
> Guide all your thoughts, and ev'ry wish controul;
> By reason rul'd, from superstition free,
> Maintain an humble chearful piety.[15]

Christian values transcended simple piety. One father emphasized modesty as an important part of the female character. According to Dr. Gregory's letter to his daughter in *The Pennsylvania Packet*, modesty was "essential" for the female sex. Gregory defined modesty as "an easy dignity in your behaviour at public places," and he advised that in conversation a female should be soft-spoken and cautious in her language. In addition, modesty implied a gentleness of character, whereas a woman who was aggressive would be frowned upon as crass and "indelicate." In fact, Dr. Gregory censured women who attempted to act like men and reproached such behavior as absolute "folly." Instead, "a fine woman, like other fine things in nature, has her proper point of view." When properly trained, Dr. Gregory concluded, a woman can achieve a virtuous character like that of Eve before the Fall: "Grace was in all her steps, Heaven in her eye, In every gesture dignity and love."[16]

Advertisements for schools and books reflected the overall trend towards greater inclusiveness of women into the educational process. Josiah Davenport of Philadelphia focused upon the basic rudiments of reading, writing, and arithmetic "intended for young ladies &c. who do or may have occasion to keep small accounts." John Jones opened a new school in 1754 that promised to teach both sexes the basics of reading, writing, and arithmetic and declared that his teaching would "do youth [a] service" by offering instruction in areas that had been "too much neglected" in prior times. Ladies as well as gentlemen "could be instructed at their respective places of abode" should they prefer their own home over that of his school. Francis Daymon's French Academy, located on Front Street in the heart of Philadelphia, promised that his instruction would offer males and females the "power to investigate every branch of science which has been conveyed to the world" in the French language.[17] These advertisements and others like them assured parents that their daughters would receive a proper education by the time they came of age.

Not everyone shared the same sentiments about expanding female education, however. For a vocal few, the wrong kind of education could actually contribute to women becoming unproductive members of society. Proponents of this attitude argued that females should receive a carefully outlined education that assisted them at becoming accomplished wives and mothers, not scholars. In their opinion, any advanced learning in the hard sciences by females would only have a deleterious effect on themselves and society. One such commentator was Leander, who penned his disapproval of higher female learning in *The Royal American Magazine*.

While claiming to be generally sympathetic to the plight of women, Leander used most of his article to soundly criticize attempts at advanced learning for women. Scientific studies, he declared, had little chance of dramatically enhancing a woman's intellectual capacity. If anything, advanced learning tended to make a woman unattractive by filling her head with notions she lacked the ability to understand: "What can be more displeasing," Leander exclaimed to his readers, "to a man of taste than *female pedantry!*" Instead of improving the character, it "deprives the lady of that sweetness, so peculiar to the gentle soul of the fair, and unfits her for the pleasure of social converse." In a society where social standing reflected one's ability to fit into accepted norms, Leander lamented how advanced education destroyed these prior conventions: "How must it disgust the refined ear, when introduced to a circle of the polite sex, to be entertained with learned discourses on abstract ideas and mixed modes!" For Leander and others of his ilk, the "austere sciences" found in higher education "hardly fit gracefully on the lips of the fair" and were not designed "to proceed from the mellifluent mouths of these amiable beings." Instead, members of the "fair sex" should be instructed in the polite branches of education rather than aspire to be "doctors in petticoats."[18]

"The Plague of a Learned Wife" illustrated the pitfalls associated with a female whose education proved to be a liability. In the story, Obadiah Oliver laments the intellectual snobbery of his wife. Claiming to be a humble tradesman, Oliver declares that he has been cursed with marrying a wife whose education has resulted in chaos on the domestic front. "I am one of those unfortunate tradesmen who are plagued with a reading wife," he announces. In his estimation, the problem has become "a very great evil" in his house. Aside from the fact that constant reading has made his wife lazy, Obadiah also claims that he fails to understand her in ordinary conversation. "Now, to tell you the truth," he confesses, "I don't take in one word in ten which comes out of her mouth, and there is no pleasure you know in hearing what you can make neither head nor tail of." Even worse, their eighteen-year-old daughter has assumed the traits of her mother, making Obadiah nervous about her prospects for marriage. He had hoped his daughter would "know better than to follow her foolish mother in what only makes her laughed at by all her acquaintances behind her back," but the prospects look bleak at best. His only solace comes in the hope that his plight might serve as a warning beacon: "I hope all unmarried tradesmen, when they have read this letter, will take special care how they venture upon a bookish woman," he concludes.[19] For Obadiah, a female education required boundaries; to transcend those boundaries risked social upheaval and chaos, both in the household and in the community.

Overall, magazines and newspapers contributed significantly to the educational process during the eighteenth century by providing critical knowledge to a reading public. The need to create a virtuous citizenry dominated the educational discussion in periodicals, and readers were inundated with models of virtuous behavior (or the lack thereof) as well as the kinds of education that would prove most valuable to improving a child's character. Periodical writers continuously emphasized morality and science as the cornerstone of a solid education. Parents who read periodicals were thus provided with an important supplement in the training of their children, and parents could improve their children's character through the knowledge they received in newspapers and magazines on a weekly or monthly basis. As one essayist decreed in *The American Museum,* the "essential part of education" was to transform "dutiful children" into "good apprentices, good husbands, good wives," and above all else, "good citizens." Another writer in *The Pennsylvania Packet* neatly summarized the central lesson to be learned by children when they waded through the various elements of a virtuous education. According to this author, happiness, the object of all societies, could only be achieved if one learned the virtues of the human character:

> If there is such a thing as happiness to be obtained on this side of the grave surely it belongs to that man who lives a life of contentment, eats the bread of industry, and sleeps the sleep of temperance; who maintains that best of blessings, a good conscience, and enjoys the gift of providence with a thankful heart; who, as a member of society, contributes every thing in his power for the good of the community to which he belongs; and, as a private man, fills every character of life with integrity and uprightness. This man is happy, this man is blessed in all his works.[20]

Periodicals in Philadelphia provided many useful functions for Americans in the eighteenth century, but perhaps none more significant than contributing to the fate of American society. The articles and essays explored in this chapter provide a glimpse of how periodicals provided society with a unique opportunity to "become American" by teaching children common traits (in this case, educating them in virtue) that would transcend colonial boundaries. By creating a forum wherein the educational direction of children could be discussed and outlined, periodicals formulated a new vision of the model American child who would become a virtuous citizen capable of contributing to the success of American society for generations to come.

NOTES

1. *The Pennsylvania Packet and General Advertiser,* August 10, 1772.

2. *Minutes of the Provincial Council of Pennsylvania,* vol. 1 (Philadelphia: Jo. Severns & Co., 1852), 34, 53.

3. Noah Webster quoted in Lorraine Smith Pangle and Thomas L. Pangle, *The Learning of Liberty: The Educational Ideas of the American Founders* (Lawrence: University Press of Kansas, 1993), 222; *The American Weekly Mercury,* March 12, 1734, and March 28, 1734; *The Independent Chronicle,* March 12, 1778.

4. *The American Magazine or Monthly View of the Political State of the British Colonies,* January 1741, 1; *The American Magazine and General Repository,* May 1769, preface; the proposal for *The Pennsylvania Mercury and Universal Advertiser* found in *The Pennsylvania Packet and the General Advertiser,* January 23, 1775; *The American Magazine and Monthly Chronicle for the British Colonies,* October 1757, 37–38.

5. *The Pennsylvania Packet and General Advertiser,* June 15, 1772; *The Pennsylvania Magazine or American Monthly Museum,* March 1775, 101–4; April 1775, 149–53; January 1776, 9–15.

6. Henry F. May, *The Enlightenment in America* (New York: Oxford University Press, 1976). The material published in American periodicals reflects the ideas found in May's book, particularly the first section on the "Moderate Enlightenment."

7. *The American Magazine, or General Repository,* June 1769, 175–76.

8. *Pennsylvania Gazette,* April 8, 1736, and March 25, 1731; *The Royal American Magazine,* February 1774, 49.

9. *Pennsylvania Gazette,* March 28, 1734; *The Pennsylvania Magazine, or American Monthly Museum,* February 1776, 65–67; *The Pennsylvania Packet and General Advertiser,* December 9, 1771, and December 30, 1771; *The Pennsylvania Magazine, or American Monthly Museum,* supplement for the year 1775, 588.

10. *The Pennsylvania Magazine,* November 1775, 503; *The American Magazine or General Repository,* January 1769, 7–8.

11. *The American Magazine and Monthly Chronicle for the British Colonies,* October 1758, 630–40.

12. This section focuses upon the definition of women's roles and their treatment as described in newspapers and magazines. For an overview of female education in the eighteenth century, see Mary Beth Norton, *Liberty's Daughters: The*

Revolutionary Experience of American Women, 1750–1800 (Boston: Little, Brown, 1980); and Linda K. Kerber, *Women of the Republic: Intellect and Ideology in Revolutionary America* (Chapel Hill: University of North Carolina Press, 1980).

13. *The Royal American Magazine,* January 1774, 9–10; May 1774, 178–79.

14. *Pennsylvania Packet or General Advertiser,* January 17, 1774.

15. *The American Magazine and General Repository,* April 1769, 122.

16. *Pennsylvania Packet,* November 28, 1774.

17. *The Pennsylvania Journal,* July 3, 1755, and December 12, 1754; *Pennsylvania Packet,* October 28, 1771.

18. *The Royal American Magazine,* April 1774, 131–32. Unfortunately, Leander never exactly defines what his version of "advanced learning" actually entailed.

19. *The American Magazine, or General Repository,* August 1769, 243–44.

20. *The American Museum, or Universal Magazine,* April 1787, 326–29; *The Pennsylvania Packet and the General Advertiser,* October 28, 1771.

Chapter 12

From Saucy Boys to Sons of Liberty
Politicizing Youth in Pre-Revolutionary Boston

J. L. Bell

Boston, the American Revolution's "cradle of liberty," was a town full of children. As in British North America as a whole, over half the population was under the age of adulthood. Children participated in political actions as early as Boston's first public protest against the Stamp Act, on August 14, 1765: an organizer described "two or three hundred little boys with a Flagg marching in a Procession on which was King, Pitt & Liberty for ever."[1] The first Bostonian to die in political violence was a young boy. Apprentices both brought on and suffered in the Massacre of 1770, and pushed their way into the Tea Party of 1773. How did those children interpret the political conflict, and what motivated many of them to participate?

The issues that white men of property debated before the Revolution had little or no immediate impact on children. "Taxation without representation" was abstract for minors who were neither taxed nor enfranchised. Securing property rights meant little to a class with little property. Though white boys could foresee those rights in their futures, defying powerful authority usually requires immediate motivations. Examining Boston children's behavior in 1765–75 suggests how basic issues of "liberty," "tyranny," and "patriotism" resonated for them. The teenagers of that decade became the soldiers, sailors, and home-front housekeepers of the war, so understanding their experiences helps to illuminate the Revolutionary movement.

The predominance of youth in Boston's population is apparent in the town's 1765 census. Out of 15,520 inhabitants, 8,119, or 52 percent, were white children under the age of sixteen. The proportion of minors under the age of twenty-one was even higher. In addition, there were probably hundreds of children of African and Native American ancestry, but little survives about their experiences.[2]

In 1765, Boston contained about equal numbers of white boys and girls under age sixteen. Children of both sexes learned to read at private neighborhood schools, but boys and girls took separate paths after the age of about seven. The town provided free education for white boys. Girls could take lessons in handwriting, crafts, dancing, and other skills, but only on a private basis.[3] Most girls prepared for adult life by doing chores at home; they rarely appear in accounts of political activity.

Of the white boys in Boston, 908 were counted in the town's five public schools in July 1765. If children were distributed evenly across the ages, that number represents about half of all boys eligible for public education. The great majority were at the three Writing Schools, which offered training in handwriting and arithmetic for future businessmen. The two Latin Schools were preparing a mere 166 boys for Harvard, and at least two-thirds of those would drop out before college. Some transferred to a Writing School, ending up among students they had taunted as "boys" instead of "gentlemen."[4]

The thousand or so school-age boys not in school were probably already at work in shops, on ships, on farms, or in mercantile counting-houses. Each year they were joined by more who had finished schooling at about age fourteen. These teenaged workers took on adult responsibilities and knowledge, but remained children under the law. Between those of school age and those in their teens, apprentices comprised the bulk of Boston boys.[5]

Young workers' indenture contracts promised them food, lodging, and clothing while they learned their vocations, but no pay. However, by tradition apprentices collected a few coins toward the end of each year. Boys who delivered newspapers carried patriotic verses asking for tips. Apprentices in shops put out handbills inviting contributions to their "New-Years box."[6] Thus, young workers had small but immediate economic interests to protect.

Boys also collected payments during their celebration of the Fifth of November, or "Pope Night." On that holiday, gangs of youths hauled around wagons displaying giant effigies of the pope, the devil, and the Stuart Pretender. As described in an account from Newburyport,

> After the [Pope Night] verses were repeated, the purser stepped forward, and took up his collection. Nearly all on whom they called, gave something.

Esquire Atkins and esquire Dalton, always gave a dollar apiece. After peram-
bulating the town, and finishing their collections, they concluded their
evening's entertainment with a splendid supper.

A traditional Pope Night crew thus had a purser, expectations of about
how much they would collect, and plans for a feast. Even small boys, not
part of the gangs, went around asking for "a little money / To buy my Pope
some drink."[7]

In Boston, Pope Night developed another tradition that overshadowed
the collection of cash. The town's youth divided into North End and
South End gangs with rival popes. By the 1760s it had become traditional
for the two big gangs to meet after dark to brawl, with the winners drag-
ging off the losers' paraphernalia to a bonfire during their feast.

Clearly, part of the appeal of Pope Night for young crowds was the
chance to be rowdy in a tightly controlled society. However, this day of
misrule was also a show of support for Protestantism and the king. As a
repudiation of the Catholics claiming the British throne, Pope Night carried a clear political message. The holiday gangs no doubt enjoyed acting
wild, but they presented themselves as British patriots, not rebels.[8]

Boston's gang rivalry thus masked a deep ideological unity. The North
and South End were not separated by great economic, religious, or ethnic
differences, merely by the Mill Creek. These colonial boys seem to have
formed gangs simply to have one group to belong to and another to fight.
Facing outsiders, they united. A nine-year-old immigrant from Ireland in
1737 recalled "my life was one continued State of warfare."[9] During the
pre-Revolutionary conflict, such town loyalty translated easily into supporting the local order against new policies from London. By 1774, young
Bostonians were so united that radicals could hide cannon in a Writing
School without one student telling the royal authorities.

Nonetheless, the Whigs resisting new parliamentary policies and taxes
felt ambivalent about recruiting youths to their cause. The danger was not
betrayal, but too much fervor. Men viewed boys as liable to get out of
hand and embarrass the town. A scuffle between "two little boys about
seven years old," a newspaper writer lamented, ". . . naturally produced a
larger one between some of the inhabitants." Organizers therefore kept
teens out of their planning sessions. Peter Edes recalled how his father
hosted colleagues before the Tea Party: "I [at seventeen] was not admitted
into their presence, my station was in another room to make punch."[10]

Yet Whigs also felt responsible for bringing up sons to value traditional freedoms. Those men, too, saw themselves as British patriots, supporting their constitution and king against corrupt government ministers. Adults therefore exposed even small boys to the consequences of ministerial policies. Thomas H. Perkins (born 1764) recalled after the Massacre how a servant took him to see the dead victims and "frozen blood in the streets." Joseph May (born 1760) saw those corpses interred. A Writing School master dismissed class so he and his scholars could attend the oration commemorating the Massacre in 1775. (The Loyalist master of a Latin School did not.)[11]

Whigs felt proud when youngsters responded to such lessons by standing up for their rights. In late January 1775, gentlemen circulated a story about South Latin School boys visiting an army general to demand their freedom to sled past his house. The capper was how the royal governor reacted to the incident. According to different versions, he said either that the boys "had only caught the spirit of the times, & that what was bred in the bone would creep out in the flesh," or that "it was impossible to beat the notion of Liberty out of the people, as it was rooted in 'em *from their Childhood*."[12] Either way, for Boston Whigs the observation reflected well on their child-rearing.

Organizers also drew girls into their cause—within the female sphere. Campaigns against luxuries and imports tied patriotism to household consumption. Females were urged to support local manufacturers by spinning yarn. Newspapers lauded the youngest attendees at spinning bees: "but eleven years old" in Jamestown, Rhode Island; "9 years old" in Braintree; "but about thirteen years of age" in Ipswich. In February 1770 the Gore family, which included daughters as young as seven, hosted a spinning bee in Boston and earned praise from the *Boston Gazette*.[13]

Friends of the royal government, who saw the opposition as a faction of manipulators, accused Whig leaders of tricking and bribing children into political acts. Loyalist judge Peter Oliver insisted that "when a Riot was to be brought on, the Factioneers would employ Boys & Negroes to assemble & make Bonfires in the Streets." William Gordon, a Roxbury minister close to the Whigs, also reported that "Boys, small and great, . . . were encouraged, and well paid by certain leaders, to insult and intimidate those who" defied the movement. Boston activists themselves acknowledged the possibility of "employing some boys to sing the Liberty Song through the streets."[14]

Men did watch over some boys' demonstrations. When a group of youths surrounded the home of a customs commissioner in March 1768, he spotted adults in the background. On February 8, 1770, a Crown informant described boys picketing an importer's shop; not only did "a Number of considerable Merchants" watch, but "Idle people, who were standing by, with Clubs and Sticks in their Hands," prevented the shopkeeper from ending the protest.[15]

Sometimes boys acted on their own, however. In September 1766, customs officials tried to search the warehouse of an uncooperative merchant. A few men gathered. Then the North Latin School let out, and "Boys came running along . . . enquiring what the Matter was." Witnesses blamed those scholars for saying that someone should summon a mob. The stalemate ended peacefully, but "in the Evening the Boys made a talk about the Informer [who had triggered the raid] and said it was one Richardson and that they knew where he lived and they they'd goe and give him three Cheers for the great Prize he'd got."[16] These jeering schoolboys were not under adult control.

Youths occasionally pushed their way into men's political actions. As a select group of Whigs tossed tea into Boston harbor in 1773, a few apprentices leaped aboard. They were told "to jump over into the flats by the side of one of the vessels [and] . . . beat up more thoroughly the fragments of boxes and masses of tea" so that nothing could be salvaged. Boys elsewhere followed the example of what was later dubbed the Boston Tea Party. In Salem, a town committee confiscated two chests of tea, and "the school boys . . . had much amusement in burning it on the Common."[17]

When crowds turned threatening or violent, however, Whigs were quick to blame youths, along with blacks and sailors. Thus, the *Boston Gazette* blamed the town's first tar-and-feathering on "a Sett of naughty Boys," though only one of the seven people the victim sued for assault was a minor. A town report dismissed the crowd that visited a governor's estate as "*liquorish Boys.*" This scapegoating was such cliché that in 1769 a royalist complained about his foes' "usual sayings . . . that it was done by Boys & Negroes, or by Nobody."[18]

If Boston's reputation was on the line, Whig leaders worked to rein in the young. Their efforts were most apparent after the August 1765 Stamp Act protests erupted into mobs trashing royal officials' houses. For one year, town fathers cracked down on Pope Night. They convinced the rival gangs to forgo their wagons and brawling, and instead to parade in ranks behind a militia general, their "captains" and "lieutenants" (young working men) in sharp new uniforms. The whole gathering then shared a banquet. Newspapers hailed this show of unity against the Stamp Act. The youths got most of the benefits of Pope Night: a day off from work, a feast, and affirmation of their patriotism.[19]

Whigs thought of children in yet another way: as a metaphor for the American colonies, with Britain as the "mother country." This image pervaded pre-Revolutionary political writing, from street songs to John Dickinson's *Letters from a Farmer in Pennsylvania.* As independence became a possibility, the metaphor gained a new meaning: the colonies were like a child who had grown up. A letter sent from Boston in 1773 argued,

> And do you really think, my good Friend, that our Mother Country, as you
> call it, is to keep her Children in Leading-strings? Are we never to go out of
> the Nursery? Does our good Mamma think we are only to be fed with Pap
> and Tea? If she does not admit we are of Age, and able to go alone, she will
> find we are come to the State of Manhood.[20]

Such rhetoric had special resonance for children coming of age themselves, even when it was not directed to them.

The image of America attaining "the State of Manhood" dovetailed with the basis of Whig ideology: that true Englishmen resisted corrupt encroachments on their liberties lest they sink into "slavery." Political activity let youths show that they were worthy of manhood. Yet if their protests became disorderly, boys were repudiated by Whig leaders and cast back down to juvenile status. Boston's youth thus faced a tough balancing act: not to falter in standing up for their rights, but not to go too far.

Understanding that background helps to make sense of children's notable political actions. Their most basic motivation seems to have been simple affiliation: being on the right side, supporting home town and king together. The hundreds of little boys marching behind a flag marked "King, Pitt & Liberty" in 1765 didn't need to understand tax policy and parliamentary factions; they simply showed the flag. Boys played little role in the nonimportation movement until the business community proclaimed certain shopkeepers "Enemies to their Country" for selling imported goods. Within weeks, schoolboys were picketing those people's shops, yelling insults at customers.[21]

Sometimes children invested normal activities with patriotic meaning, known perhaps only to themselves. Thirteen-year-old Anna Green Winslow attended a party in April 1772 where the host "brought in the talk of Whigs & Tories & taught me the difference between them." At the end of May she visited "Libberty Assembly Hall," the big Manufactory building on Tremont Street, "to see a piece of cloth cousin Sally spun for a summer coat for unkle." Winslow had never learned to spin, so to show support for the factory "Miss Gridley & I did ourselves the Honour of dancing a minuet in it."[22]

Boys used the language of traditional rights, like their fathers, when they felt those rights were being violated. Shooed away from a customs man's house, young protesters replied "they would not, Kings high Way" —invoking their freedom to travel public roads. The South Latin School committee who visited the general in January 1775 reportedly framed their grievance as "the invasion of their rights made by one of his servants; that he had spoiled their sport by tossing a quantity of ashes over a spot of ground which they & their fathers before them had taken possession of" for sledding.[23]

Pope Night gangs lampooned the new customs commissioners in 1767, but what most galvanized youths seems to have been the arrival of army regiments the next year. Friction grew between soldiers and locals, and children felt the danger. On an errand in March 1770, John and Samuel Appleton ran into troops hot from brawls with workers. John pleaded, "Soldier, spare my life!" "No, damn you, we will kill you all," replied one redcoat, smacking the twelve-year-old with his sheathed cutlass.[24]

Youths found ways to protest the presence of the royal army. In January 1769, newspapers reported, "some boys were the other evening playing at foot ball near the province house when either by accident or design; they threw down one of the centry boxes." Pvt. James McKaan described another collision with young footballers that December:

> The Mobb increased more, and at lenth Struck the Ball against this Deponant and hit him on the Head, and rebounded over a Wall upon which A Young Lad jumped over the Wall after it (altho this Deponant told them that no one should go after it).

This tussle ended with the football players seeking a warrant against the private for trying to grab the "Young Lad." Boston youths had started to treat petty confrontations as part of a larger struggle against tyranny.[25]

In early 1770, boys took the lead in picketing importers' shops. These demonstrations occurred only on Thursdays, when the public schools closed after a short morning session. Youngsters carried pageantry reminiscent of Pope Night, displaying "a large Wooden head carved and painted."[26] Though adult Whigs watched, boys themselves seem to have designed these protests.

On February 22, the young picketers set up their signs in the North End. Ebenezer Richardson—the same customs officer whom the North Latin boys had jeered in 1766—tried to knock down the signs. The youngsters followed Richardson to his house. He chased them off. They responded by throwing garbage and then stones. His windows broken, Richardson fired a musket at the crowd. His shot hit two boys: Sammy Gore and Christopher Seider.[27]

What brought those two boys to the front of that mob? Gore was a paint merchant's son who had just turned nineteen. The *Boston News-Letter* reported that he "happened to be there as a Spectator," but he was from a politically active family. His father, brother, and brother-in-law had all dined as Sons of Liberty the previous August. Less than a week before Sammy was wounded, the Gores had hosted their spinning bee.[28]

The bigger puzzle is Seider. He was probably just under eleven years old. His parents were German immigrants who attended Anglican churches, and he worked for a Loyalist family. The *News-Letter* said Seider "was going from School, [and] ran down with the rest of the Boys" after hearing noises. Yet he quickly joined in the violence, "stooping to take up a Stone" when he was shot. One clue to what might have inspired Seider is that his pockets held "several heroic pieces," including "*Wolfe's Summit of human Glory*"—most likely a poem about Gen. James Wolfe, patriotic hero of Quebec.[29]

After Seider died, Whigs praised the little boy's "manly spirit," but the funeral they organized highlighted his youth. Four or five hundred boys walked in pairs in front of six more carrying the pall over the small coffin. Newspapers estimated that thirteen hundred people—8 percent of all Bostonians—walked in this procession. Thirty carriages and other vehicles brought up the rear. John Adams wrote in his diary for February 26, "My Eyes never beheld such a funeral. The Procession extended further than can be imagined. . . . [T]he Ardor of the People is not to be quelled by the Slaughter of one Child and the Wounding of another."[30]

The ardor of the people rekindled a week later, on the night of March 5. Bostonians, already hot from brawls between soldiers and ropemakers, heard that the sentry at the customs office had clubbed an apprentice: another boy attacked by another ministerial employee. Angry men surrounded the sentry on King Street, and the violence spiraled. By the end of the night seventeen-year-old Samuel Maverick was dead and two other apprentices were wounded in what became known as the Boston Massacre.

Whigs made the most of child-victims Seider and Maverick; men shooting children, particularly a child as young as ten, looked like convincing evidence of tyranny. Printers tallied the two weeks of deaths with six small coffins, those for Seider and Maverick labeled with the victims' ages. In 1771 Paul Revere displayed a picture of "Seider's pale Ghost fresh-bleeding." Phillis Wheatley wrote a poem about the boy. At least three broadsides retold the Seider killing while the royal authorities arranged a pardon for Richardson.[31]

From 1771 through the end of the war, Boston commissioned a memorial oration on the Massacre's anniversary. For years that event ended with a collection for survivor Christopher Monk, disabled at age seventeen or, as John Hancock declaimed, "cut off in the gay morn of manhood." In 1775, Dr. Joseph Warren extended the circle of young victims to include wholly imaginary children of the dead men: "take heed, ye orphan babes, lest, whilst your streaming eyes are fixed upon the ghastly corpse, *your feet slide on the stones besplattered with your father's brains.*"[32] Such rhetoric could only have heightened children's fears.

In fact, the violence on King Street in 1770 had been sparked not by politics but by working boys' hopes for a little cash. Sometime in late 1769, according to shoemaker George R. T. Hewes, barber John Piemont promised one of his apprentices the fee for shaving an army captain. The grace period for the officer to pay "had expired, but the money could not be got, though frequent applications had been made for it. . . . [F]inally the last application was made" on March 5. That application took the form of barber's boy Edward Garrick shouting that the captain "owed my fellow Prentice." Garrick's words show that he sought to collect not for his master, but for another boy. He showed no grudge against the army; not only did Piemont's lads shave officers, but the shop employed a moonlighting soldier, and the apprentices had just visited his barracks.[33]

Regardless, the sentry on King Street got sick of Garrick's grousing and, as the boy testified, "struck me with his Gun under my Ear." That assault quickly made the apprentices turn their financial issue into a political grievance. Garrick's coworker demanded of the soldier "what he meant by thus abusing the people." The barber's boys then gathered an inflamed crowd, and the shootings followed.[34]

A few patterns emerge from this tumult of activity. Boston youngsters seem to have joined the Whig movement early on out of local loyalty and the desire to prove themselves worthy Englishmen (and Englishwomen). In political actions they could show their patriotism, revile town enemies, and get away with a little mischief. After 1768, encounters with soldiers gave youngsters experiences they interpreted as "abusing the people." In 1770 children gained real fears and grievances as they saw their peers killed and disabled by royal employees, all of whom escaped hanging.

In 1774, after the Tea Party, London sent troops back into Boston and closed its harbor to Atlantic trade. The Massachusetts countryside turned militant. Children in the occupied town supported the provincial military effort through silence. In September, two of the Boston militia's cannons were hidden from the army in the South Writing School, where over two hundred boys studied. One concealer recalled, "The guns remained in that box for a fortnight, and many of the boys were acquainted with the fact, but not one of them betrayed the secret."[35]

By then, personal and political issues had so intertwined that some children imbibed the values of liberty without learning the issues that adults were arguing over. One was Ebenezer Fox, born in Roxbury in 1763 and bound out to work on a farm. "Almost all the conversation that came to my ears related to the injustice of England," he recalled.

> I, and other boys situated similarly to myself, thought we had wrongs to be redressed; rights to be maintained; and, as no one appeared disposed to act the part of a redresser, it was our duty and our privilege to assert our own rights.

Fox had absorbed the Whig ideology. Yet when he acted on those values by running away on the night of April 18, 1775, he knew so little about current events that he assumed the anxious crowds along the road were hunting for him.[36]

When war finally came, the little boys who marched against the Stamp Act in 1765 were of prime age to be soldiers. Some younger boys took war as a chance to assume adult freedoms. On April 19, thirteen-year-old Benjamin Russell and several friends left their Writing School and followed the redcoat reinforcements out of town, attaching themselves to the provincial camp by the end of the day. Teenagers enlisted with and without their parents' consent. Thirteen-year-old Daniel Granger of Andover was so small that when he was singled out for praise, his captain "sat me down on his Knees."[37] These boys took on men's roles in the fight for liberty, leaving the symbolic battles of childhood behind.

NOTES

1. Dirk Hoerder, *Crowd Action in Revolutionary Massachusetts, 1765–1780* (New York: Academic Press, 1977), 98.

2. J. H. Benton Jr., *Early Census Making in Massachusetts, 1643–1765* (Boston: Charles E. Goodspeed, 1905), 74–75. The census used age sixteen as a dividing line because of militia laws, but twenty-year-old males were still legally "boys."

3. Robert Francis Seybolt, *The Private Schools of Colonial Boston* (Cambridge, MA: Harvard University Press, 1935).

4. *Reports of the Record Commissioners of the City of Boston* [hereafter *Boston Records*] (Boston: Rockwell & Churchill, 1881–1909), 16:181; E. Jennifer Monaghan, "Readers Writing: The Curriculum of the Writing Schools of Eighteenth-Century Boston," *Visible Language* 21 (1987): 167–214; Henry F. Jenks, *Catalogue of the Boston Latin School* (Boston: Boston Latin School Association, 1886), 1:39.

5. For simplicity, I refer to all working boys as "apprentices," although not all were formally indentured.

6. Stephen W. Nissenbaum, *Christmas in Early New England, 1620–1820: Puritanism, Popular Culture, and the Printed Word* (Worcester, MA: American Antiquarian Society, 1996), 106–9.

7. Joshua Coffin, *A Sketch of the History of Newbury, Newburyport, and West Newbury* (Boston: Samuel G. Drake, 1845), 251; Samuel Eliot Morison, *Harrison Gray Otis, 1765–1848: The Urbane Federalist* (Boston: Houghton Mifflin, 1969), 8.

8. J. L. Bell, "Du Simitière's Sketches of Pope Day in Boston, 1767," in *The Worlds of Children, 1620–1920: Proceedings of Dublin Seminar for New England Folklife, 2002* (Dublin Seminar, 2004), 217.

9. Gardner Weld Allen, "Captain Hector McNeill, Continental Navy," *Massachusetts Historical Society Proceedings* [hereafter *MHSP*], 55 (1922): 60. McNeill felt the situation had improved by 1773—for Scotch-Irish Protestants.

10. William Pencak, *War, Politics, and Revolution in Provincial Massachusetts* (Boston: Northeastern University Press, 1981), 121–22; Oliver Dickerson, comp., *Boston under Military Rule, 1768–1769* (Boston: Chapman & Grimes, 1936), 105; Peter Edes to Benjamin C. Edes, February 16, 1836, *MHSP,* 12 (1871–73), 175.

11. Pauline Maier, *From Resistance to Revolution: Colonial Radicals and the Development of American Opposition to Britain, 1765–1776* (New York: Knopf, 1972); Thomas Handasyd Perkins, "To My Children," July 18, 1846, 6–7, Thomas Handasyd Perkins Papers, Massachusetts Historical Society; James Spear Loring, *The Hundred Boston Orators,* 4th ed. (Boston: John P. Jewett, 1852), 20–23; "Extracts from the Diary of John Tileston," *New England Historical & Genealogical Register* [hereafter *NEHGR*] 20 (1866): 11; Jenks, *Catalogue of the Boston Latin School,* 2:100.

12. John Elliott to Jeremy Belknap, January 30, 1775, in *The Belknap Papers: Massachusetts Historical Society Collections,* 6th series, 4 (1891): 77–78; "Letters of John Andrews, Esq., of Boston, 1772–1776," *MHSP* 8 (1864–65): 398–99.

13. Dickerson, *Boston under Military Rule*, 85–86, 116; *Boston Gazette*, February 26, 1770.

14. *Peter Oliver's Origin and Progress of the American Rebellion: A Tory View* (San Marino, CA: Huntington Library, 1961), 89; William Gordon, *The History of the Rise, Progress, and Establishment, of the Independence of the United States of America* (London: the author, 1788), 1:277; Dickerson, *Boston under Military Rule*, 5–6.

15. John Richard Alden, *General Gage in America* (Baton Rouge: Louisiana State University Press, 1948), 156; "Narrative of Proceedings at Boston from February 7th to March 14th 1770," New England Papers (10:3:70–1), Sparks Manuscripts, Houghton Library, Harvard University.

16. George G. Wolkins, "Daniel Malcom and the Writs of Assistance," *MHSP*, 58 (1924–25): 46–47, 56. On Richardson, see J. L. Bell, "'A Wretch of Wretches Prov'd with Child': From Local Scandal to Revolutionary Outrage," *New England Ancestors* 6.1 (Winter 2005): 22–24.

17. [Benjamin Bussey Thatcher], *Traits of the Tea Party* (New York: Harper & Brothers, 1835), 262–63; Susan Smith, "Memoir of Col. David Mason—by his daughter Susan Smith . . . ," (reel 4, frames 272–80), Shaw Family Papers, Library of Congress.

18. *Boston Gazette*, December 18, 1769; *Legal Papers of John Adams*, L. Kinvin Roth and Hiller R. Zobel, eds. (Cambridge, MA: Harvard University Press, 1965), 1:41; *An Appeal to the World; or, A Vindication of the Town of Boston* (1769), quoted in *The Writings of Samuel Adams*, Harry Alonzo Cushing, ed. (New York: G. P. Putnam's Sons, 1908), 1:424; John Mein to Joseph Harrison, November 5, 1769, New England Papers (10:3:51), Sparks Manuscripts.

19. Hoerder, *Crowd Action in Revolutionary Massachusetts*, 117–18.

20. *Berrow's Worcester* (UK) *Journal*, January 27, 1774.

21. *Boston Gazette*, February 26, 1770.

22. *Diary of Anna Green Winslow: A Boston School Girl of 1771*, Alice Morse Earle, ed. (Boston: Houghton-Mifflin, 1894), 58–59, 72.

23. *Legal Papers of John Adams*, 2:416. Elliott to Belknap, January 30, 1775, *Massachusetts Historical Society Collections*, 6th series, 4:77–78.

24. *Legal Papers of John Adams*, 3:139. Clashes with soldiers similarly politicized shoemaker George R. T. Hewes. See Alfred F. Young, *The Shoemaker and the Tea Party: Memory and the American Revolution* (Boston: Beacon Press, 1999), 34–36.

25. Dickerson, *Boston under Military Rule*, 50. James McKaan, deposition, July 24, 1770, in transcripts from the Colonial Office, Great Britain (CO5/88/459), at the Library of Congress.

26. John Boyle, "Boyle's Journal of Occurrences in Boston, 1759–1778," *NEHGR* 84 (1930): 262.

27. *Boston Evening-Post*, February 26, 1770.

28. William H. Whitmore, "Genealogy of the Families of Payne and Gore," *MHSP* 13 (1873–75): 417–24; *Boston News-Letter,* March 1, 1770. This newspaper was accused of having "partially related" the shooting the week before, and may therefore have slanted this report to please the Whigs. "An Alphabetical List of the Sons of Liberty who dined at Liberty Tree, Dorchester, Aug. 14, 1769," *MHSP* 11 (1869): 140.

29. Seider was baptized on March 18, 1759. H. Hobart Holly, "Some Germans of Germantown in Massachusetts," *NEHGR* 138 (1984): 229; Wilford W. Whitaker and Gary T. Horlacher, *Broad Bay Germans: 18th-Century German-Speaking Settlers of Present-Day Waldoboro, Maine* (Rockport, ME: Picton Press, 1998), 282–83; *Boston Post-Boy,* February 26, 1770; *Boston Evening-Post,* February 26, 1770; *Boston News-Letter,* March 1, 1770; *Legal Papers of John Adams,* 2:418.

30. *Boston Gazette,* February 26, 1770; *Boston News-Letter,* March 1, 1770.

31. *Boston Gazette,* March 11, 1771; Robert C. Kuncio, "Some Unpublished Poems of Phillis Wheatley," *New England Quarterly* 43 (1970): 297.

32. Massacre orations reprinted in Hezekiah Niles, comp., *Principles and Acts of the Revolution in America* (Baltimore: William Ogden Niles, 1822), and transcribed at http://chnm.gmu.edu/courses/zagarri/hist499/oration.html, accessed June 12, 2005.

33. [Thatcher], *Traits of the Tea Party,* 118–19; a garbled version of Hewes's story appears in [James Hawkes], *A Retrospect of the Boston Tea-Party* (New York: S. S. Bliss, 1834), 29–30; Depositions #16 and 38 in *A Short Narrative of the Horrid Massacre in Boston* (Boston: John Doggett Jr., 1849), 45, 57–58.

34. *Legal Papers of John Adams,* 3:50; *A Short Narrative of the Horrid Massacre,* 57–58.

35. William Tudor, *The Life of James Otis, of Massachusetts* (Boston: Wells and Lilly, 1823), 454–55; "Letters of John Andrews," 362.

36. Ebenezer Fox, *The Revolutionary Adventures of Ebenezer Fox, of Roxbury, Massachusetts* (Boston: Munroe & Francis, 1838), 17–18, 22.

37. Joseph T. Buckingham, *Specimens of Newspaper Literature: With Personal Memoirs, Anecdotes, and Reminiscences* (Boston: Charles C. Little & James Brown, 1850), 2:3; John Greenwood, *The Revolutionary Services of John Greenwood of Boston and New York, 1775–1783* (New York: De Vinne, 1922), 7, 9; "A Boy Soldier under Washington: The Memoir of Daniel Granger," *Mississippi Valley Historical Review* 16 (1930): 539, 543.

"Though I Was Often Beaten for My Play"
The Autobiography of John Barnard

*Our image of New England children—and their parents, for that matter—
tends to be rather severe. The following excerpt from the autobiography of a
well-known eighteenth-century Massachusetts minister, John Barnard, suggests that this perception does not tell the whole story about New England
boyhood. Although it is certainly filled with piety and theological musings, it
also reveals a version of colonial childhood that resembles in at least a few
ways more modern childhoods. (From "Autobiography of the Rev. John
Barnard," Collections of the Massachusetts Historical Society, 3rd Ser., 5
[1836]: 178–182)*

I, JOHN BARNARD was born at Boston, 6th Nov. 1681; descended from rep-
utable parents, viz. John and Esther Barnard, remarkable for their piety
and benevolence, who devoted me to the service of God, in the work of
the ministry, from my very conception and birth; and accordingly took
special care to instruct me themselves in the principles of the Christian
religion, and kept me close at school to furnish my young mind with the
knowledge of letters. By that time I had a little passed my sixth year, I had
left my reading-school, in the latter part of which my mistress made me a
sort of usher, appointing me to teach some children that were older than
myself, as well as smaller ones; and in which time I had read my Bible
through thrice. My parents thought me to be weakly, because of my thin
habit and pale countenance, and therefore sent me into the country, where
I spent my seventh summer, and by the change of air and diet and exercise
I grew more fleshy and hardy; and that I might not lose my reading, was
put to a school-mistress, and returned home in the fall.

In the spring of my eighth year I was sent to the grammar school,
under the tuition of the aged, venerable, and justly famous Mr. Ezekiel
Cheever. But after a few weeks, an odd accident drove me from the school.

There was an older lad entered the school the same week with me; we strove who should outdo; and he beat me by the help of a brother in the upper class, who stood behind master with the [master's book] open for him to read out [of]; by which means he could recite his [lesson] three and four times in a forenoon, and the same in the afternoon; but I who had no such help, and was obliged to commit all to memory, could not keep pace with him; so that he would be always one lesson before me. My ambition could not bear to be outdone, and in such a fraudulent manner, and therefore I left the school. About this time, arrived a dissenting minister from England, who opened a private school for reading, writing, and Latin. My good father put me under his tuition, with whom I spent a year and a half. The gentleman receiving but little encouragement, threw up his school, and returned me to my father, and again I was sent to my aged Mr. Cheever, who placed me in the lowest class; but . . . in a few weeks he advanced me to [the higher class], and the next year made me the head of it.

In the time of my absence from Mr. Cheever, it pleased God to take to himself my dear mother, who was not only a very virtuous, but a very intelligent woman. She was exceeding fond of my learning, and taught me to pray. My good father also instructed me, and made a little closet for me to retire to for my morning and evening devotion. But, alas! how childish and hypocritical were all my pretensions to piety, there being little or no serious thoughts of God and religion in me.

Just as I had completed my eighth year, my father saw cause to take a second wife, a virtuous woman, an excellent wife, and an extraordinary good mother-in-law [stepmother], in whom God graciously very much made up my loss; who, though she could not be supposed to have the love of me which she had of her own children by my father, yet was she constant in her dutiful regard to and care of me and a younger brother. I remember to have heard persons of figure, who knew her, say to me when I was grown up a young man, that they never knew but two good mothers-in-law, and mine was one of them. My honored father died in December, 1732, having just completed his 78th year; my good mother-in-law outlived him twenty-six years, and died January the last day, in 1758, being in her 94th year.

Though my master advanced me, as above, yet I was a very naughty boy, much given to play, insomuch that he at length openly declared, "You Barnard, I know you can do well enough if you will, but you are so full of play that you hinder your classmates from getting their lessons, and therefore, if any of them cannot perform their duty, I shall correct you for it." One unlucky day, one of my classmates did not look into his book, and therefore could not say his lesson, though I called upon him once and again to mind his book; upon which our master beat me. I told master the reason why he could not say his lesson was, his declaring he would beat me if any of the class were wanting in their duty; since which this boy would not look into his book, though I called upon him to mind his book, as the class could witness. The boy was pleased with my being corrected, and persisted in his neglect, for which I was still corrected, and that for several days. I thought, in justice, I ought to correct the boy, compel him to a better temper; and therefore, after school was done, I went up to him, and told him I had been beaten several times for his neglect; and since master would not correct him I would, and I should do so as often as I was corrected for him; and then drubbed him heartily. The boy never came to school any more, and so that unhappy affair ended.

Though I was often beaten for my play, and my little roguish tricks, yet I don't remember that I was ever beaten for my book more than once or twice. One of these was upon this occasion. Master put our class upon turning *Æsop's Fables* into Latin verse. Some dull fellows made a shift to perform this to acceptance; but I was so much duller at this exercise that I could make nothing of it; for which master corrected me, and this he did two or three days going. I had honestly tried my possibles to perform the task; but having no poetical fancy, nor then a capacity opened of expressing the same idea by a variation of phrases, though I was perfectly acquainted with prosody, I found I could do nothing; and therefore plainly told my master, that I had diligently labored all I could to perform what he required, and perceiving I had no genius for it, I thought it was in vain to strive against nature any longer; and he never more required it of me. Nor had I any thing of a poetical genius till after I had been at College some time, when upon reading some of Mr. Cowley's works, I was highly pleased, and a new scene opened before me.

I remember once, in making a piece of Latin, my master found fault with the syntax of one word, which was not so used by me heedlessly, but designedly, and therefore I told him there was a plain grammar rule for it. He angrily replied, there was no such rule. I took the grammar and showed the rule to him. Then he smilingly said, "Thou art a brave boy; I had forgot it." And no wonder; for he was then above eighty years old.

While I was a schoolboy, I experienced many signal deliverances from imminent danger, on the land, and in the waters. I mention two signal deliverances; the one in the year 1692, in my eleventh year, I fell from a scaffold at the eaves of the old North Meeting House, eighteen feet high, between two pieces of timber that lay on the ground, without touching them. I lay upon the ground until somebody ran to my father's house, about two hundred feet off, and acquainted him with my fall; who came and took me up, without any apparent signs of life in me, and carried me home; where, by the blessing of God upon the means used, in some hours I recovered breath and sensation, and had no bone broken nor dislocated, though I complained of inward ails; but through the divine mercy soon got well.

The other is a more remarkable instance of the goodness of God to me. In June, 1693 . . . [a] malignant distemper, called the scarlet fever . . . spread in Boston, of which many persons died, and that within two or three days of their being taken ill. It pleased God I was seized with it, and through the rampancy of the fever, and a violent pain at my heart, which rendered every breath I drew to be as though a sword had pierced me, I was so bad that life was despaired of. On the third night (I think,) it seemed to me that a certain woman, wife of a doctor, who used to supply my father's family with plasters upon occasion, came and brought me some small dark-colored pills, and directed me to put one in my mouth, and hold it there till it grew mellow, then squeeze it flat betwixt my thumb and finger and apply it to my right nipple; it would soak in, and before I had used them all so, I should be well. I followed the prescription, and when I had used the third pill, my pain and fever left me, and I was well. My tender father, very early the next morning, came into my bedchamber to inquire how it was with me. I told him I was quite well, and intended to get up presently, and said the pills Mrs. (naming her) had given me last night had perfectly cured me. He said to me, "Child, I believe she was not here; I heard nothing of it." To confirm him I said, "Sir, I have the remaining four pills now in my hand," and put my hand out of bed to show them, but they dropped out of my hand into the bed. I then raised myself up to look for them, but could not find them. He said to me, " I am afraid, child, you are out of your senses." I said to him, "Sir, I am perfectly awake, and in my senses, and find myself truly well." He left the room with the supposition that I was delirious, and I saw by his countenance that he was ready to give me over for lost. He then inquired of all the house whether that woman had been at the house the day or evening before. They all let him know that they had not seen her here. He betook himself to his closet and in about an hour came to me again; [I] continued firm in the story I had told him. He talked to me of some other things, and found by my answers that I was thoroughly awake, and as he now thought, under the power of no distraction was better satisfied, and left me with a more placid countenance. By noon I got up, and was perfectly recovered from my sickness. I thought I would have given ever so much to know what the pills were, that others might receive the benefit of them. Finding that the above said woman had not been at our house and I was perfectly healed, I could not help thinking that a merciful God had sent an angel, as he did Isaiah to Hezekiah, to heal me; and to this very day, I cannot but esteem it more than an ordinary dream, or the wild ramblings of a heated imagination. It seemeth to me a sort of heavenly vision. And what less can you . . . make of it? The kind offices of the ministering spirits are, doubtless, more than we are aware of. However, thus has God mercifully appeared for my help, when I was brought very low, and in this manner rescued me from the jaws of death. Forever blessed be his holy name! But to return.

From grammar school I was admitted into the college, in Cambridge. . . .

John entered Harvard at the age of sixteen; he graduated four years later, and despite his self-professed lack of seriousness, he became a diligent and respected Congregational minister, serving a congregation in Marblehead, Massachusetts, for many years. He died in 1770 at the age of ninety-eight.

"A Bookish Inclination"
Benjamin Franklin Grows Up

Benjamin Franklin—publisher, editor, scientist, inventor, diplomat, politician, and revolutionary—was one of the best-known Americans of his time. But before he became famous he was a boy struggling to make his way in a hard world. His autobiography, which he wrote on and off throughout the last twenty years of his life, began with a brief history of the Franklin family. His father, Josiah, had married twice and fathered seventeen children; Ben, born in 1706, was the youngest son. The following excerpt describes his education, his pastimes, and his attempts as a youth to find gainful and worthy employment—including disagreements with his father and brother about the nature of that employment. (From Iowa State University's Eserver.org, at http://eserver.org/books/franklin/, accessed July 30, 2005)

My elder brothers were all put apprentices to different trades. I was put to the grammar-school at eight years of age, my father intending to devote me, as the tithe of his sons, to the service of the Church. My early readiness in learning to read (which must have been very early, as I do not remember when I could not read), and the opinion of all his friends, that I should certainly make a good scholar, encouraged him in this purpose of his. My uncle Benjamin, too, approved of it, and proposed to give me all his short-hand volumes of sermons, I suppose as a stock to set up with, if I would learn his character. I continued, however, at the grammar-school not quite one year, though in that time I had risen gradually from the middle of the class of that year to be the head of it, and farther was removed into the next class above it, in order to go with that into the third at the end of the year. But my father, in the meantime, from a view of the expense of a college education, which having so large a family he could not well afford, and the mean living many so educated were afterwards able to obtain—reasons that he gave to his friends in my hearing—altered his first intention, took me from the grammar-school, and sent me to a school for writing and arithmetic, kept by a then famous man, Mr. George Brownell, very successful in his profession generally, and that by mild, encouraging methods. Under him I acquired fair writing pretty soon, but I failed in the arithmetic, and made no progress in it. At ten years old I was taken home to assist my father in his business, which was that of a tallow-chandler and [soap]-boiler; a business he was not bred to, but had assumed on his arrival in New England, and on finding his dying trade would not maintain his family, being in little request. Accordingly, I was employed in cutting wick for the candles, filling the dipping mold and the molds for cast candles, attending the shop, going of errands, etc.

I disliked the trade, and had a strong inclination for the sea, but my father declared against it; however, living near the water, I was much in and about it, learnt early to swim well, and to manage boats; and when in a boat or canoe with other boys, I was commonly allowed to govern, especially in any case of difficulty; and upon other occasions I was generally a leader among the boys, and sometimes led them into scrapes, of which I will mention one instance, as it shows an early projecting public spirit, tho' not then justly conducted.

There was a salt-marsh that bounded part of the mill-pond, on the edge of which, at high water, we used to stand to fish for minnows. By much trampling, we had made it a mere quagmire. My proposal was to build a wharff there fit for us to stand upon, and I showed my comrades a large heap of stones, which were intended for a new house near the marsh, and which would very well suit our purpose. Accordingly, in the evening, when the workmen were gone, I assembled a number of my play-fellows, and working with them diligently like so many emmets [an ant-like insect], sometimes two or three to a stone, we brought them all away and built our little wharff. The next morning the workmen were surprised at missing the stones, which were found in our wharff. Inquiry was made after the removers; we were discovered and complained of; several of us were corrected by our fathers; and though I pleaded the usefulness of the work, mine convinced me that nothing was useful which was not honest.

I continued thus employed in my father's business for two years, that is, till I was twelve years old; and my brother John, who was bred to that business, having left my father, married, and set up for himself at Rhode Island, there was all appearance that I was destined to supply his place, and become a tallow-chandler. But my dislike to the trade continuing, my father was under apprehensions that if he did not find one for me more agreeable, I should break away and get to sea, as his son Josiah had done, to his great vexation. He therefore sometimes took me to walk with him, and see joiners, bricklayers, turners, braziers, etc., at their work, that he might observe my inclination, and endeavor to fix it on some trade or other on land. It has ever since been a pleasure to me to see good workmen handle their tools; and it has been useful to me, having learnt so much by it as to be able to do little jobs myself in my house when a workman could not readily be got, and to construct little machines for my experiments, while the intention of making the experiment was fresh and warm in my mind. My father at last fixed upon the cutler's trade, and my uncle Benjamin's son Samuel, who was bred to that business in London, being about that time established in Boston, I was sent to be with him some time on liking. But his expectations of a fee with me displeasing my father, I was taken home again.

From a child I was fond of reading, and all the little money that came into my hands was ever laid out in books. Pleased with the *Pilgrim's Progress,* my first collection was of John Bunyan's works in separate little volumes. I afterward sold them to enable me to buy R. Burton's *Historical Collections*; they were small chapmen's books, and cheap, 40 or 50 in all. My father's little library consisted chiefly of books in polemic divinity, most of which I read, and have since often regretted that, at a time when I had such a thirst for knowledge, more proper books had not fallen in my way since it was now resolved I should not be a clergyman. Plutarch's *Lives* there was in which I read abundantly, and I still think that time spent to great advantage. There was also a book of De Foe's, called an *Essay on Projects,* and another of Dr. Mather's, called *Essays to do Good,* which perhaps gave me a turn of thinking that had an influence on some of the principal future events of my life.

This bookish inclination at length determined my father to make me a printer, though he had already one son (James) of that profession. In 1717 my brother James returned from England with a press and letters to set up his business in Boston. I liked it much better than that of my father, but still had a hankering for the sea. To prevent the apprehended effect of such an inclination, my father was impatient to have me bound to my brother. I stood out some time, but at last was persuaded, and signed the indentures when I was yet but twelve years old. I was to serve as an apprentice till I was twenty-one years of age, only I was to be allowed journeyman's wages during the last year. In a little time I made great proficiency in the business, and became a useful hand to my brother. I now had access to better books. An acquaintance with the apprentices of booksellers enabled me sometimes to borrow a small one, which I was careful to return soon and clean. Often I sat up in my room reading the greatest part of the night, when the book was borrowed in the evening and to be returned early in the morning, lest it should be missed or wanted.

And after some time an ingenious tradesman, Mr. Matthew Adams, who had a pretty collection of books, and who frequented our printing-house, took notice of me, invited me to his library, and very kindly lent me such books as I chose to read. I now took a fancy to poetry, and made some little pieces; my brother, thinking it might turn to account, encouraged me, and put me on composing occasional ballads. One was called *The Lighthouse Tragedy*, and contained an account of the drowning of Captain Worthilake, with his two daughters: the other was a sailor's song, on the taking of *Teach* (or Blackbeard) the pirate. They were wretched stuff, in the rub-street-ballad style; and when they were printed he sent me about the town to sell them. The first sold wonderfully, the event being recent, having made a great noise. This flattered my vanity; but my father discouraged me by ridiculing my performances, and telling me verse-makers were generally beggars. So I escaped being a poet, most probably a very bad one; but as prose writing has been of great use to me in the course of my life, and was a principal means of my advancement, I shall tell you how, in such a situation, I acquired what little ability I have in that way.

There was another bookish lad in the town, John Collins by name, with whom I was intimately acquainted. We sometimes disputed, and very fond we were of argument, and very desirous of confuting one another, which disputatious turn, by the way, is apt to become a very bad habit, making people often extremely disagreeable in company by the contradiction that is necessary to bring it into practice; and thence, besides souring and spoiling the conversation, is productive of disgusts and, perhaps enmities where you may have occasion for friendship. I had caught it by reading my father's books of dispute about religion. Persons of good sense, I have since observed, seldom fall into it, except lawyers, university men, and men of all sorts that have been bred at Edinborough.

A question was once, somehow or other, started between Collins and me, of the propriety of educating the female sex in learning, and their abilities for study. He was of opinion that it was improper, and that they were naturally unequal to it. I took the contrary side, perhaps a little for dispute's sake. He was naturally more eloquent, had a ready plenty of words; and sometimes, as I thought, bore me down more by his fluency than by the strength of his reasons. As we parted without settling the point, and were not to see one another again for some time, I sat down to put my arguments in writing, which I copied fair and sent to him. He answered, and I replied. Three or four letters of a side had passed, when my father happened to find my papers and read them. Without entering into the discussion, he took occasion to talk to me about the manner of my writing; observed that, though I had the advantage of my antagonist in correct spelling and pointing (which I ow'd to the printing-house), I fell far short in elegance of expression, in method and in perspicuity, of which he convinced me by several instances. I saw the justice of his remark, and thence grew more attentive to the manner in writing, and determined to endeavor at improvement.

About this time I met with an odd volume of the *Spectator*. It was the third. I had never before seen any of them. I bought it, read it over and over, and was much delighted with it. I thought the writing excellent, and wished, if possible, to imitate it. With this view I took some of the papers, and, making short hints of the sentiment in each sentence, laid them by a few days, and then, without looking at the book, try'd to compleat the papers again, by expressing each hinted sentiment at length, and as fully as it had been expressed before, in any suitable words that should come to hand. Then I compared my *Spectator* with the original, discovered some of my faults, and corrected them. But I found I wanted a stock of words, or a readiness in recollecting and using them, which I thought I should have acquired before that time if I had gone on making verses; since the continual occasion for words of the same import, but of different length, to suit the measure, or of different sound for the rhyme, would have laid me under a constant necessity of searching for variety, and also have tended to fix that variety in my mind, and make me master of it. Therefore I took some of the tales and turned them into verse; and, after a time, when I had pretty well forgotten the prose, turned them back again. I also sometimes jumbled my collections of hints into confusion, and after some weeks endeavored to reduce them into the best order, before I began to form the full sentences and compleat the paper. This was to teach me method in the arrangement of thoughts. By comparing my work afterwards with the original, I discovered many faults and amended them; but I sometimes had the pleasure of fancying that, in certain particulars of small import, I had been lucky enough to improve the method or the language, and this encouraged me to think I might possibly in time come to be a tolerable English writer, of which I was extremely ambitious. My time for these exercises and for reading was at night, after work or before it began in the morning, or on Sundays, when I contrived to be in the printing-house alone, evading as much as I could the common attendance on public worship which my father used to exact on me when I was under his care, and which indeed I still thought a duty, though I could not, as it seemed to me, afford time to practise it.

When about sixteen years of age I happened to meet with a book, written by one Tryon, recommending a vegetable diet. I determined to go into it. My brother, being yet unmarried, did not keep house, but boarded himself and his apprentices in another family. My refusing to eat flesh occasioned an inconveniency, and I was frequently chid for my singularity. I made myself acquainted with Tryon's manner of preparing some of his dishes, such as boiling potatoes or rice, making hasty pudding, and a few others, and then proposed to my brother, that if he would give me, weekly, half the money he paid for my board, I would board myself. He instantly agreed to it, and I presently found that I could save half what he paid me. This was an additional fund for buying books. But I had another advantage in it. My brother and the rest going from the printing-house to their meals, I remained there alone, and, despatching presently my light repast, which often was no more than a bisket or a slice of bread, a handful of raisins or a tart from the pastry-cook's, and a glass of water, had the rest of the time till their return for study, in which I made the greater progress, from that greater clearness of head and quicker apprehension which usually attend temperance in eating and drinking.

And now it was that, being on some occasion made asham'd of my ignorance in figures, which I had twice failed in learning when at school, I took Cocker's book of Arithmetick, and went through the whole by myself with great ease. I also read Seller's and Shermy's books of Navigation, and became acquainted with the little geometry they contain; but never proceeded far in that science. And I read about this time Locke *On Human Understanding,* and the *Art of Thinking,* by Messrs. du Port Royal.

While I was intent on improving my language, I met with an English grammar (I think it was Greenwood's), at the end of which there were two little sketches of the arts of rhetoric and logic, the latter finishing with a specimen of a dispute in the Socratic method; and soon after I procur'd Xenophon's *Memorable Things of Socrates,* wherein there are many instances of the same method. I was charm'd with it, adopted it, dropt my abrupt contradiction and positive argumentation, and put on the humble inquirer and doubter. And being then, from reading Shaftesbury and

Collins, become a real doubter in many points of our religious doctrine, I found this method safest for myself and very embarrassing to those against whom I used it; therefore I took a delight in it, practis'd it continually, and grew very artful and expert in drawing people, even of superior knowledge, into concessions, the consequences of which they did not foresee, entangling them in difficulties out of which they could not extricate themselves, and so obtaining victories that neither myself nor my cause always deserved. I continu'd this method some few years, but gradually left it, retaining only the habit of expressing myself in terms of modest diffidence; never using, when I advanced any thing that may possibly be disputed, the words certainly, undoubtedly, or any others that give the air of positiveness to an opinion; but rather say, I conceive or apprehend a thing to be so and so; it appears to me, or I should think it so or so, for such and such reasons; or I imagine it to be so; or it is so, if I am not mistaken. This habit, I believe, has been of great advantage to me when I have had occasion to inculcate my opinions, and persuade men into measures that I have been from time to time engag'd in promoting; and, as the chief ends of conversation are to *inform* or to *be informed,* to *please* or to *persuade,* I wish well-meaning, sensible men would not lessen their power of doing good by a positive, assuming manner, that seldom fails to disgust, tends to create opposition, and to defeat every one of those purposes for which speech was given to us, to wit, giving or receiving information or pleasure. For, if you would inform, a positive and dogmatical manner in advancing your sentiments may provoke contradiction and prevent a candid attention. If you wish information and improvement from the knowledge of others, and yet at the same time express yourself as firmly fix'd in your present opinions, modest, sensible men, who do not love disputation, will probably leave you undisturbed in the possession of your error. And by such a manner, you can seldom hope to recommend yourself in pleasing your hearers, or to persuade those whose concurrence you desire. Pope says, judiciously,

> Men should be taught as if you taught them not,
> And things unknown propos'd as things forgot;

farther recommending to us

> To speak, tho' sure, with seeming diffidence.

And he might have coupled with this line that which he has coupled with another, I think, less properly,

> For want of modesty is want of sense.

If you ask, *Why less properly?* I must repeat the lines,

> Immodest words admit of *no defense,*
> For want of modesty is want of sense.

Now, is not want of sense (where a man is so unfortunate as to want it) some apology for his want of modesty? and would not the lines stand more justly thus?

> Immodest words admit *but* this defense,
> That want of modesty is want of sense.

This, however, I should submit to better judgments.

In Search of the Historical Child
Questions for Consideration

Thirty years ago the historian Ross W. Beales Jr. went "In Search of the Historical Child." The resulting essay, one of the most frequently cited articles in the historiography of childhood, confronted the long-held assumption that "colonial Americans . . . regarded their children as 'miniature adults' and recognized no stage of development like twentieth-century adolescence."[1] In other words, for colonial youngsters childhood was a stage through which they must pass very quickly on their way to righteous and responsible adulthood. From Alice Morse Earle to Michael Zuckerman, Beales argued, historians had almost universally placed too much emphasis on stiff family portraits and harsh Puritan sermons and ignored more homely evidence—not to mention common sense—to reduce the arc of colonial children's lives.[2]

At the end of his brief survey of the literature and sources on colonial children, Beales concluded that "notions of 'miniature adulthood' and the absence of adolescence in colonial New England are, at best, exaggerations." Most historians agree. We now believe, with Beales, that colonial youth did experience a "prolonged 'adolescence' or 'youth,'" during which they came of age in appropriate ways for their time and place. Beales offered a long excerpt from a 1720 essay in which the Puritan Benjamin Coleman called youth the "chusing" or "fixing time," when

> you commonly chuse your *Trade*; betake your selves to your business for life, show what you incline to, and how you intend to be imploy'd all your days. Now you chuse your *Master* and your Education or Occupation. And now you dispose of your self in *Marriage* ordinarily, place your *Affections*, give away your hearts, look out for some *Companion* of life, whose to be as long as you live.

"This," he concluded, "is the work of your Youth." Of course, that is the work of youth in almost any society.

Although Beales went in search of his historical child in New England, the question can be asked of children in all of the American colonies. And although we no longer think of colonial children and youth as "miniature adults," the questions of what it meant to be a child and an adult, and how young Americans passed from one stage of their lives to another, remain important to historians of all times and places. Indeed, those questions are, in one way or another, at the center of most histories of childhood and youth. This is especially true when one assumes that childhood and youth are, in fact, "constructions"—variable sets of assumptions and ideals that shape what people expect of children and what children can expect from society.

The essays, documents, and illustrations in this anthology offer a number of different points of view on childhood, youth, parenting, education, coming of age, and many other issues related to growing up in colonial America. They also show that Europeans, Africans, and Native Americans —and the ethnic groups within those major racial categories—experienced markedly different childhoods. The following questions are designed to help readers examine these primary and secondary sources more closely, and, like Beales, to conduct their own "search for the historical child."

1. What evidence can you find in this volume to support the idea that, in fact, Beales was *wrong,* and that colonial children really were "miniature adults"? In other words, what experiences and traditions would suggest to historians that colonial Americans did not consider childhood as a separate stage of life? What evidence can you find that *supports* Beales's argument?

2. We tend to think of people who lived in the past as being quite different from us. Sometimes it's even hard to imagine from black and white photos stashed in the back of a hall closet what it was like to have been alive in the 1940s. It is even harder to get a sense of real people's lives in the 1640s! Nevertheless, connections can be made. List some of the attitudes, policies, and practices—from children, parents, teachers, public officials, and others—regarding children that would seem familiar to Americans in the early twenty-first century.

3. If childhood and youth are, indeed, "constructions," how did the diverse ethnic and racial groups who came together in colonial America construct

different childhoods for their offspring? How were they similar? How did their constructions change over time?

4. Although all societies note and often celebrate various ways in which their children "come of age," there are often differences in what societies deem important enough to commemorate. Modern Americans, for instance, might list the onset of puberty, high school or college graduation, religious confirmation, obtaining a driver's license, and taking a full-time job as typical stages in a person's "coming of age." How did colonial Americans mark their sons' and daughters' coming of age? How did that vary from place to place, from time to time, and from ethnic group to ethnic group?

5. An underlying theme of this anthology is that childhood in a colony was different from childhood in a more established, settled place. Some of the essays, documents, and illustrations make this point quite explicitly; others provide more subtle evidence. What circumstances led to the creation of a unique form of childhood in the American colonies?

6. We can all name the most important people and organizations in our lives: they are normally our parents, teachers, and coaches, and our schools, clubs, and churches. If they had been asked, who and what would colonial children have listed as their most important influences? How did that vary by place, ethnicity, and gender?

7. Children's historians spend a great deal of their time discussing the differences between the experiences of boys and girls as they grow into men and women. In most societies, gender plays an important role in the ways that children and youth are prepared by their parents and by the communities in which they live to be adults. How did the training and other experiences of boys and girls in colonial America differ? How was it similar?

8. Historians of children and youth normally choose one of two approaches in their research. Some write about institutions and ideas—schools, for instance, or childrearing practices. Others try to write from the points of view of children, insisting that children's thoughts and words are as valid as those of adults. What attitudes, beliefs, and interests peculiar to colonial children and youth—distinct from those of their parents—can you glean from the essays and sources in this anthology?

9. One of the terms mentioned in the introduction is "agency," which refers to the extent to which children (or any other person, for that matter) can control or at least shape certain elements of their lives. How did colonial children and youth exert agency? How did their opinions, decisions, and actions help determine the course of their lives?

10. Historians have to balance the rhetoric of published sources with the actual events in the lives of people who lived in the past. One reason why historians accepted the "miniature adult" idea for so long was that they placed too much confidence in the rather harsh language of Puritan sermons and colonial laws. How do the primary sources in this anthology support or contradict the arguments made in the essays? What other topics than those presented in this volume do the sources address?

NOTES

1. Beales, "In Search of the Historical Child," 379–98.
2. See, for instance, Earle, *Child Life in Colonial Days,* 50, 62; Zuckerman, *Peaceable Kingdoms,* 72.

Suggested Readings

The historiography of American colonial childhoods dates to the publication of Alice Morse Earle's *Child Life in Colonial Days* in 1899. Morse was a writer and amateur historian who, in a short but prolific career, published many books about daily customs and material artifacts in early America. Like her other books, the heavily illustrated *Child Life in Colonial Days* reflected an antiquarian rather than an analytical interest in the past. But Earle's book was the only study of children, as such, to appear for many decades. There have been several groundbreaking studies of colonial families and attitudes toward children, including a number by some of the most celebrated colonial historians of the last fifty years. But most explore family dynamics in general rather than children's lives in particular, and, as in so much colonial historiography, New England dominates the other colonies. For instance, in *The Puritan Family*, Edmund Morgan suggested that "spiritual tribalism" led Puritans to develop family relationships shaped by a series of duties and rights, obligations and privileges. One of the best known and most often assigned books on colonial social history is John Demos's *Little Commonwealth*, which exploded at least a few of the harsh myths about Puritan attitudes and behavior and used material artifacts, court records, estate inventories, and other classic social history sources to outline the homely lives and family ties of early New Englanders. More recently, Anne Lombard, in *Making Manhood*, argued that New England boys were brought up in a world dominated by fathers and raised to embody the virtues of moderation, responsibility, and conformity. A few historians have explored similar topics for other colonies. Helena Wall cut across colonial boundaries in *Fierce Communion*, which traced the intervention of community interests and standards in several issues, including marriage and childrearing. One of the few books dealing specifically with southern families and children, Daniel Blake Smith's *Inside the Great House*, examined the shift from patriarchal to child-centered concepts of family life during the second century of settlement in the Chesapeake region.

A number of books on colonial social history, including the New England town studies of the 1960s and 1970s, although they provided useful information about children, treated them only as parts of the larger demographic, cultural, economic, and religious themes with which they were concerned. A few historians reserved a chapter or two to colonial childhood; for instance, in her survey of "everyday life" in the late colonial period, Stephanie Grauman Wolf argued that eighteenth-century Americans—at least the wealthy, literate portion of the population—began to project the attitudes and assumptions of a childhood that we would recognize as "modern."

But only a handful of books was devoted entirely to the experiences of children or even adults' attitudes toward children. There were a few notable exceptions. Philip Greven tackled the prickly topics of religion, emotion, and childrearing in *The Protestant Temperament,* suggesting that colonists applied a spectrum of attitudes toward childrearing, religion, and discipline, from the strict "evangelical" approach of New Englanders to the "genteel" attitude of southern planters. In *Children in the House,* Karin Calvert suggested that the furniture and other material artifacts related to children show that colonial parents' first priority was to get their children into upright and independent positions. More recently, Judith S. Graham focused on a single family—the frequently stricken but close-knit brood of the Boston judge, merchant, and diarist Samuel Sewall—to lighten traditional representations of dour Puritan parenting.

A few historians have explored facets of the lives of young Native Americans and slaves. Although her fascinating look at the contrasting cultures of New England revolved around families, Gloria Main's *Peoples of a Spacious Land* also included a couple of chapters about growing up in English and Native American settlements. A recent book on New England Indians offered a chapter on young Native Americans working as indentured servants in Rhode Island, while Philip D. Morgan's magisterial study of eighteenth-century slavery briefly fit children into its discussion of slave families. In South America, Mark Szuchman placed children in their family and community contexts in his study of late colonial and early national Argentina.

The following bibliography includes full citations for all of the secondary sources mentioned in the essays, as well as other books of interest to historians of children and youth and of colonial America.

General Children's History

Ariès, Phillipe. *Centuries of Childhood: A Social History of Family Life.* New York: Knopf, 1962.

Bremner, Robert, ed. *Children and Youth in America: A Documentary History.* Vol. 1, *1600–1865.* Cambridge, MA: Harvard University Press, 1970.

Buckley, Thomas, and Alma Gottlieb, eds. *Blood Magic: The Anthropology of Menstruation.* Berkeley: University of California Press, 1988.

Cunningham, Hugh. "The Employment and Unemployment of Children in England c. 1680–1851." *Past and Present* 126 (1990): 115–50.

———. "Histories of Childhood." *American Historical Review* 103 (October 1998): 1195–1208.

Graff, Harvey J. *Conflicting Paths: Growing Up in America.* Cambridge, MA: Harvard University Press, 1995.

———. *Growing Up in America: Historical Experiences.* Detroit, MI: Wayne State University Press, 1987.

Hawes, Joseph W., and N. Ray Hiner, eds. *American Childhood: A Research Guide and Historical Handbook.* Westport, CT: Greenwood Press, 1985.

Heywood, Colin. *A History of Childhood: Children and Childhood in the West from Medieval to Modern Times.* Cambridge, UK: Polity Press, 2001.

Illick, Joseph E. *American Childhoods.* Philadelphia: University of Pennsylvania Press, 2002.

King, Wilma. *Stolen Childhood: Slave Youth in Nineteenth-Century America.* Bloomington: Indiana University Press, 1995.

Mintz, Steven. *Huck's Raft: A History of American Childhood.* Cambridge, MA: Belknap Press of Harvard University Press, 2004.

Schwartz, Marie Jenkins. *Born in Bondage: Growing up Enslaved in the Antebellum South.* Cambridge, MA: Harvard University Press, 2000.

Sommerville, C. John. "Bibliographic Note: Toward a History of Children and Youth." *Journal of Interdisciplinary History* 3 (Autumn 1972): 439–47.

Sutton, John R. *Stubborn Children: Controlling Delinquency in the United States, 1640–1981.* Berkeley: University of California Press, 1988.

Turner, Victor. *The Ritual Process: Structure and Anti-Structure.* Chicago: Aldine Publishing Company, 1969; reprint, Aldine de Gruyter, 1997.

Van Gennap, Arnold. *Rites of Passage.* Chicago: University of Chicago Press, 1960.

Wallach, Glenn. *Obedient Sons: The Discourse of Youth and Generations in American Culture, 1630–1860.* Amherst: University of Massachusetts, 1997.

Walvin, James. *A Child's World: A Social History of English Childhood, 1800–1914.* Harmondsworth, UK: Penguin, 1982.

General Colonial History

Axtell, James, ed. *The Indian Peoples of Eastern America: A Documentary History of the Sexes.* New York: Oxford University Press, 1981.

Bragdon, Kathleen J. *Native People of Southern New England, 1500–1650.* Norman: University of Oklahoma Press, 1996.

Carrasco, David, ed. *The Oxford Encyclopedia of Mesoamerican Cultures. The Civilizations of Mexico and Central America.* 3 vols. New York: Oxford University Press, 2001.

Craton, Michael. "Jamaican Slave Mortality: Fresh Light from Worthy Park, Longville, and the Tharp Estates." *Journal of Caribbean History* 3 (1971): 1–27.

Deetz, James, and Patricia Scott Deetz. *The Times of Their Lives: Life, Love, and Death in Plymouth Colony.* New York: Freeman, 2000.

Dexter, Harry Martyn, and Morton Dexter. *The England and Holland of the Pilgrims.* London, 1906; reprint, Whitefish, MT: Kessinger Publishing, 2004.

Ditz, Toby. "Shipwrecked; or, Masculinity Imperiled: Mercantile Representations of Failure and the Gendered Self in Eighteenth-Century Philadelphia." *Journal of American History* 81 (1994): 51–80.

Dunn, Richard. "A Tale of Two Plantations: Slave Life at Mesopotamia in Jamaica and Mount Airy in Virginia, 1799–1828." *William and Mary Quarterly* 34 (1977): 32–65.

Edwards, Bryan. *The History, Civil and Commercial, of the British Colonies in the West Indies.* Vol. 2. New York: AMS Press, 1966 [1819].

Fischer, David Hackett. *Albion's Seed: Four British Folkways in America.* New York: Oxford University Press, 1989.

Greene, Jack P. *Interpreting Early America: Historiographical Essays.* Charlottesville: University Press of Virginia, 1996.

Greven, Philip J. *Four Generations: Population, Land, and Family in Colonial Andover, Massachusetts.* Ithaca, NY: Cornell University Press, 1970.

Hall, Douglas. *In Miserable Slavery: Thomas Thistlewood in Jamaica, 1750–86.* Mona, Jamaica: University of the West Indies Press, 1989; reprint, 1999.

Hawke, David Freeman. *Everyday Life in Early America.* New York: Harper and Row, 1988.

Henretta, James A., et al., eds. *The Transformation of Early American History: Society, Authority, and Ideology.* New York: Knopf, 1991.

Higman, B. W. *Slave Population and Economy in Jamaica, 1807–1834.* New York: Cambridge University Press, 1976.

Langdon, George. *Pilgrim Colony: A History of New Plymouth, 1620–1691.* New Haven, CT: Yale University Press, 1966.

León-Portilla, Miguel. *The Aztec Image of Self and Society: An Introduction to Nahua Culture.* Salt Lake City: University of Utah Press, 1992.

Lockhart, James. *The Nahuas after the Conquest. A Social and Cultural History of the Indians of Central Mexico, Sixteenth through Eighteenth Centuries*. Stanford, CA: Stanford University Press, 1992.

Lovejoy, Paul E., and David V. Trotman. "Enslaved Africans and Their Expectations of Slave Life in the Americas: Towards a Reconsideration of Models of 'Creolisation.'" In Verene A. Shepherd and Glen A. Richards, eds., *Questioning Creole: Creolisation Discourses in Caribbean Culture*. Kingston, Jamaica: Ian Randle Publishers, 2002, 67–91.

McAndrew, John. *The Open-Air Churches of Sixteenth-Century Mexico: Atrios, Posas, Open Chapels, and Other Studies*. Cambridge, MA: Harvard University Press, 1965.

Miller, Perry. *The New England Mind: The Seventeenth Century*. Cambridge, MA: Harvard University Press, 1983.

Mintz, Sidney W. *Sweetness and Power: The Place of Sugar in Modern History*. New York: Penguin Books, 1985.

Morgan, Philip D. *Slave Counterpoint: Black Culture in the Eighteenth-Century Chesapeake and Lowcountry*. Chapel Hill: University of North Carolina Press, 1998.

Nissenbaum, Stephen. *The Battle for Christmas*. New York: Knopf, 1996.

Nwokeji, Ugo. "African Conceptions of Gender and the Slave Traffic." *William and Mary Quarterly* 58 (2001): 47–68.

Oaks, Robert. "Philadelphians in Exile: The Problem of Loyalty during the American Revolution." *Pennsylvania Magazine of History and Biography* 96 (1972): 298–325.

Petley, Christer. "Slavery, Emancipation, and the Creole World View of Jamaican Colonists, 1800–1834." *Slavery & Abolition* 26 (2005): 93–114.

Piersen, William Dillon. "White Cannibals, Black Martyrs: Fear, Depression, and Religious Faith as Causes of Suicide among New Slaves." *Journal of Negro History* 62 (1977): 147–59.

Powell, Sumner Chilton. *Puritan Village: The Formation of a New England Town*. Middletown, CT: Wesleyan University Press, 1963.

Rubertone, Patricia. *Grave Undertakings: An Archaeology of Roger Williams and the Narragansett Indians*. Washington, DC: Smithsonian Institution Press, 2001.

Rutman, Darrett B., and Anita H. Rutman. *A Place in Time: Middlesex County, Virginia, 1650–1750*. New York: Norton, 1984.

Silverman, David J. "The Impact of Indentured Servitude on the Society and Culture of Southern New England Indians, 1680–1810." *New England Quarterly* 74.4 (1991): 622–66.

———. "Indians, Missionaries, and Religious Translation: Creating Wampanoag Christianity in Seventeenth-Century Martha's Vineyard." *William and Mary Quarterly* (2005): 141–75.

Silverman, Kenneth. *The Life and Times of Cotton Mather*. New York: Columbia University Press, 1985.

Simmons, William. *Spirit of the New England Tribes: Indian History and Folklore, 1620–1984.* Hanover, NH: University Press of New England, 1986.

Spruill, Julia Cherry. *Women's Life and Work in the Southern Colonies.* Chapel Hill: University of North Carolina Press, 1938.

Stannard, David E. *The Puritan Way of Death: A Study in Religion, Culture, and Social Change.* New York: Oxford University Press, 1977.

Stratton, Eugene Aubrey. *Plymouth Colony, Its History & People, 1620–1691.* Salt Lake City, UT: Ancestry Publishing, 1986.

Thornton, John. "Cannibals, Witches, and Slave Traders in the Atlantic World." *William and Mary Quarterly* 40 (2003): 273–94.

Vickers, Daniel. *Farmers and Fishermen: Two Centuries of Work in Essex County, Massachusetts, 1630–1830.* Chapel Hill: University of North Carolina Press, 1994.

Wolf, Stephanie Grauman. *As Various as Their Land: The Everyday Lives of Eighteenth-Century Americans.* New York: HarperPerennial, 1993.

Zuckerman, Michael. *Peaceable Kingdoms: New England Towns in the Eighteenth Century.* New York: Knopf, 1970.

Books and Articles on Colonial Children and Families

Axtell, James. *The School upon a Hill: Education and Society in Colonial New England.* New Haven, CT: Yale University Press, 1974.

Beales, Ross W., Jr. "In Search of the Historical Child: Miniature Adulthood and Youth in Colonial New England." *American Quarterly* 27 (October 1975): 379–98.

Benes, Peter, ed. *Families and Children: Dublin Seminar for New England Folklife Annual Proceedings.* Boston: Boston University, 1985.

Brewer, Holly. *By Birth or Consent: Children, Law, and Revolution in England and America, 1550–1820.* Chapel Hill: University of North Carolina Press, 2002.

Calvert, Karin. *Children in the House: The Material Culture of Early Childhood, 1600–1900.* Boston: Northeastern University Press, 1994.

Crane, Elaine Forman. "The World of Elizabeth Drinker." *Pennsylvania Magazine of History and Biography* 103 (January 1983): 3–28.

Demos, John. *Circles and Lines: The Shape of Life in Early America.* Cambridge, MA: Harvard University Press, 2004.

———. "Developmental Perspectives on the History of Childhood." *Journal of Interdisciplinary History* 2 (1971): 315–27.

———. *A Little Commonwealth: Family Life in Plymouth Colony,* 2nd ed. New York: Oxford University Press, 2000.

Earle, Alice Morse. *Child Life in Colonial Days.* New York: Macmillan, 1899.

"The Family in Early American History and Culture." Special Issue. *William and Mary Quarterly,* 3rd ser., 39 (January 1982).

Fliegelman, Jay. *Prodigals and Pilgrims: The American Revolution against Patriarchal Authority, 1750–1800.* Cambridge: Cambridge University Press, 1982.

Forbes, Susan. "Quaker Tribalism." In Michael Zuckerman, ed., *Friends and Neighbors.* Philadelphia: Temple University Press, 1982.

Frost, J. William. *The Quaker Family in Colonial America: A Portrait of the Society of Friends.* New York: St. Martin's, 1973.

Fryer, Darcy R. "In Pursuit of Their Interest: Communal Oversight of Economic and Family Life among the Eighteenth-Century South Carolina Lowcountry Gentry, c. 1730–1789." Ph.D. diss., Yale University, 2001.

Glover, Lorri. *All Our Relations: Blood Ties and Emotional Bonds among the Early South Carolina Gentry.* Baltimore: Johns Hopkins University Press, 2000.

Graham, Judith S. *Puritan Family Life: The Diary of Samuel Sewall.* Boston: Northeastern University Press, 2000.

Grassby, Richard. *Kinship and Capitalism: Marriage, Family, and Business in the English-Speaking World, 1580–1740.* New York: Cambridge University Press, 2001.

Greven, Philip J. *The Protestant Temperament: Patterns of Child-rearing, Religious Experience, and the Self in Early America.* New York: Knopf, 1977.

———. *Spare the Child: The Religious Roots of Punishment and the Psychological Impact of Physical Abuse.* New York: Knopf, 1991.

Griffin, Dorothy Gail. "The Eighteenth-Century Draytons of Drayton Hall." Ph.D. diss., Emory University, 1985.

Gutman, Herbert. *The Black Family in Slavery and Freedom, 1750–1925.* New York: Random House, 1976.

Hecht, Tobias, ed. *Minor Omissions: Children in Latin American History and Society.* Madison: University of Wisconsin Press, 2002.

Herbert, T. Walter. *Dearest Beloved: The Hawthornes and the Making of the Middle-Class Family.* Berkeley: University of California, 1993.

Herndon, Ruth Wallis, and Ella Wilcox Sekatau. "Colonizing the Children: Indian Youngsters in Servitude in Early Rhode Island." In Colin G. Calloway and Neal Salisbury, eds., *Reinterpreting New England Indians and the Colonial Experience.* Boston: Colonial Society of Massachusetts, 2003, 137–76.

Hoffer, Peter Charles, and N. E. H. Hull. *Murdering Mothers: Infanticide in England and New England, 1558–1803.* New York: New York University Press, 1981.

Hunt, Margaret. *The Middling Sort: Commerce, Gender, and the Family in England, 1680–1780.* Berkeley: University of California Press, 1996.

Jabour, Anya. *Marriage in the Early Republic: Elizabeth and William Wirt and the Companionate Ideal.* Baltimore: Johns Hopkins University Press, 1998.

Joyce, Rosemary A. "Girling the Girl and Boying the Boy: The Production of Adulthood in Ancient Mesoamerica." *World Archaeology* 31 (2000): 473–83.

Levy, Barry. *Quakers and the American Family: British Settlement in the Delaware Valley.* New York: Oxford University Press, 1988.

Lipsett-Rivera, Sonya, ed. Special Issue on the Children in the History of Latin America. *Journal of Family History* 23 (1998).

Lombard, Anne S. *Making Manhood: Growing Up Male in Colonial New England.* Cambridge, MA: Harvard University Press, 2003.

Main, Gloria. *Peoples of a Spacious Land: Families and Cultures in Colonial New England.* Cambridge, MA: Harvard University Press, 2001.

Morgan, Edmund. *The Puritan Family: Religion and Domestic Relations in Seventeenth-Century New England.* New York: Harper and Row, 1966.

Narrett, David E. *Inheritance and Family Life in Colonial New York City.* Ithaca, NY: Cornell University Press, 1992.

Ozment, Steven. *Ancestors: The Loving Family in Old Europe.* Cambridge, MA: Harvard University Press, 2001.

Plane, Ann Marie. "Childbirth Practices among Native American Women of New England and Canada, 1600–1800." In Peter Benes, ed., *Medicine and Healing: The Dublin Seminar for New England Folklife Annual Proceedings 14 and 15 July 1990.* Boston: Boston University Press, 1992, 13–24.

———. *Colonial Intimacies: Indian Marriage in Early New England.* Ithaca, NY: Cornell University Press, 2000.

Pleck, Elizabeth. *Domestic Tyranny: The Making of Social Policy against Family Violence from Colonial Times to the Present.* New York: Oxford University Press, 1987.

Pollock, Linda. *Forgotten Children: Parent-Child Relations from 1500–1900.* Cambridge: Cambridge University Press, 1983.

Premo, Bianca. *Children of the Father King: Youth, Authority, and Legal Minority in Colonial Lima.* Chapel Hill: University of North Carolina Press, 2005.

Romero, R. Todd. "'Ranging Foresters' and 'Women-Like-Men': Physical Accomplishment, Spiritual Power, and Indian Masculinity in Early Seventeenth-Century New England." *Ethnohistory* 53 (Spring 2006).

Roth, Randolph. "Child Murder in New England." *Social Science History* 25.1 (2001): 101–47.

Scott, Anne Firor. "Sisters, Wives, and Mothers: Self-Portraits of Three Eighteenth-Century Women." In Nancy Hewitt, ed., *Women, Families, and Communities: Readings in American History,* vol. 1. Glenview, IL: Scott, Foresman, 1990.

Shammas, Carole, Marylynn Salmon, and Michel Dahlin. *Inheritance in America: From Colonial Times to the Present.* New Brunswick, NJ: Rutgers University Press, 1987.

Slater, Peter G. *Children in the New England Mind: In Death and in Life.* Hamden, CT: Archon Books, 1977.

———. "'From the Cradle to the Coffin': Parental Bereavement and the Shadow of Infant Damnation in Puritan Society." In N. Ray Hiner and Joseph Hawes, eds., *Growing Up in America: Children in Historical Perspective.* Chicago: University of Illinois Press, 1985.

Smith, Daniel Blake. *Inside the Great House: Planter Family Life in Eighteenth-Century Chesapeake Society.* Ithaca, NY: Cornell University Press, 1980.

Sommerville, C. John. *The Discovery of Childhood in Puritan England.* Athens: University of Georgia Press, 1992.

Stearns, Peter, and Carols Stearns. "Emotionology: Clarifying the History of Emotions and Emotional Standards." *American Historical Review* 90 (October 1985): 813–36.

Stein, Max. *The Pre-Columbian Child.* Culver City, CA: Labyrinthos, 1992.

Stone, Lawrence. *The Family, Sex, and Marriage in England, 1500–1800.* New York: Harper and Row, 1977.

Szuchman, Mark D. *Order, Family, and Community in Buenos Aires, 1810–1860.* Stanford, CA: Stanford University Press, 1988.

Thompson, Angela. "Children in Family and Society: Guanajuato, Mexico, 1780–1840." Ph.D. diss., University of Michigan, 2000.

Twinam, Ann. *Public Lives, Private Secrets: Gender, Honor, Sexuality, and Illegitimacy in Colonial Spanish America.* Stanford, CA: Stanford University Press, 1999.

Vinovskis, Maris A., and Gerald F. Moran. *Religion, Family, and Life Course: Explorations in the Social History of Early America.* Ann Arbor: University of Michigan Press, 1992.

Wall, Helena M. *Fierce Communion: Family and Community in Early America.* Cambridge, MA: Harvard University Press, 1995.

———. "Notes on Life since *A Little Commonwealth*: Family and Gender History since 1970." *William and Mary Quarterly,* 3d. ser., 57 (2000): 808–25.

About the Contributors

Mariah Adin is a Ph.D. candidate in history at Fordham University. Her research centers on Dutch colonial New York, particularly on the legal contexts of the life and culture of the inhabitants of New Amsterdam.

J. L. Bell is an editor and the administrator of the Friends of the Longfellow House in Cambridge, Massachusetts. He has delivered papers at meetings of the Dublin Seminar for New England Folk Life and of the New England Popular Culture Association and maintains the website Boston1775.net.

Audra Abbe Diptee is a member of the Department of History at Carleton University. Her work has been published in *Slavery and Abolition* and in *Immigrants and Minorities*. Her current research, funded by the Social Science and Humanities Research Council of Canada, examines gender, age, and ethnicity in the slave trade to Jamaica in the late eighteenth century.

Dorothy Tanck de Estrada is a Professor at Centra de Estudios Históricos of El Colegio de México in Mexico City. She is the author of five books and sixty articles and book chapters. She was awarded the 2001 Howard F. Cline Memorial Prize for best work of ethnohistory by the Conference on Latin American History of the American Historical Association for her book, *Pueblos de indios y educación en el México colonial, 1750–1821.*

Darcy R. Fryer earned her Ph.D. in early American history at Yale University in 2001. She taught at Columbia for a year and worked as an assistant editor on the *Papers of Benjamin Franklin*. She currently teaches history at the Brearley School in Manhattan.

Philip J. Greven is Professor Emeritus at Rutgers University. In addition to many articles, chapters, and reviews, he is the author of *Four Generations: Population, Land, and Family in Colonial Andover, Massachusetts*; *The Protestant Temperament: Patterns of Child-rearing, Religious Experience, and the Self in Early America*; and *Spare the Child: The Religious Roots of Punishment and the Psychological Impact of Physical Abuse.*

C. Dallett Hemphill is Professor of History at Ursinus College. A recipient of fellowships from the NEH and the ACLS, he is the author of *Bowing to Necessities: A History of Manners in America, 1620–1860*. He is currently researching a book on sibling relations in America from 1600 through 1860.

Lauren Ann Kattner, who received her Ph.D. at the University of Texas at Austin, is an instructor in the humanities and American civilizations at Columbus (Ohio) State Community College. The author of several book chapters and encyclopedia entries, she is at work on a book entitled "Confronting Slavery: German Catholics in Pennsylvania and the South, 1719–1836."

James Marten is Professor and Chair of the Department of History at Marquette University. Among his books are *The Children's Civil War* and two edited volumes: *Children and War: A Historical Anthology* and *Childhood and Child Welfare in the Progressive Era: A Brief History with Documents.*

John J. Navin is Associate Professor of History and Associate Dean of the College of Humanities and Fine Arts at Coastal Carolina University. He has published essays on New England children in *Murder on Trial, 1620–2002*, and in the forthcoming *The Human Tradition in the Atlantic World, 1500–1850.*

Keith Pacholl is an Assistant Professor of history at the University of West Georgia. His dissertation, written at the University of California at Riverside, is "Bearers of the Word: Religion and Print in Early America." He has published essays and articles on the Revolutionary War era in several anthologies and encyclopedias.

R. Todd Romero is a member of the History Department at the University of Houston. His first book, *Making War and Minting Christians: Masculinity, Religion, and Colonialism in Early New England*, will be published by the University of Massachusetts Press.

Helena Wall is Warren Finney Day Professor of History at Pomona College. She has received research fellowships from the NEH, the Charles Warren Center at Harvard, and the Huntington Library, and is the author of *Fierce Communion: Family and Community in Early America*. She is currently working on two book-length projects: *A Twice-Told Tale: Reconsidering Colonial New England* and *"The Boundaries of Sorrow": The Precariousness of Life in Early America*.

Parnel Wickham is Professor and Chair of the Department of Special Education at Dowling College. His work on the history of mental retardation in the English-speaking colonies of America has been published in *Journal of Health and Human Resources Administration*, *Research in the Sociology of Health Care*, and *Disability, Handicap, and Society*.

Index

Printed in the United States
201899BV00001B/9/A